Balanced Living

Balanced Living

Don't Let Your Strength Become Your Weakness

ROBERT MARSDEN KNIGHT

WIPF & STOCK · Eugene, Oregon

BALANCED LIVING
Don't Let Your Strength Become Your Weakness

ISBN 13: 978-1-55635-838-8

www.wipfandstock.com

Manufactured in the U.S.A.

The mature person is not someone for whom there are no more scandals or mysteries.

—Thomas Merton

Contents

Introduction

"It was hard to have a conversation with
anyone; there were too many people talking."

—Yogi Berra

So what's this book about? To and for and by whom is it written?

The answer to the first question is easy enough. It's about balance, about how our lives work better the more balanced they are, in all sorts of ways. Conversely, when our lives are out of balance is when we are likely to get sick, in some way or other—mentally, emotionally, morally, or spiritually, even socially. When our lives are out of balance, our strengths are working against us. We have taken them or they have taken us too far. Thus, our problem or problems are not the result of some insufficiency, some deficit, a lack of something or other on our part. At least, that is usually not the case. Rather, when we are failing or falling or perhaps sabotaging ourselves, whatever the goal, it is because of too much of a good thing. Throughout this book, I explore balance as a key to good mental health, good moral and spiritual health, emotional well-being, and even social functioning. That is my thesis, and I develop it, throughout most this book, in a variety of ways.

The last three questions? They're a bit more involved, because they are all tied together, one with the other. For example, I have written this book out of my own experience, personally and professionally, over the past thirty-five years. Let me explain that part first. Over most of my adult life, I have, as a minister, worked as a counselor and teacher. I have primarily studied and practiced and taught the art and science of psychotherapy in the context of my vocation as a Christian minister. Actually, I'm a Baptist, faintly disguised as a Christian! Nonetheless, this is who I am and what I have been doing, now, for a long time. This book is written out of the concreteness of my experience, of my life and work.

In the "Prologue" to *The Canterbury Tales,* Chaucer describes the Clerk, a symbol of a learned person in the Middle Ages, with these words: "Gladly would he learn and gladly teach."[1] I have had some excellent teachers along the way. Mine has been a privileged education, both formally and informally. In fact, I've been educated quite beyond my intelligence. I have also been afforded the opportunity to teach others. We learn both ways, as it were, from both sides of the desk. In fact, if we are open to the possibility, we may learn even more as a teacher than as a student, since teachers usually incur greater responsibility in the learning process. Anyone who has ever done much teaching might likely agree, if one is inclined to understand education as dialogue. That is surely how I have come to see it. I have learned a lot, certainly about psychotherapy at its best, from some good counselors, teachers, and supervisors, as well as from clients, students, supervisees, and parishioners.

My approach in this book is descriptive and interpretive, rather than argumentative. Whether counseling is of value, or how much so, is debatable. Since the process tends to be fairly subjective, it is sometimes hard to determine "success" or "outcome" in the way such is often measured. Some years ago, *Consumer Reports* featured a survey of subscribers, "the largest survey ever to query people on mental health care." This survey indicated what some might consider a positive outcome. At least that is what *Consumer Reports* concluded. I find such a survey interesting, since we usually turn to *Consumer Reports* when we are shopping for a new car or refrigerator or air conditioner. To summarize: "Four thousand of our readers who responded had sought help from a mental health provider or a family doctor for psychological problems, or had joined a self-help group. Most were highly satisfied with the care they had received. Most had made strides toward resolving the problems that led to treatment, and almost all said life had become more manageable. This was true for all the conditions we asked about, even among the people who had felt the worst at the beginning."[2] Be that as it may, it is not my intent to argue for or against the value of counseling in this book. Instead, I describe and interpret my experience as a client and as a counselor, how I under-

1. Geoffrey Chaucer, "Prologue," *The Canterbury Tales* (London: Penguin Books, 2003).

2. "Does Therapy Help?" *Consumer Reports,* November 1995, 734–39.

stand the process to work when it works, and how I teach and train other counselors.

That, itself, seems somewhat ironic in the larger context of my life. I grew up in a small-town, middle-class environment where what I am describing in this book, in terms of my primary vocation as an adult, was quite unknown to me or anyone else I knew in my childhood and adolescence. Growing up, I expect I may have known what a psychiatrist was, as well as a psychologist or a social worker, but hardly a pastoral counselor or a marriage and family therapist. Still, I didn't know anyone who practiced any of these professions; I never observed any such folk at work. In my youth, there were no guidance counselors in the schools, at least where I lived. They began to appear about the time I graduated from high school. That was in 1961. In those days, children who had problems in school were seen as "dumb" or "bad." They were hardly considered to have any sort of "disability," much less being "challenged" in whatever way. If you had a personal or family problem, it was your minister or family doctor, perhaps a teacher or a coach, or maybe a Scout or youth group leader whom you might have approached to try to talk with about your problem, in search of some help. Not that I, nor anyone else I knew, ever did. If I had any such problems, I was as unaware of them as I was surely sheltered in my family and church and community. My parents, as well as the other adults in my life, obviously worked hard at hiding such things from me and other children of my circumstances. Perhaps they were even trying to hide such things from themselves?

For example, I'm remembering a friend who may have been the smartest kid in high school. At least she made the best grades. That may have been because, apart from school, she never went anywhere. She surely had lots of time to study, because otherwise, her mother, a single parent, wouldn't let her out of the house. I expect her mom had been diagnosed paranoid schizophrenic. Looking back upon what must have been a painful adolescence for this girl, what I am aware of is just how unaware I was of what was going on in her life, even though everyone knew something wasn't quite right in their family. Whatever it may have been was never mentioned. Again, I would learn only years later that the legendary coach, who taught me and generations of other boys in our town how to play basketball, was a sick alcoholic. As a kid, that was not something of which I was ever aware. Somehow, I missed it, even as there were plenty of folk in our town who were just as invested in trying to "protect" this winsome and gifted fellow. Today we would call that "enabling."

If it sounds as though I was culturally or otherwise deprived, that may be so, except I heard the prominent psychiatrist and popular author, the late Scott Peck, lecture on one occasion. He shared a touching personal story from his adolescence. It seems that he was a student at a prestigious New England prep school, hardly the cultural backwater of anywhere. He said he wanted to leave the school. When he talked to several different people at the school, all of whom were authority figures, they all tried to talk him out of it. They assured him that if he left, he would be sabotaging his fast track to Harvard and assured success for the rest of his life. "And then," he said, "I went to a math teacher whom I had heard had worked on the atomic bomb. If that were so, I figured he must be the smartest person in the school. I told him my problem, and he just listened. I asked him what I should do. And for the longest time he didn't answer. It looked like he was struggling, that he was thinking real hard about what was so troubling to me. And then, finally, he said, 'I don't know. I don't know what you should do.'"

"I made my decision," Peck said. "I left the school. And when I reflect on that experience, I think that man may have saved my life. Looking back on it, I think I was that depressed. And my logic seemed to be, if the smartest guy in a school full of smart people didn't know what I should do, maybe there wasn't as much wrong with me as I thought. Maybe what I wanted to do wasn't so bad, so crazy after all."

It wasn't until I was a seminary student that I became exposed to the value of counseling. It was encouraged in that environment. Even if one isn't aware of "having any problems," if you will, being a minister is a vulnerable vocation, where one needs to be rather aware and highly sensitized to what is going on with oneself and others, both intra- and interpersonally. Such exposure, even confrontation, is promoted in an environment where persons are being shaped and formed to function effectively and responsibly as professional clergy in the service of the church. That was certainly true when and where I went to seminary.

Still, my seeking counseling wasn't quite that abstract. In those days I was supporting myself, a wife, and a child; working full-time; and going to seminary full-time. I had overworked most of my life and had become rather adept (or perhaps adapted?) at doing so. In fact, I had come to pretty much define myself on such terms, complete, of course, with a fair amount of ego recognition, not to mention a pretty good dose of "Look how hard I'm working" martyrdom to go with it.

If I had always managed the stress in my life fairly well, by this time in my life I seemed to have met my match. I wasn't doing such a good job. Before, most of my authority figures had usually just told me how great I was and cheered me on. Now, for the first time in my life, there were people I admired and respected, my mentors and even some peers, who were starting to say things to me like, "Who do you think you are?" and "What do you think you're doing?" It was sufficient to get my attention, or at least I had matured enough by then to hear what they were saying, and I sought professional help from a pastoral counselor. I began to learn some things about myself of which I had been quite unaware, and I began to change rather significantly with respect to how I looked at myself and others. I would describe the experience as positive and healing, leading to substantive change and growth in my life. That process has continued over many years.

While I learned to appreciate the value of counseling as a seminary student, I hardly thought that doing such work would be how I would spend most of my ministry. This also suggests an interesting irony, because there were others among my peers who clearly sensed a calling to such a vocation and were preparing to serve as chaplains and pastoral counselors in specialized ministry settings. My experience was otherwise. While in seminary, I read the autobiography of the famous Baptist preacher Harry Emerson Fosdick, entitled *The Living of These Days*.[3] It was striking to me to read about Fosdick as a student at Union Theological Seminary in New York City in the early years of the 20th century, including his honest telling of what had been, for him, a "nervous breakdown" during that time in his life. Still, as he described his recovery and his growing sense of vocation, of a calling, it seemed quite confirming to me. Nurtured, as was I, in the life of the church, it seemed as though the church had affirmed and called forth Fosdick's gifts in much the same way it had called forth mine. He too had gone to seminary, not so much to become a minister, as to learn, along the way of formal theological study, that indeed a minister was who he was called to be and the work he was called to do. Thinking he would likely be a theologian and teacher, Fosdick discovered in seminary that he was not, in fact, a scholar, but more of a generalist, that his were

3. Harry Emerson Fosdick, *The Living of These Days* (New York: Harper and Row, 1956).

the gifts of a preacher and a pastor. Similarly, God was working in my life and experience in a comparable setting, more than a half-century later, in quite the same way. I graduated from seminary, and I was ordained to the vocation of pastor with a deep sense of calling that this was who I had become and was becoming and what I would do with my life.

However, the doors that opened for me were in more specialized ministries. First, I started as a campus minister in a university setting, and then I worked as a prep school chaplain. Initially, this was a bit disconcerting. I wondered if I were somehow mistaken with respect to what I was supposed to be doing with my life. Nevertheless, I proceeded to walk through the only doors that seemed open, both of which prioritized the ministry of counseling. I pursued continued specialized training in psychotherapy, although not in the most formal and traditional of ways. Among other opportunities, this included my participation in the "Synanon game," an intense and highly confrontational form of group therapy in the setting of a rather ominous federal prison. Such that, even today, I get calls, not infrequently, from fellow-therapists asking me to see some character they find themselves uncomfortable working with.

I was then offered a position as director of a community mental health clinic, a public agency where I worked for many years and was afforded extensive opportunity to develop my skills and credentials as a mental health professional, both as a pastoral counselor and as a marriage and family therapist. During those years, I developed a private counseling practice with a group of family physicians, was invited to teach in two different graduate programs in clinical counseling, and began to consult with private industry, the military, and public sector organizations.

It would be many years later, as something of a surprise—what is it C. S. Lewis called it? *Surprised By Joy!*—that I would be called to serve as pastor of a congregation, back to where I had thought I was headed when I finished seminary. Sometimes our journey in this life seems to take some side roads. That can be confusing, even discouraging. Often, however, when we look back on our lives, with the perspective of enough time or distance, we can discern some providence and likely some grace in it all. That is certainly true for me, and it is out of my experience that this book is written. I am not trying to argue for or against the value of counseling in anyone's life. Rather, I am trying to describe and interpret much of what I have learned along the way, as a client, therapist, teacher, consultant, and supervisor.

I often explain that I entered seminary in search of some answers, but what I was given were some different questions. There was a time in my life when I didn't understand what that meant, but I do now. Truth is like that. It usually has more than one side to it. How you see things has a lot to do with where you're standing. As often as not, the kind of answers we get in life have to do with the kind of questions we ask.

As to or for whom this book is written, it is necessary for me to reframe that question, which is not surprising for a therapist. We do that a lot. I am reminded of my buddy, the late Grady Nutt, a gifted minister who made a living and quite a reputation as a humorist. Even today, you can still see Grady on *Hee Haw* reruns on television. Some years before his untimely death, Grady wrote a neat little book. I can't recall the title, but it had to do with youth and their self-concept. It was a book about self-esteem, from a Christian way of seeing things. Grady told me he wrote the book three times. "The first time," he said, "I wrote it for my professors, those who had mentored and taught me, so they would know I had read the right books, that I knew what I was supposed to know. The second time, I wrote it for my peers, so they would think much the same thing, so they would respect me and what I had learned. But then, I finally sat down at the kitchen table and pictured my next door neighbor, a little twelve-year-old boy named Maury"—I think that was the name—"and I wrote the book for him, as though he were sitting across from me and we were having a conversation. The last time I wrote that book, I wrote it for Maury."

That is how I understand the writing of this book. It is not, however, an imagined conversation. It is hardly a conversation I would like to have with anyone. Rather, what I have written in these pages, and faithfully so, are the kinds of conversations I have been having with all sorts of people over the past thirty-five years. These include my counselors, teachers, supervisors, colleagues, peers, and friends, as well as clients who have invested themselves, including their time and their money, in and with me, who have sought my help and my presence in the struggles and celebrations of their lives. This group also includes students I have taught, counselors and aspiring counselors I have supervised, and folk in the congregation I now serve. This book is nothing more and nothing less than that: an extended conversation over many years with many different people. If it is a book about counseling, and certainly counseling from the perspective of a Christian minister, it is because that is who I am and what it is I have been doing for so long.

Therefore, if I were to characterize this book, it is at least two things: it is authentic, and it is provincial. In the sense that what I have shared in these pages is neither fictional nor hypothetical, even as it reflects the culture and ethos of where I have lived and worked and the people I have lived and worked with; where and when I was born, to whom I was born and by whom I was reared; where I went to school; the fact that I have by now lived beyond half a normal lifetime, that I am male and Euro-American, and that the only language I speak is English; that I am heterosexual, a spouse, a parent; that I grew up in the small-town coal-mining culture of the Midwest and have lived most of my adult life in the South; that I am a person of modest ability and achievement and have developed, over the course of my living, some sense of gratitude for the given-ness of my life, for both the friendships extended and the opportunities afforded me, as well as my share of failures, rejections, and disappointments.

Is this a textbook? Not in the highly technical or scholarly sense. Hardly. It's too shallow for that. What is it they say? "Deep down, we're all shallow!" Is it a self-help book? Perhaps. I would think that experienced therapists and any number of other kinds of people-helpers, professional or otherwise, might find this book at least interesting, perhaps even helpful here and there. Since I primarily teach and train counselors in the process of developing their skills, those who aspire to do such work might particularly find this book of value. Readers who have been in therapy, who are consumers of, or are perhaps potential consumers of mental health services might, as well, find this book informative.

My suggestion is that anyone reading this book think of it in terms of overhearing a conversation. Some years ago, the winsome Disciples scholar and preacher Fred Craddock wrote an important book with a catchy title, *Overhearing the Gospel*.[4] Overhearing can be a valid, helpful, and important way of learning anything. It tends to be indirect, which is often how we learn some important things, at least initially. In particular, it allows one to maintain a certain distance. It doesn't require quite the level of involvement. Indeed, such a way of learning can often be less threatening, certainly if one is not so sure he is all that interested in learning, or learning about whatever.

I invite readers to take such a stance with regard to this book. It may, after all, be the best way to read it, certainly when I speak from such an

4. Fred Craddock, *Overhearing the Gospel* (Nashville: Abingdon, 1978).

explicit Christian point of view. If one is not a Christian, nor inclined to be one, for whatever reasons, to overhear whatever I am saying here to others who share a similar faith and values commitment might be the best approach.

Years ago, I read Claude Steiner's *Scripts People Live.*[5] It is, I think, my favorite of all the books on Transactional Analysis (TA). Among other important things Steiner says in that book, he claims that healthy relationships are characterized by "no secrets, no Rescues, no power-plays." Rescuing, capitalized as it is, is some more TA jargon. It is doing or trying to do for anyone else what they can do for themselves, and/or may not have asked you to do for them. You're on your own when it comes to the meaning of power-plays or secrets. However, I am claiming that in writing this book I have heeded Claude Steiner's insistence that there be no secrets. By that, I mean that the best psychotherapists have no hidden power or powers, no secret or inside information. If your counselor happens to know something you may not, that does not mean that you can't or don't have a right to know it, too. If you are not a therapist, and it seems as though I am talking, in this book, to another therapist, or she is talking to me, I would invite you to overhear, or perhaps even to enter into the conversation. We will all likely be the better for it. Indeed, I believe I illustrate rather thoroughly in these pages that the best learning, the best insight, and the best understanding goes both ways, between client and counselor, between student and teacher, between supervisee and supervisor.

There is a logic to this book, in terms of progression. However, it can be read cafeteria style, as in pick what you want. To extend that analogy, we often take too much, and sometimes the combination of things may seem rather strange. Be that as it may, the first chapter in this book is a discussion of a variety of issues related to mental health services in general and psychotherapy in particular. In this chapter, I interpret various mental health professions, in relation to counseling, and conclude with a brief interpretation of various counseling theories and approaches to psychotherapy.

In chapters two through five, I develop the concept of balance as integral to good mental health, emotional well-being, moral and spiritual health, and social functioning. If this book were a golf course, chapter two would be what is called "the signature hole." If you don't play golf, that

---

5. Claude Steiner, *Scripts People Live* (New York: Grove Press, 1974).

analogy may not mean much. Let me explain. In this chapter, I interpret the function of balance in the context of a Hebrew-Christian view of sin and the classical Greek concept of what is tragic. I explain how I have learned to pay attention to matters of balance out of my training and experience as a therapist and relate this to a variety of tensions or dualities common to the lives of most people. If this chapter may seem the most accessible, easier or lighter reading, it's likely because, in my judgment, one wouldn't necessarily need to be a professional counselor or a pastoral theologian to appreciate it. However, the latest research suggests that only thirty-one percent of college graduates today are functionally literate; one of the criteria being that functional literacy is "the ability to read a complex book and extrapolate from it."[6] I don't consider this book "complex" in any way, even though the most common criticism I've heard over the years, in the congregation I serve, is that my sermons are "too intellectual." Unfortunately, if that's the case, we're in real trouble, when it comes to the "dumbing down" of America, even at church!

Chapter three, "Balanced Families," provides an introduction to what is called family systems theory, with which any credentialed marriage and family therapist would be familiar. I illustrate and interpret this theory in relation to both marriage and parenting.

Chapter four draws on the Myers-Briggs Type Indicator and the significance of balance in relation to the polarities presented in that instrument. The MBTI is, among any number of personality inventories, one that seems to be quite popular in our culture: the tendencies of the extrovert and the introvert, the intuitive and the senser, the thinker and the feeler, the judger and the perceiver. What I have done with these various temperament traits is to discuss them, beyond a general introduction, as they impact upon the person and the work of a counselor. I discuss this in some detail since the Myers-Briggs provides an appropriate framework in which to consider these matters. For example, what seem to be the relative strengths and weaknesses of various therapists and the particular style they might reflect in terms of personality type? Since I tend to be more of an intuitive than a senser, in Myers-Briggs-ese, it strikes me that this book, in general, might likely appeal more to another intuitive than to a senser, or perhaps make more sense, particularly in terms of *how* it is

---

6. *The Post and Courier,* December 26, 2005, 1A.

written. This is because sensers and intuitives sometimes have problems trying to understand each other.

Chapter five, "Balanced Religion," is explicitly theological, from my perspective as a Christian minister and pastoral counselor. Years ago, I taught in an all-boys prep school, The Baylor School in Chattanooga, Tennessee. It was a pretty macho kind of place, as one might expect. Sports were a big deal. In fact, all students were required to participate in either interscholastic athletics or physical education. As a result, almost everyone on the faculty coached something or other. As legend had it, if a boy were to approach a coach, asking, "Are we going to practice today? It looks like it's going to rain," the coach would say, "Son, it never rains after three o'clock at Baylor!" In fact, nearly every teacher in the school was called "coach," including the few women who taught there. There was the chemistry "coach," the glee-club "coach," the Latin "coach," who, by the way, *was* the highly succesful football coach (not that I've known many football coaches who've taught Latin). Since I was the school chaplain, the kids called me "the God coach." Come to think of it, that's not such a bad way to think of a minister, at least this one. In "Balanced Religion," I discuss a variety of ways that Christian faith can get pretty sick for lack of balance. Conversely, a balanced faith tends to reflect a reasonably healthy relationship with God, oneself, and others.

I need to add that when I speak theologically, I commonly use the term Hebrew-Christian, or merely Christian. Today, Islam, which is also a monotheistic religion and is rooted in a similar theological tradition, has become a prominent reality for many. However, I have hardly studied the Qur'an in the way I have studied the Hebrew Bible, our Christian Old Testament, nor have I been privileged to have the kind of positive relationships with any Muslims as I have had with several Jews. Consequently, I don't know the religion of Islam in any way comparable to my understanding of Judaism and classic Hebrew thought, out of which any faithful interpretation of Christian faith must be understood. This is but another of my limitations, and I am the poorer for it. Nevertheless, those are my circumstances, and this is why, throughout this book, I can only legitimately offer my understanding and interpretation of Hebrew-Christian theology and ethics.

In the last chapter, I tend to three different matters that are important to me as a counselor and a minister. The first concerns the various stages of human development, in particular, the work of Erik Erikson.

The second has to do with certain values I see as implicit in a constructive counseling process, of which I suspect many therapists aren't often
aware. Finally, I reflect upon the person and the work of a therapist as a
paradigm for "doing" theology from my perspective as a Christian.

As to whatever in this book may be original, that is debatable. Not
much, I suspect. There is little here that I haven't learned from someone,
and I have tried to be faithful in acknowledging who such people are,
for they have blessed my life. Anything else is my responsibility. In the
words of Rocky Balboa: "I think I invented it."[7] Likewise, I would hardly
describe this book as controversial or sensational, in the sense of how
such characteristics often help sell books, whether they are ever read or
not. When it comes to any kind of psychotherapy, much less the matter of
Christian faith, the field is awfully broad. Different people, even among
the best counselors or ministers, often understand, interpret, or go about
their work in ways that would seem so different. Not that there is anything wrong with this.

When I was in seminary, my friend and classmate Michael Hester
once said. "You don't take courses. You take teachers." Since he, unlike
myself, came from an educated family, I took him at his word. I figured
he knew something I didn't. My experience so far has proven him right,
so I have presented in the pages of this book how I best understand the
work of the effective counselor and the counseling process, what makes
the most sense to me, how good therapists seem to operate, and what
their work looks like, at least as I have experienced it as a client and have
studied, practiced, and taught this science, which is even more of an art. I
won't even claim that what I advocate is the "best" way, nor is it hardly the
only way to do counseling. However, it is my way, and I'll stand by it.

Dr. Hester's observation has been a helpful reminder across the years
whenever I have attended a professional conference, lecture, or workshop.
However much or however little the presenter may seem to know or not
know about whatever the topic, I can likely learn something from her if I
believe: "You don't take courses; you take teachers." Often when I attend
such meetings, I'm amused to overhear conversations taking place during
a break, conversations concerning what is "wrong" with the presentation,
about what the presenter apparently "doesn't know" or "isn't doing right,"
according to whomever and his particular source of knowledge or expe-

7. *Rocky*, directed by John G. Avildsen, Chartoff-Winkler Productions, 1976.

rience. This seems to be a favorite pastime among my professional colleagues in such settings, where everyone present surely knows more and can present such material better than anyone else in attendance. What's that definition of an expert? "A 'little spert' away from home!" Unless the operative word is "different," rather than "more," or "better," or "right," or "wrong." I have found that this way of thinking tends to make my life more enjoyable than it might be otherwise. I learn a lot more, sometimes even rather serendipitously, when I pay more attention to *how* someone understands and interprets something, particularly when it concerns something I'm supposed to know, or at least think I know a lot about.

I'm remembering a college English teacher who was famous for saying, "This book either 'finds' you, or it doesn't." So it is or will be, I suspect, with this book, at least for those who choose to read it. I have thought of how I might have written it differently, even better, not that I ever could, mind you, because then, you see, it would be a different book, and it would hardly be mine. It was, in fact, my church history professor in seminary, Glenn Hinson, who taught me how to read a book. Since I had been in school for a while, you'd think I might have learned that by then, but not so. Dr. Hinson explained that most educated people have been taught to read books critically. Sometimes that has to do with what we like. More often, it seems, critical reading has even more to do with what we don't like, with whatever it is we can find that is "wrong," in whatever way or other, with what has been written. Not that this is necessarily a bad thing. Still, Dr. Hinson claimed that the fairest way to read a book is to ask oneself, "Does this book do what it sets out to do? Does it accomplish what it claims its purpose to be?" And not that Dr. Hinson wasn't and isn't a bona fide intellectual, critical thinker, and genuine scholar. Still, I would see him as even more of a Christian, in the deepest and best sense of what that means. There is, in his suggestion, indeed a touch of grace. There may even be those who read this book who will extend some of the same to me.

I also want to comment on this important matter. Counseling is inherently microcosmic, in that therapists deal, almost exclusively, with one person or, in the case of those of us who work out of a systemic orientation, one family (or whatever the system) at a time. Throughout my professional life, I have, however, tried to be a responsible participant in the larger world of social, moral, and political affairs. In recent years this has included, in particular, my role as president of the Charleston (SC)

Chapter of Americans United for the Separation of Church and State. Since, ironically, the more secular a government, the more vitally religion tends to flourish. Similarly, at least from a Christian perspective, imposed religion ends up defeating its very purpose. If the healing of persons, families, and organizations is the preoccupation of this book, the healing of society is no less important. And while I can't, given my obvious limitations, imagine writing a credible book on society, public morality, or politics, in any macrocosmic sense, some of what I suggest in this book is, I believe, relevant to the humanizing and civilizing of the larger society in which we live, locally, nationally, and globally.

For nearly twenty years, I wrote a column, "Healthy Living," in the Summerville (SC) *Journal-Scene*, which dealt primarily with personal and family matters. In more recent years I have written a periodic "Dear Abby" column in the Sunday "Faith and Values" section of the Charleston (SC) *Post and Courier*. Readers send in questions, which I then attempt to answer. I initially thought the focus of the questions would tend toward matters of personal and family life. However, they have instead reflected more social, political, or ethical concerns, questions regarding the religion and politics of sexual orientation, for instance, whether the Bible should be taught in our public schools, should the government be concerned with the financial affairs of popular televangelists, etc. Consequently, what I've just noted stands out rather starkly when I look back over the writing of this book and how it hardly attends, in any overt way, to such social, political, and ethical matters.

For example, it's hard for me to imagine that one could read the Gospels of the Christian New Testament and not realize that Jesus has so much to say, in such a penetrating way, regarding the problem of economic disparity. As Jesus seems to frame it, it is less a "poverty" problem, than a problem of "wealth." This is about as scandalous an observation as anyone could possibly make regarding the consumerist culture of modern and postmodern America. The fact that I have not attended to this seminal concern of Jesus, in any explicit way, even in the chapter on "Balanced Religion," is glaring, at least to me, as a Christian. It's like Thanksgiving without the turkey, Christmas without the tree, the Fourth of July without the flag, a birthday party without the cake. Something important would seem to be missing.

Recently, I was on a panel of representatives of various world religions at a College of Charleston symposium. Each of us was asked, "What is the most pressing moral concern in your particular religious tradition?" I was prepared to answer, "Ecology," since it's hard to imagine sustaining much of any quality of life apart from adequate clean air and water. However, I changed my response to "Exploitation," because I see that concept being more comprehensive regarding a variety of concerns, certainly from the ethical perspective of Christian faith, including, for example, the abuse of power with respect to political and social violence, racism, sexism, and economic and environmental exploitation. In this book, however, I have hardly tended to such matters.

I originally wrote this book in 1996. In the ensuing years, I have played with it and picked at it in various ways, while submitting it to various publishers. Of the several rejections I've received, some have been cordial; some, just as impersonal. Upon Wipf & Stock offering me a contract to publish *Balanced Living*, I have not revised it in any substantive way. Consequently, the book strikes me as being dated in some respects—most notably, some of the references. Still, I believe it also retains a certain relevance and timeliness, perhaps even timelessness. In "Bowen Natural Systems Theory," for example (which I reference or allude to in various parts of the book, most notably in the chapters on "Balanced Families" and "Balance and Personality Type"), social, cultural, and economic factors are minimized, compared to such important interpersonal dynamics as "differentiation" and "reactivity," whatever the system.

Readers will note that I have used feminine and masculine pronouns alternately, and quite as arbitrarily, except when referring to a particular male or female. It's just another way of trying to play fair among all of us, at least males and females, in the human family. If you understand this, the alternate and arbitrary gender of the pronouns may not, then, seem quite as confusing, or perhaps even as annoying as they might otherwise.

Among the several people I wish to acknowledge and thank for their help with this project, I mention Patricia Day and Vada Simpkins, who once served our church faithfully and took on even more responsibility than usual in helping me with this effort, as have Lee Alderman and Debbie Ritter in recent years. The graduate students in my family therapy courses at Webster University and The Citadel have inspired this book, as they have persisted in asking: "When are you going to write all this stuff down?" The majority of students I teach work in some of the most difficult human service jobs. In addition, they are pursuing their master's degrees, after which they won't make a lot more money, while continuing to serve, as it were, "on the front lines." As helping professionals, they will continue to work with primarily an economically vulnerable population in our society. I find that inspiring. My students have heard most of the less religious stuff I've written about here, in some form or other. I've been talking with them, even as they have been talking with me about these things for years. On the other hand, the more explicit Christian teaching in this book has grown, over the past fourteen years, out of my ministry as pastor of First Christian Church, "Charleston's Historic Disciples Congregation."

For now, I offer to you, the reader, what I often say to folk in the life of our church, as well as to students, clients, friends, and my kids, people I care for most: "Stay loose and tough and rest in some grace."

1

Counseling and Psychotherapy

"[Famous golf teacher] Mr. [Harvey] Penick used to charge five dollars an hour for his lessons, and people were always after him to raise his fees. He would say, 'I use small words, so how can I charge big prices.'"

—Tom Kite[1]

IN THIS BOOK, I USE COUNSELING AND PSYCHOTHERAPY SYNONYMOUSLY. Not that a card-carrying psychoanalyst would typically think of herself as a counselor. Hardly. Many therapists are known to be rather picky about such things. Or that a high school guidance counselor or a counselor on the staff of the Department of Vocational Rehabilitation might likely think of himself as a psychotherapist. Most psychiatrists don't think of themselves as counselors. In fact, this seems to be a rather common distinction: that psychotherapy, or therapy, is associated with the medical profession, whereas counseling tends to be more often associated with such fields as education and ministry.

A common connotation is that psychotherapy has to do with more serious forms of psychopathology, with what one might consider "deeper" problems. Also, psychotherapy is often associated with psychoanalysis, or with more psychodynamic approaches to counseling, in particular, as this may have to do with the function of the unconscious. It is debatable whether this association is promoted or not by those who work out of such a theoretical orientation. Still, the average layperson often thinks of any form of counseling as psychoanalysis. For example, whenever there is a cartoon in the *New Yorker* poking fun at therapists or their patients, it will picture someone lying on a couch talking about their dreams or their

---

1. Don Wade, ed., *"And Then Jack Said to Arnie . . ."* (Raleigh: Contemporary Books, 1991), 144.

fantasies, or perhaps freely associating. Many clients have said to me, "I guess I need to be here. I've never had any psychoanalysis, but my wife said I needed to talk to someone." However, psychoanalysis is actually a specific form of psychotherapy, though not necessarily an approach that is held in particularly high regard by various other therapists who are just as highly trained and whose work with their clients may be quite as demanding or difficult.

Here is something else to keep in mind. Medically trained counselors, such as psychiatrists and psychiatric nurses, usually refer to their clients as "patients," while most other psychotherapists generally refer to their patients as "clients." I once treated a clinical psychologist. Our work together was fruitful, and he claimed that, among several things about me and what I did with him that he found helpful, one thing that was important to him was how I related to him, neither as a client nor as a patient, but as a "person."

Therefore, I am not willing to distinguish between counseling and psychotherapy in any way that suggests that counseling is a somehow inferior professional function or role. That line of thinking tends to reinforce a kind of professional snobbery, or elitism, which is all too common among mental health professionals. Essential to being a competent and ethical professional counselor is not only the acknowledgement of one's capability, but also a clear sense of one's limitations. For example, to refer a client to another therapist for any number of reasons, not least of which because of a patient's particular need does not necessarily imply that the referring counselor is in any way inferior. No one mental health professional, or any such grouping of professionals, is competent in treating all human problems. Indeed, any counselor astute and ethical enough to realize this and make appropriate referrals is likely among the more competent mental health professionals who offer their services, whatever they may call themselves.

I am, for example, a Fellow of the American Association of Pastoral Counselors. I am also an Approved Supervisor of the American Association for Marriage and Family Therapy. If I were to claim which of these credentials has traditionally reflected a more rigorous and demanding regimen of training, it would be that of the pastoral counselor. Because of this, I can hardly distinguish between the two in any way which suggests that counseling is somehow inferior to therapy. Ironically, if psychotherapy connotes a more psychodynamic, or what some might consider a more analytical approach to understanding and helping people, and counseling suggests less of such an emphasis, then most credentialed pastoral counselors tend to be psychotherapists, while many marriage and family therapists function more often as counselors. I'm afraid such distinctions between psychotherapy and counseling tend to be rather arbitrary at best, if not self-serving at worst.

Also, in this book, I use mental health synonymously with emotional health, with social health and functioning, as well as with moral and spiritual health. I think this is a valid way of understanding people in more holistic terms, except where mental health, or illness, refers specifically to organicity, to matters of brain tissue, body chemistry, or genetics. Even then, when dealing with what might seem to be more definitive matters, one still may find it difficult to distinguish such concerns from other factors of overall functioning that involve the emotional, social, moral, and spiritual dimensions of persons. Optimal mental health services value the expertise, the perspective, and the emphases of competent professionals trained in a variety of disciplines. This includes those who have studied biochemistry, genetics, and brain function, those who have studied dogs and rats and pigeons, as well as those who have read the Bible, Sophocles' *Antigone*, Augustine's *Confessions*, and Shakespeare's *King Lear*.

Trying to define psychotherapy, in any abstract sense, is difficult, if not nigh impossible, since it is understood in so many different and quite valid ways by a variety of mental health professionals who approach their work from a wide range of perspectives. What's that great line about preachers? "They're like manure. When you spread 'em around, they do some good. But when you put 'em in a pile, you know what you've got!" The same might surely be said of counselors—or as one of my cynical friends prefers to say, "cancelers." I'm afraid he may be right, at least when we take ourselves too seriously. Some therapists would emphasize the cognitive aspects of counseling; others, the affective or emotional; while still others, the behavioral. Some would focus on change, others on growth, and then again, others would place a high value on insight. In a textbook, *Current Psychotherapies*, co-edited with Danny Wedding, Raymond Corsini lists nine different counseling functions: "listening, questioning, evaluating, interpreting, supporting, explaining, informing, advising, and ordering."[2]

2. Raymond Corsini and Danny Wedding, eds., *Current Psychotherapies* (Itasca: F. E. Peacock Publishers, Inc., 1989), 2.

I was taught by a clinical psychologist who first supervised my counseling that the purpose of therapy was to help people change, according to
some mutually agreed upon goal(s) between the client(s) and the counselor. He claimed that what some call "growth" or "progress" or "improvement" is usually ambiguous and often manipulative. That is, people can
grow or progress or improve in becoming even more adept at how they
manipulate, control, avoid, or sabotage themselves. The importance of
change is clearly emphasized in the managed care environment of today's
mental health service delivery, specifically, behavioral change. Insurance
companies and other third-party providers demand treatment plans from
mental health professionals, who wish to be paid for their services by such
providers. The treatment plans spell out in rather specific detail how a
patient is going to be different, in what ways, and on what time frame, and
certainly in what manner this can and will be measured.

Change, under these conditions, refers specifically to a reduction in
the symptoms that brought the client to the counselor in the first place. In
addition, change will refer to some sort of prediction, if not a guarantee,
that further treatment will no longer be needed. In fact, I actually proved
myself something of a prophet nearly 30 years ago when a symposium of
graduate students in clinical counseling asked me what I thought would
be the more important issues in counseling in the future. My response?
"Who's going to pay for it?" Whenever this is the prime consideration
in providing mental health services, measurable behavioral change will
be the goal, whether we like it or not. Therefore, therapists who frame
their work in terms of helping clients feel better, become more assertive,
have an improved self-concept, have greater insight into their problems,
or mature spiritually will tend to have more difficulty negotiating with the
"bottom line" mentality of today's managed care, in which the "business"
of mental health service delivery is just that.

Ironically, while I was taught that observable and measurable change
on the part of clients was the goal of counseling, I worked for many years
in a community mental clinic that served an emotionally, socially, and
economically vulnerable population, in which the most important goal
seemed to be helping patients stay out of the hospital.

It was in this context that I first began to understand support as a
crucial function of counseling, working with folk whose lives might not
change a great deal, even under the most optimal of conditions. If such support were withdrawn, or not available, however, clients would tend to de-

compensate and regress disproportionately to whatever growth or change one might likely notice in the opposite direction. If the quality of their lives would surely deteriorate, often fairly rapidly, without adequate support, then providing that same level of support normally did not tend to produce significant improvement. I have also observed a similar pattern with many so-called "higher functioning," or "private practice" patients: for many, the continued presence of a capable and caring therapist in their lives helps them to at least maintain their level of functioning, while the absence of such tends to produce a rather predictable pattern of deterioration. Therefore, I highly value the supportive function of counseling.

At this juncture, let me raise a concern over which I have some ambivalence. Those who have worked in public outpatient mental health settings know of what I speak: de-institutionalization, or keeping people out of the hospital, has been a primary goal for a number of years. The rationale is that this is both more cost-effective and more humane. As regards the latter, I'm not so sure. For example, I have had many patients over the years describe their hospitalizations to me in more positive, less negative terms. It seemed to me, from listening to many such patients, that while they were in the hospital, as much as they may have resisted and resented going, their diet was better, their hygiene and health care were better, and certainly their socialization seemed to improve. While such patients are often quite isolated socially, even or likely in their home community or families, they have frequently described having closer and more significant friendships in the hospital, in terms of both other patients, as well as staff. As a result, I have some doubts that keeping people out of the hospital is always the most humane consideration, even if it is more cost-effective.

As for trying to define psychotherapy in any abstract sense, I won't. I have chosen, rather, to use more of a descriptive approach, which is more concrete, more specific than general. I will offer such examples and illustrations throughout this book. For now, let me offer two. The first involves a young woman, her husband, and her children. I saw them some years ago, and I was able to intervene in their lives in some ways that were helpful. This is not always the case for any counselor, and while I could surely describe and interpret this family and their circumstances, as well as my work with them, on more clinical terms, I'll let this young woman tell her own story. I think it important for those of us who are therapists to try to understand our clients, as much as possible, on their terms and in their words.

In this case, I asked this young woman to write her story, since she was obviously bright and articulate and had shared with me her plans to eventually attend college and become a high school English teacher. In this piece, she has changed the names of her husband and children and some of their actual circumstances for the sake of their anonymity. Here's how she tells her story:

"A CLIENT'S CASE STUDY"

It's hard to write about something that seems to have happened EONS ago! I've only been in therapy for a year and a half, but in that time I've learned so much about myself that it makes my head spin. I've really grown up a lot.

When I first called to make an appointment with Dr. Knight I was a desperate 23-year-old with two small children and a faltering marriage. I was suffering with postpartum depression, and I didn't want to have anything to do with my four-month-old daughter. I was fearful at times of hurting her, and I felt horrible for even thinking such a thing. My husband, Bob, was afraid to go to work in the morning for fear of what he would find when he came home. He insisted that I find a way to deal with it or he would divorce me. That was scary enough to make me seek counseling. Even though I did not think I was "crazy," I had started to worry that I might be.

From the time I found out I was pregnant with Jennifer I didn't want her. I wanted to have an abortion, but after discussing this with Bob, I decided not to. He said that I'd better make that decision on my own and soon, because he didn't think he could live with me if I aborted his baby after the first four or six weeks. I felt coerced into the decision to keep the baby, and then I felt guilty for having wanted to end the pregnancy in the first place.

The reason I didn't want to have a second baby was directly related to experiences with my son, Jason. Although I very much wanted to have Jason and had planned to be the perfect mom, after he was born three and half years ago I had many negative feelings toward him. He was colicky and I never took time away from him. So, in spite of the fact that I wanted and loved him very much, some-

6

times I just hated this precious baby for taking away my freedom. I even secretly wished that he would die or be kidnapped. Can you imagine the guilt a mother feels over such a thought? How, I thought, would I ever handle this type of feeling toward a baby that I hadn't wanted in the first place? Needless to say, I was pretty depressed throughout most of the pregnancy.

When Jennifer was born two years ago Jason was not quite 20-months old, and he was my world. I didn't want to share that world with this or any other baby. In the delivery room, when the nurse tried to hand her to me, I said, "Give it to him (Bob)." I was only in the hospital for two days during which I had to take care of Jenny, but when I came home I focused 90 percent of my energy on Jason again. I only spent time with her when she needed to be fed, and then I would look down at her and wish that she would go away. I told Bob that I wanted to put her up for adoption. He said he'd leave me if I did, but I was afraid I'd hurt her. I resented her for breaking apart my marriage and thought, "If only she weren't here, I could pick up the pieces of my life and put it all back together."

I didn't know what to expect from a therapist at our first session, and I was nervous. Bob had told me not to tell him that I had expressed a fear of hurting my child. He said Dr. Knight would call the Department of Social Services and they would take the kids away from us. Although that was exactly what I wanted for Jenny, I didn't want to lose Jason, and I was sure that if they took one of the kids they would take both. Also, if they took the kids away, Bob would surely leave me. So, what was I supposed to tell this guy anyway?

I was afraid he'd think I was a terrible person for having such bad feelings, but from where I stood I had a lot to lose if I didn't talk to him. So I did tell Dr. Knight my feelings. Instead of judging me, like I had expected him to, he simply told me that it was not unusual to have such negative feelings, even toward my child, and that I was not a "bad" person. Then he asked me where I thought those feelings were coming from. I didn't know at that point. I thought he was going to give me the answers. Instead he gave me reassurance and the guidance to find my own answers.

Through the course of my therapy I learned things about myself I never would have guessed. Although I had always known that I

7

was a perfectionist, I didn't realize that this would eventually be my downfall. After all, I was brought up thinking that if it's worth doing, it's worth doing right. Through my school years I strove to be the perfect student. My mom and dad knew that I was smart and talented, so they pushed me to develop "to my full potential." If my little sister brought home a 'B' on her report card, they told her it was wonderful because they knew school was hard for her. If I brought home the same 'B', I was told that it was okay, but they were sure that it would be an 'A' next time. Dad had even occasionally asked, "Why is this only an 'A'? Why not an 'A-plus'?" Although looking back I can see that he never meant to hurt me, it was hard to always feel that I wasn't quite "good enough" at anything.

After I got married I tried to be the perfect wife. The only thing I had to go on was what I saw my mom do as I was growing up. She seemed very strong to me, but always dissatisfied. She did everything she was supposed to do (cooking, cleaning, laundry, etc.) without ever outwardly complaining. Instead of telling dad when she was not happy about a situation, she just shrugged her shoulders and worked harder at doing everything herself. Mom gave 200 percent to the marriage and never seemed to expect dad to contribute anything. He seemed to give very little of himself to anyone.

Now that I had kids, I was driven to be the perfect mom, and once again my model was my own mother. I felt the perfect mom was someone who adored her children and had the patience to smile all the time, no matter what they did or said. She stayed home full-time so she could devote herself to her children and do all those special "mom" things—baking cookies, arts & crafts, teaching her three-year-old to read. Mine had done all those things, and she always put her children first. Even her own needs came second to those of her family. Taking care of everyone else seemed to keep her going. Now I realize it probably just tore her apart.

Being the perfect wife and mother didn't seem like such a difficult task at first, even though I had set my standards very high. I wasn't a career woman and Bob's salary was adequate to support us, so I thought I was all set. What I didn't realize is that 24 hours a day, seven days a week, 52 weeks a year is a long time to spend with anyone, even your own kids! After all, on only one paycheck Bob and I seldom went out on "dates" without the kids, and I never went anywhere alone. Every time the kids got on my nerves I'd convince myself that I must find some new method of child rearing, because the one I had certainly wasn't working. I never believed anyone who told me I had great kids. I thought they were just awful.

But the problem wasn't with my kids, it was with me. Along with prolonged exposure to them, I was into self-deprivation. Since I was such a bad mom, I certainly didn't deserve to have time and nice things for myself. So I never bought myself anything new, not even clothes (which I desperately needed after three years and two pregnancies). There was always something that the kids or Bob needed more than what I needed. I was sacrificing for my family, and that was how it should be, I thought.

Along with all of that, I had also put upon myself the added responsibility of mothering my own mom. Although she and dad lived 800 miles away, I felt that I was her only emotional support system. My sister was still in high school and dad just didn't seem to care about mom anymore. So when she called, I tried to be attentive to her needs and to give her the support she was crying out for. Trips "home" to visit became a nightmare for me because then I had to be the perfect daughter, on top of everything else, for my parents' sake. It's odd that part of my pain came from trying to ease the pain mom was in because she, too, tries to be everything to everybody.

After my first few sessions with Dr. Knight I started to think he was the crazy one. He kept telling me that I was doing the best that I knew how, and that I was not "bad" or "crazy". He said that I needed time to myself and that I did deserve to do some nice things for just me. And then I'd go home to Bob who would say something like, "What are you getting for my $80 an hour, anyway?" He'd say that I didn't seem to be getting any better, and that I was wasting a lot of money just to have someone to talk to. I wanted to stop therapy at that time because I felt that I had failed. Bob was right, I was wasting his money.

The next time I saw Dr. Knight I told him that this would be our last appointment because therapy was obviously doing nothing for me. He said that was fine, if it was really what I thought I should do. But about four days later I found myself calling to make another appointment. I did need someone to talk to, and he was the only one I could open up to without fearing rejection. He really listened to me. He made me listen to myself.

After a few more sessions I had started to take Dr. Knight's advice, and I put both kids into a Mother's Morning Out program at a local church once a week. I also started to believe that I wasn't a bad person and that I might be able to put my life together again. Bob was still threatening me with divorce once in awhile and it was very hard to live with that looming over my head. Once I felt that I could really stand behind my words if I had to, I mustered the courage to counter one of his threats. When he said divorce, I said, "Fine. If that's really what you want, just give me six months to get on my feet with the kids and you're out." I told him that I didn't want to divorce him but that I didn't want him to be miserable either. I could no longer live with the day-to-day fear that he would take off. He didn't know what to say, so I asked him to come with me to see Dr. Knight. He agreed, even though he was sure it wouldn't help. I was the one with the problem, he said.

Those next three or four sessions were spent trying to explain to Bob just what I was going through, how I was beating myself up for not being the perfect everything. I also had to enlist Dr. Knight's help to convince him that I did deserve to buy some things for myself. Bob was of the "I-Earned-It-So-I'll-Decide-How-It's-Spent" school. He felt that since I wasn't bringing any money in, I shouldn't feel free to spend his. Also, he thought that since I had chosen to be a full-time wife and mother, I should never complain. I should have known what I was getting into. I had time away from the kids when they were sleeping and that should be plenty. I didn't need anything else, he thought. Once I got a third party—and a man, at that—who suggested that I did contribute my fair share to the family, that I did need an occasional break from the kids and that I deserved to spend some of the money he made, he started to listen. His acceptance of all of this took a little more time, but once it kicked in, our marriage started to get back on track.

One of the first things I learned in therapy was that I needed to start asserting myself. Even when I was ready to put that lesson into practice, Bob wasn't quite ready for it. All of a sudden, it seemed, I'd tell him what I wanted instead of just going along with whatever he said. And although he had always complained when I just sighed "Fine" to everything, it was hard for him to stop and consider my opinions and to not criticize my way of doing things. We had to make many compromises. I learned to stand up for myself and Bob learned to back down sometimes. I juggled the budget so that we could both have some spending money of our own without going into debt, and he stopped demanding to know where every single penny went. We made sure there was money put aside for babysitters, and we took time away from the kids, both together and separately.

Once I got used to taking time for myself I started to feel less guilty about not being perfect at everything I tried to do. I joined a woman's club. I started working out at a local gym, and I began to buy myself some new clothes. I even bought some things for myself "just because I wanted to!" I was treating myself better, looking better and feeling better about myself than I ever had. The kids didn't get on my nerves nearly as often, and when they did I dealt with it, without blaming myself for their behavior. In short, I became a better mom by letting myself off the hook for not being perfect.

One of the hardest lessons I've learned has been to "let go" of the family I grew up in. Compared to dealing with my husband and kids, learning to stop being "daddy's little girl" and "mommy's best helper" was near to impossible! After all, I'd been stuck in those roles for the past 23 years. But eventually I realized that my primary responsibility was to the family Bob and I have created, not to my parents. I care about and love my mom and dad very much, but it is not my job to take care of them emotionally. Since this has occurred to me, my trips "home" have been much more pleasant. I've taken that pressure off myself. My main concern is now with "my" family. Our last trip to my parent's house was even fun! The kids and I really enjoyed ourselves, even though Bob couldn't get off work and come with us.

This story has a happy ending for our whole family. Right around the time Jennifer turned a year old, she and I finally "bonded". Our relationship grew, and although I regret having missed out emotionally on most of her time as an infant, we have made up for that lost time over the past year. I truly love my daughter, and that is something I had not let myself do for a long time.

Bob and I have benefited from the changes we've made, too. Our marriage is stronger than ever, thanks to his adaptability and to our more even exchange of give-and-take. I've become a better, stronger person. I understand and accept the fact that I am only human and, at times, less than perfect. I've learned to recognize when I need a break, and now I take one. Jason calls it my "Mommy-time" and, at three-years-old, even he thinks it's a reasonable request—most of the time.

All in all, my kids have probably gained the most from my experiences in therapy. They now have a mom who is happy with her life. They can now learn, by examples that I can now set, to feel good about themselves. I have to agree with Dr. Knight when he tells me that this is the best gift I could ever give to my kids.

This, I submit, is not an unusual scenario for any experienced family counselor. It may sound a bit "glowing," as this woman reflects upon her experience in therapy. Still, it was actually rather dramatic, for when she first came to see me she was in considerable emotional pain over the situation she was in. To her credit, she was a "quick study." Her husband also deserves a great deal of credit, as he was hardly as recalcitrant as some spouses can be. Also, they were both young, young enough at the time to be my own children, and, despite the stress in their lives, shared a significantly deep commitment to one another in their marriage. Therefore, in this case, they offered a lot to work with.

I, of course, made a clinical and ethical decision that she was not going to hurt her child. I did so on the basis of considerable experience in working with clients who have presented similar problems and such symptoms. My approach to treatment with this woman was also predicated on a diagnosis that this woman's problem was not a lack of integrity, nor was she lacking in effort. To the contrary, hers was a bit too much of such a good thing. If her story is a not uncommon example of the function of constructive counseling, as any experienced therapist knows, just as many stories don't turn out with quite as happy an ending.

Counseling is often a lot like playing baseball. In the major leagues even the best hitters fail nearly 70 percent of the time, and few pitchers have a .500 record. A good therapist develops a sense of perspective and some patience, certainly with her clients, not to mention himself. Indeed, there are other apt illustrations of counselors doing considerable good in what would seem to be far less normative ways.

For example, Dr. Corsini recalls being a prison psychologist many years ago. An inmate about to be paroled stopped by his office to thank him for "changing my life." Dr. Corsini couldn't remember the fellow, and when he checked the man's file, all that was indicated was that he had given this inmate an intelligence test a few years back. The guy explained how his life had changed, describing all sorts of positive things, including the fact that he had begun hanging out with a different class of friends, that he had started back to church, that he had pursued a trade while still in prison, and that he had lined up an opportunity to start college when he was released. This man seemed rather rehabilitated, and Dr. Corsini couldn't quite compute how all of this had come about, if indeed he, as a prison psychologist, had contributed in any significant way to such positive change. When he asked how he had been of help, the inmate replied, "You told me I had a high I.Q."

Dr. Corsini submits this as an example of psychotherapy in one sentence, only eight words long. [3] Therefore, I won't venture an abstract definition of counseling. I would rather use more of a descriptive approach. Though I will commit to this: I, like Dr. Corsini, prefer to think of psychotherapy in broader, less narrow terms. If that is an error in judgment, then that is the direction in which I wish to make it. There are lots of different kinds of people, broadly construed as mental health professionals, doing important, helpful work in lots of different ways which I would certainly consider counseling, or if you prefer, psychotherapy. I have a friend who is a voice teacher, and he often describes his work in the language of a therapist. Be that as it may, I hope my understanding of this dynamic people-helping enterprise becomes clearer as I describe it throughout this book, primarily in terms of how I, as a client, have been served by competent counselors, what I have learned over the years, how I go about my work as a therapist, as well as how and what I teach others.

For now, I want to look first at certain characteristics of various mental health professionals and then briefly outline some ways to interpret various theories of counseling. I would expect this to be of some help to consumers, or perhaps to potential consumers of mental health services. Indeed, parishioners in the church I currently serve as pastor often ask me for a referral for counseling, or for a particular kind of mental health evaluation for themselves, a family member, or a friend. What I will be

---

3. Ibid., 4.

talking about here is in response to the kinds of questions they commonly ask about mental health services and providers.

WHO ARE THE MENTAL HEALTH PROFESSIONALS?

By mental health professional, I am referring to people with certain educational credentials, training, and experience, who in most states are now licensed to practice counseling and who are paid for their services. These include psychiatrists and psychiatric nurses, psychologists, clinical social workers, pastoral counselors, marriage and family therapists, and other mental health counselors.

THE MEDICAL PERSONNEL

Psychiatrists are physicians. They have completed medical school and a residency in psychiatry and are licensed to practice medicine. They are the only mental health professionals authorized to prescribe medication, though in some states clinical psychologists can prescribe certain medication as well. Because of their training and expertise, they are essential to the delivery of mental health services. In public and private mental health clinics, they are usually the clinical directors and supervise all diagnoses, treatment plans, and clinical work, either directly or indirectly. Some psychiatrists serve a general population of people. Others specialize in working with children and adolescents, or adults, while still others have particular specialties, such as the treatment of alcoholism or other drug addictions, the treatment of sexual dysfunction or pathology, or the treatment of various other more specific problems.

Other kinds of physicians also practice psychiatry. These may include family doctors, internists, obstetricians and gynecologists, pediatricians, and neurologists. I, in fact, have a teaching colleague who is an osteopath. He is a highly trained and experienced mental health professional who currently teaches on the psychiatry faculty of our state's major medical school. Physicians other than psychiatrists may also prescribe appropriate psychotropic medications, such as anti-depressants and tranquilizers. They may also provide counseling to patients. Indeed, if one were to review the prescriptions written by family physicians over any particular interval, it would not be surprising to note that psychotropic medications would be at or near the top of the list. Ours is, after all, a depressed, highly stressed, and often conflicted society.

What is important to remember, in this context, is that the only mental health providers authorized to prescribe psychotropic medication are those who are physicians (or sometimes clinical psychologists). At the same time, in terms of training and expertise in psychotherapy, in whatever forms it may take, psychiatrists are not necessarily trained any better than other mental health professionals. Some are, of course, highly skilled therapists and emphasize that kind of work in their practice. Others are not particularly capable counselors and seldom do much in the way of psychotherapy.

For example, in public mental health centers and hospitals, psychiatrists generally do very little counseling. They normally supervise the clinical work of other staff, and they provide diagnoses and supervise treatment plans. This is also not uncommon for psychiatrists in private practice, where they may function primarily as medical providers and consultants. In fact, the other day a young man called for an appointment at our church-subsidized counseling center, which I supervise. He said his psychiatrist only saw him for 15-minute appointments to evaluate and monitor the medication he had prescribed for this patient. The young man said that his psychiatrist had agreed that he needed more extensive psychotherapy, which the doctor either wasn't willing or able to provide. It is likely that, if the doctor did see this patient for typical hour-long sessions of therapy, his fee would be prohibitive for this particular patient. Therefore, the first thing the therapist who sees this young man at our center will do will be to get an appropriate release of information form signed to protect this client's confidentiality. Then she can ethically and legally call this young man's psychiatrist and consult with him regarding this patient, thereby hopefully providing appropriate therapeutic continuity in a professionally cooperative relationship with the psychiatrist's diagnosis and treatment plan. Private psychiatric fees for counseling may be beyond what many patients can afford. Other therapists often provide a high-quality service that is less costly. In psychotherapy, patience is crucial. Physicians are often in a hurry.

I first studied family therapy, years ago, with a psychiatrist named Oliver Bjorkesten. Dr. Bjorksten offered an interesting analogy. He said, "In medicine, diagnosis is the hard part, and the treatment is usually much easier." By that, he meant that if you can figure out what is going on with the patient, the options for treatment are usually fairly limited. For most illnesses, given the proper diagnosis, the subsequent treatment is often pretty standard. "In psychotherapy, however," Dr. Bjorkesten explained, "it tends to be just the opposite. The diagnosis is usually pretty easy; it's the treatment that is the hard part."

My clinical experience over the years has certainly confirmed Dr. Bjorksten's observation. Most well-trained and experienced counselors can usually figure out pretty quickly what is going on with a patient who presents for therapy. Counseling tends to be a much more subjective process, that of relating to and connecting with a client in such a way (or ways) that he can connect with and make sense of, what it is that "fits," that the particular client may find helpful, that she can use. Such a process of relating usually takes time.

For a number of years now, outpatient public mental health centers have utilized what I call a case manager model. Tasked with treating a large clientele of chronically and often quite seriously mentally ill patients, this case manager model seems to be the most efficient and cost-effective. Here psychiatrists, or other kinds of physicians, supervise all clinical work. They assess patients, diagnose, supervise treatment plans, and write prescriptions. The rest of the work might likely include individual, family, or group counseling, medication monitoring, occupational and socialization therapy, and social work services to patients, including home visits, advocacy programs, and other supportive services. This is usually carried out by others, such as psychiatric nurses, social workers, and pastoral and clinical counselors.

Psychiatric nurses also have medical training. However, they are not authorized to write prescriptions, even though experienced psychiatric nurses usually know a lot of psychiatry. They are often "in tune" with the way the physicians they work with think. As a non-medically trained therapist, I have always found good psychiatric nurses quite helpful, particularly in interpreting medically related issues to me. Psychiatric nurses have a license to practice their profession as R.N.'s. Many will often have advanced degrees, such as a bachelor's degree in nursing, or perhaps a master's degree in counseling, social work, or nursing. Some psychiatric nurses are gifted therapists. I am thinking of four different nurses with whom I worked for many years. All were exceptionally capable counselors. Two of these nurses had master's degrees in mental health disciplines beyond their nursing credentials. Another went beyond her nursing degree to earn a doctorate in counseling psychology.

I have also known some psychiatric nurses who were more like Nurse Ratched in *One Flew Over the Cuckoo's Nest*. They were pretty hurtful people, and not because they didn't care. They were just so parental and patronizing in how they related to patients. In terms of Dr. Corsini's list of counseling functions, they did much less "listening" than they did "ordering," perhaps even scolding, or at least complaining about their patients. For example, "I just can't get John to take his medicine." As if that is anyone's business but John's. Whenever any mental health professional goes around talking about what he "can't get so-and-so to do," she is in more trouble than he usually realizes. Passive-aggressive patients tend to exploit such a style. Cooperation on the part of clients, for their own sake, is more likely to happen the less parental, and certainly the less patronizing their counselors tend to be, even if the counselors are nurses or medical doctors.

In this context, I would also mention that physician's assistants (P.A.'s) are also employed rather extensively these days, certainly in public mental health centers, as well as in private practice. They are also permitted to write prescriptions.

Some of the graduate students I teach in a clinical counseling program or supervise for licensure in our state as professional counselors or marriage and family therapists are nurses. I always encourage students and supervisees who don't have a medical background to work in an inpatient psychiatric unit or an outpatient mental health clinic, where they will have the opportunity to work alongside psychiatrists and psychiatric nurses, even if but for a few years. That learning experience is invaluable for anyone who wishes to be a competent counselor. There is nothing quite as fruitful in developing one's clinical competence as being part of a multi-disciplinary team of mental health professionals. When you staff cases together, and where effective clinical supervision is provided in such settings, the learning curve is extended.

Prior to pastoring a church, I have always worked as a psychotherapist in a medical context, both in a public mental health clinic and in a group practice of family physicians. Family medicine is an ideal setting for the practice of counseling, certainly when the physicians involved believe in its value, support it, and are available for consultation. My life and work have been enriched over the years by this association, and I would not want to practice apart from being quite closely aligned with an appropriate consulting physician. I think this is the safest and soundest approach.

Also, I have noticed over the years that patients are often less threatened at coming for counseling to a family doctor's office. Less stigma seems to be attached to that setting, at least for some people, and they are often not as defensive about seeking such help. This is important in a culture where mental health problems still tend to be stigmatized.

I also have found the attitudes of clients toward psychotropic medication intriguing. For some, this seems to be their primary interest: "Just give me my medicine; I don't want to talk to anyone." Still, I would say that even more patients seem resistant to medication, as in "If I have to take medicine I must be weak or really sick," or, "If I just had more faith I wouldn't have to take this medicine." So let me speak, here, to this issue, and I will do so in terms of a general discussion of depression.

Because depression, in the common lexicon, is such a generic term and is used so broadly, I have found it helpful to explain depression this way. Clients, students, and supervisees have told me that they find this explanation helpful. I think of depression as a both/and kind of thing. It can be, and often is, a physical illness quite unrelated to what one might consider any identifiable psychological problem(s) in a person's life. I call this endogenous, or clinical, depression. Some clinical depression is a result of other forms of illness, or perhaps a symptom of other forms of medical treatment. It is not uncommon for chronic, debilitating illness to cause or contribute to depression. Post-partem depression is common among women, and some women experience depression related to menopause and other gynecological factors.

The development of antidepressant medications in the last thirty-five years has been rather dramatic. Antidepressants generally don't produce serious side effects and can be prescribed diagnostically. That is, certain symptoms would suggest certain antidepressant medication that would seem most appropriate. It is sometimes necessary to experiment to find the right medication and the right dosage. What is important to remember is that the kind of depression I am here describing requires proper medication. You can go to counseling forever, but if your depression is biochemical, counseling, no matter how good, is not likely to relieve your symptoms.

Much of the research on depression, from this perspective, suggests hereditary factors, chemical factors, and genetic tendencies to being depressed. Also, I think it is important to keep in mind that when speaking of depression and medication, some depression may never be "cured," only managed or controlled, much like other chronic and quite serious illnesses, such as diabetes or hypertension. Fortunately, there is medication to help in this effort.

At the same time, there is another kind of depression that I consider psychological. Some might call it situational or circumstantial. It may be the result of trauma, recent or distant. It may be associated with a loss, a failure, or a disappointment, perhaps a part of one's grieving. Then again, psychological depression may have as its source some unresolved conflict in one's life. If one wants to take it even further, such depression may be the result of shaming, or of guilt. Some people's depression seems to be learned, or perhaps attributable to cultural factors, family dynamics, and/or lifelong patterns of how certain people have adapted to try to survive in their circumstances.

I knew a psychiatrist some years ago who defined depression as "hurt feelings." If such a statement may be too broad, and likely too shallow as well, there is still some truth to it. Under these circumstances, counseling can be helpful in alleviating or managing depression, although appropriate medication may still be needed or helpful. Sometimes people are psychologically depressed to such a degree that appropriate medication can help reduce their symptoms, thus making them, as we say, "more available" to make use of psychotherapy as a helpful mode of treatment. Sometimes both things are at work at the same time: there are psychological features that would likely explain the depression, and the person is also clinically depressed as the result of biochemical factors.

Some years ago, I had an agitated, or manicky depression. Psychologically, it was quite understandable. I had suffered a loss, actually something of a trauma, and likely a sense of failure, too. I was conflicted between the way my life was working, how I had planned and prepared for it to be, and how I believed it ought to be, or at least how I wanted it to be. Such a set of circumstances is a pretty classic scenario of what I call psychological depression. While I was able to maintain my general level of functioning, my symptoms persisted for several years.

The primary symptom of my depression was that I couldn't sleep. Because I couldn't sleep, by the end of the day I was pretty tired, so I would fall asleep before my usual bedtime, only then to wake up in a few hours and not be able to go back to sleep for the rest of the night, or sometimes until just an hour or so before I had to get up again to go to work. This is a vicious and debilitating syndrome. However, psychologically, it is rather explainable. My primary psychic defenses involve rationalizing and intellectualizing. I could understand why I would likely be depressed and rationalize that things were not as bad as they could be, that I was strong and capable, had integrity, was loved and cared for, that I would likely get better . . . and so on . . . and so forth . . . . In the meantime, however, and certainly in the middle of the night, when I should have been getting good rest, my defenses had broken down, and I was agitating. I was bouncing off the walls.

My family doctor prescribed an antidepressant that had tranquilizing properties, appropriate for such an agitated depression. I was not able to tolerate the normal dosage; it left me feeling hung over in the morning. Therefore, it was necessary to titrate it down to a dosage I could handle. The result was that I began to be able to get a good night's sleep, to feel and function better. I continued to take the medication for several years.

Then, one night, I must have forgotten to take the medicine. I don't recall. I do know that it was not some dramatic gesture, as in, "I'm tired of taking this medicine. I'm going to flush it down the toilet." It wasn't that at all. For whatever reason, I just didn't take it, and I slept the night through. I slept well. And the next night . . . and the next . . . and I haven't taken the medicine since. I have continued to sleep well for many more years than those I was depressed.

So what happened? Did the medicine finally do its work, over several years, and heal me? Psychologically, did I eventually, over several years, resolve the conflict in my life? Was that the source of my healing? Did I ultimately need emotional or spiritual healing? In the meantime, did the medication help to treat the symptoms? Did it at least give me a decent night's sleep so that I could function better, and also so that I was better able to make use of the therapy I had sought during that time in my life? Was my healing miraculous? If so, was the miracle somehow manifested through medicine and counseling?

Normally, we think of being depressed as having the blues, as being "down," as being lethargic, lacking in will and purpose, focus and energy. Sometimes, though, agitation or anxiety can be a symptom of depression. This is often misdiagnosed, and tranquilizers are commonly prescribed. Unlike antidepressants, tranquilizers may be addictive.

My family doctor was, in this instance, perceptive and informed. His diagnosis and treatment, both psychologically and medically, were right on target. Also, we often distinguish between affective and cognitive illness, if that is how you wish to define them. Some would disagree, claiming that mental health problems are not illnesses, but that is not the point here. The term "affective" typically refers to emotions, while cognitive involves thinking. Generally, we think of depression as an affective illness, but if you have ever been depressed, then you are aware, perhaps, that at least one symptom of such depression is that your thinking generally starts to get pretty crazy. In particular, when you are depressed you often get rather paranoid. You start wondering what people are thinking or saying about you, or perhaps even what they are doing, or going to do to you, or what other bad things might possibly happen. At least I do, and I have found this to be true with most people, even among those who otherwise are not particularly paranoid. The cognitive component of depression, an affective illness, is certainly something I have noticed and urge both clients and therapists to pay attention to.

While we are on this subject, let me briefly address the problem of suicide. I would delineate with regard to suicide in much the same way I think of depression in general. Psychologically, suicide is the ultimate passive-aggressive behavior, in that it "gets back at" whomever, literally or symbolically. It is like the person is saying, "Now you'll know how much I am hurting, or have been hurt," since family and friends of suicide victims are usually devastated whenever a loved one takes his life. From this perspective, suicide is when one escalates her sense of powerlessness or hopelessness or rage to violence, violence turned on oneself in such a way as to also hurt others. Still, many suicides occur when persons are psychotic.

I believe there is yet another way to think of suicide, and that is when a person is so depressed for so long that the emotional pain seems quite unbearable. Here, it would seem, suicide becomes a desperate seeking of relief from the pain of depression. Most experienced mental health professionals have worked with clients who have taken their lives, and they might likely interpret such suicides from any one or a combination of these perspectives.

These interpretations, as attempts to try to understand suicide, I would distinguish from suicides as a political statement, or from suicides connected with terminal or extreme debilitating illness apart from depression. Then again, suicide is usually ranked second to accidental death in fatalities among young people. For example, I recall a teenager telling me once that she had been driving her car at night on a highway outside of town with her car lights turned off. The difference between a suicide and an accident is not always clear. This is certainly true of many teenage suicides, and it likely applies to others as well, where suicidal ideation and carelessness are in collusion. Sometimes, I think, suicide can be understood as an over-reaction to a dramatic experience of trauma, of loss or failure or sense of despair.

As someone has defined it, suicide is "a permanent solution to a temporary problem," when all sense of perspective is lost. In this sense, then, it is not necessarily something someone may have pondered over a long and painful period of time. This interpretation would certainly apply, I think, to many teenage suicides.

PSYCHOLOGISTS

Psychologists come in various shapes and sizes. Most psychologists who practice psychotherapy are either clinical or counseling psychologists. Most have doctoral degrees (either a Ph.D., an Ed.D., or a Psy.D.) and are licensed to practice in the state where they work. Some educational psychologists also practice counseling, and many are especially adept at diagnosing and treating various learning disorders. As for their training as psychotherapists, psychologists aren't trained any better or any different from other mental health professionals. Some are highly skilled counselors, while others are not gifted as such. Some are not all that interested in counseling; they prefer teaching and/or research, or work in administration in both public and private mental health agencies. Some psychologists do not even work in the mental health field, but are employed in industry, in fields such as marketing or advertising.

It is worth noting here that, whatever the mental health discipline, developing strong counseling skills is not usually done in school, regardless of the degree program, apart from required clinical internships. One learns to be a capable therapist while doing counseling in a clinically supervised setting. Thus, the quality of one's supervision is extremely important. In the state where I work, for example, students who complete a master's degree in counseling are required to pass an examination and work under approved supervision for approximately two years before they can be licensed as either a professional counselor or a marriage and family therapist, or both.

For psychologists and social workers, the demands of clinical supervision are usually even more extensive. When I say "approved supervision," in my state those who supervise post-graduate students seeking to be licensed as professional counselors or marriage and family therapists have to be licensed themselves as supervisors, a level of training and experience that extends beyond the license of LPC or LMFT. Nurses may have a similar post-graduate level of clinical training in counseling. And, of course, psychiatrists complete a several-year residency beyond medical school. During their residency, their work is clinically supervised. Many pursue even more advanced and specialized training beyond that. Still, I would say that the best therapists continue to seek supervision and training beyond the levels I have just described in an effort to develop and refine their counseling skills, and anyone with a license or recognized credential in a mental health discipline is required to complete regular units of continuing education.

Psychologists are the experts in testing, just as psychiatrists are the experts in medicine. Psychologists are trained to administer and interpret psychological instruments at a level superior to other mental health professionals. Clinical psychologists are also trained to diagnose and treat the most serious forms of mental illness. In the state where I work, psychologists have been at the forefront in supporting legislation that would create "practice laws." The best example of a practice law is law that provides that properly credentialed psychologists might be the only mental health professionals licensed to do psychological testing or make certain psychological diagnoses. If this sounds like someone is trying to "protect his or her turf," practice laws are also designed to protect consumers of mental health services.

Where it gets stickier is if it means that only pastoral counselors can discuss moral and spiritual problems with clients, or if only properly credentialed marriage and family therapists can offer this service. Obviously, there are many psychiatrists, psychologists, social workers, nurses, and other kinds of physicians who address such issues with patients, whether they are particularly credentialed to do so or not. To deny them this right would be like saying that no physician besides a psychiatrist can prescribe an antidepressant. So then, practice laws, designed to protect the consumer, are not without some ambiguity.

CLINICAL SOCIAL WORKERS

Social work school is a professional school, like medical school, law school, seminary, or divinity school. Social work school is where one goes, upon at least graduation from college, to be trained to practice the profession of social work. Thus, social work training is practitioner-oriented. While social workers don't have uniquely specialized training as part of a mental health discipline, in the sense that physicians study medicine, psychologists have a certain expertise in testing, or clergy study theology, social workers do stand in a rich historical tradition, because professional social work remains at the heart of human services and the helping professions.

Not all social workers practice psychotherapy. Some study and serve as advocates for social policy, while others work in children's homes and adoption agencies, in hospitals and nursing homes, for the health department or the department of social services, in alcohol and other drug abuse treatment programs, in public schools, in prisons, in homeless shelters and nutrition programs. They may work not primarily as counselors, but as caseworkers, or as executives, directors, managers, and supervisors. Some social workers teach and/or do research in graduate or professional schools or in public or private institutions.

Social workers who do specialize in counseling are commonly referred to as clinical social workers, are credentialed as such, and are licensed to practice their profession. Many also have other mental health credentials, such as those of a marriage and family therapist, an addictions specialist, or a geriatrics specialist. I know some social workers who are good therapists.

Even those who don't practice as such are generally well trained in understanding the nuances of rather sophisticated clinical work. For example, I have a social worker colleague on the staff of a rather large and historic church-related children's home. He works almost exclusively with placing children in foster homes and with adoptive families, as well as in trying to arrange appropriate home settings for children with various emotional and social problems. Even though he does not consider himself a therapist, whenever he and I have consulted over the years concerning a child and/or family, it is clear to me that he has a high level of expertise in understanding and supporting the work I do. We have worked well together with families he has referred to me.

PASTORAL COUNSELORS

Credentialed pastoral counselors are normally ordained clergy who have graduated from college and seminary and frequently hold an additional specialized degree in their field or a related mental health discipline. Credentialed pastoral counselors have completed several years of clinical supervision of their work as therapists, and they are required to pass an examination. The American Association of Pastoral Counselors (AAPC) credentials such clergy. In some states, pastoral counselors are licensed as such. In other states, they may be licensed as professional counselors. Many are also credentialed and licensed as marriage and family therapists. Some hold appropriate credentials and are licensed as psychologists.

The training of clergy in counseling isn't any different from psychotherapy training in other mental health disciplines, except that pastoral counselors have expertise in understanding and treating human problems as they relate to moral and spiritual issues in a way that other mental health professionals do not, unless they have had comparable training in theology and ethics. Pastoral counseling is an interdisciplinary profession, integrating theology and the behavioral sciences. When one considers that psychotherapy, as we know it, isn't very old—after all, Sigmund Freud only died in 1939—it is worth noting, I think, that Hebrew-Christian pastoral counselors, at least, stand in a moral tradition of faith and reason, a way of believing and thinking and behaving that extends over some 3000 years.

More than 30 years ago, the theologian Thomas Oden was writing extensively on the theology of contemporary psychotherapy. Subsequently he extended that interest, or perhaps disillusionment, certainly with a fee-based approach to a kind of pastoral counseling tied too closely to ostensibly secular therapeutic models. Oden turned to studying the roots of pastoral care and counseling, what some would call "spiritual formation" in the history of the Church, extending back even into the patristic period, which dates from the first five centuries of Christian history. [4] Contemporary pastoral counseling can certainly be traced to an emphasis on being more available to people as a counselor in the ministry of the Puritan divine Richard Baxter, in the 17th century, to the first attempts at

---

4. Thomas C. Oden, *Care of Souls in the Classic Tradition* (Philadelphia: Fortress Press, 1981). cf. also John T. McNeill, *A History of the Cure of Souls* (New York: Harper and Row, 1951).

writing and studying verbatim accounts of pastoral encounters (counseling?) on the part of Ichabod Spencer in the nineteenth century, to the seminal influence of Anton Boisen on the clinical training of clergy in mental hospitals in the twentieth century. [5] It is this perspective that the pastoral psychotherapist brings to the interdisciplinary nature of quality mental health services these days.

In a 1991 Gallup poll of a thousand men and women, 66 percent said they would prefer to receive counseling from someone who represented their spiritual values, and 81 percent said they wanted their spiritual values respected and integrated into the counseling process.[6] My experience suggests that this matter can be understood at an even deeper level. If you have ever worked in a psychiatric hospital or an outpatient mental health clinic and have had the opportunity to observe, or perhaps even try to relate to (or even restrain!) someone who has become psychotic, if you have ever listened to the verbiage, the content is almost always explicitly and outrageously sexual or religious or both. This suggests that these may, indeed, be the deepest and perhaps the most conflicted issues in people's lives.

I once heard a female therapist say that any counselor who works with women and does not talk with them about food is derelict, given all the crazy messages women receive in our culture about food, in contradiction to how they are supposed to look. Her example was your average woman's magazine, filled with the most attractive pictures of beautiful-looking women and beautiful-looking food, as if the two somehow go together, which they usually don't. Perhaps the same rationale might be applied to most people and their religion, for which the current politically correct term seems to be "spirituality." Freud seemed to think that most people's problems had to do with either sex or death, at least in their more primal imagery. However, I remember Sam Keen saying some years ago that anyone in America today can talk about sex. What is most terrifying for most people, he claimed, is the very thought of God! In this sense, then, religion or, if you prefer, spirituality has to do with concerns of ultimacy in any of our lives.

Yes, I know that most ministers do counseling, but that is not what I'm talking about when I speak of pastoral counselors as mental health

5. E. Brooks Holifield, *A History of Pastoral Care in America* (Nashville: Abingdon, 1983).

6. American Association of Pastoral Counselors White Paper, 2001.

professionals. Credentialed pastoral counselors have specialized training and clinically supervised experience quite beyond that of your journeyman parish pastor. In fact, parish clergy who do "too much" counseling in their pastoral role are generally asking for trouble, not the least of which is that of "dual relationships," where the line between pastor, friend, and therapist becomes unethically blurred. Most experienced, well-trained, and astute pastors know this. Some large congregations have a minister on staff who specializes in pastoral care and counseling. Sometimes denominations or an ecumenical consortium of congregations in a community will support a pastoral counseling center that has its own identity, apart from any one congregation.

I recall an article I read years ago in the *Journal of Pastoral Care* in which a clinical psychologist, who had practiced as a mental health professional for a number of years, sensed a more focused call to ministry, had attended seminary, and had been ordained as a Lutheran pastor. He was sure that his finest pastoral gift would be that of counseling individuals and families in the parish he served, only to realize—and not too soon—that this was not likely something he should be doing to any great extent with people he related to socially in many and various ways in the life of that congregation.

When I accepted a call to serve as a parish pastor some years ago, I closed my private counseling practice where I had worked for many years. When people today ask me if I do any counseling, I explain that within the congregation I serve I do pastoral care: I visit people in the hospital and in nursing homes, I visit shut-ins, I do fairly limited pre-marital counseling with couples who ask me to perform their marriage, and I am certainly available to folk, in our congregation and in the community, to meet with people in a crisis and to refer them for more extensive counseling if that is needed. Parish ministers need to be able diagnosticians, in the sense of having some idea of what a person's needs seem to be in terms of appropriate counseling. They also need to know their local resources and be able to access them. The ministry of referral is extremely important, as that is frequently how folk get to a mental health professional, by way of referral from a clergyperson whose judgment they trust. Parish clergy and chaplains commonly intervene in the crises of people's lives, at times when they may be quite vulnerable, and parish clergy certainly need to have a clear sense of what their limitations in counseling parishioners are.

Even though I currently pastor a congregation, and that is my primary employment, I continue to teach graduate students in family therapy as an adjunct professor. I supervise selected post-graduate students for licensure as professional counselors, and I am frequently asked to consult with other mental health professionals on particular cases. I also supervise a small family counseling center designed to serve a less affluent clientele, folk whose financial resources are limited, who don't have insurance or cannot afford a co-payment, and for whom customary private-practice counseling fees are too costly. The congregation I serve graciously subsidizes this service.

I got the idea for this ministry over years of private practice as a therapist, working with clients I admired and was challenged to work with, but who could not afford my fee. Therefore, the service our church provides is unique, since we are not taking money out of the pocket of the psychologist down the street who is trying to make a living but could not do so seeing the clients we serve at such reduced fees. In our church's counseling ministry, I don't do the counseling. I supervise the clinical work of post-graduate students who are pursuing licensure in our state as professional counselors and marriage and family therapists.

In the context of any discussion of pastoral counseling, I would also want to address the important work of chaplains in hospitals, nursing homes, jails and prisons, the military, industry, colleges and schools, and police and fire departments. The emphasis in their ministry is perhaps best understood as being somewhere between that of a parish pastor and a pastoral counselor. While they are not trained to do intensive and extensive psychotherapy, their training exceeds that of most parish pastors in terms of their crisis intervention, assessment, and referral skills. Chaplains in medical settings, of course, have specialized training in issues involving medical ethics and in ministering to those who are grieving, as well as patients and families facing serious and/or terminal illness.

MARRIAGE AND FAMILY THERAPISTS

For more than a half-century now, the mental health discipline of marriage and family therapy has developed as a specialty. Consequently, today most states have a license for the practice of such. In fact, this may be the primary professional identity of a counselor: as a marriage and family therapist. There are numerous graduate training programs throughout the country in this specialty. Other helping professionals who have completed sufficient training and who are credentialed and licensed as marriage and family therapists may include clergy, school and clinical counselors, occupational and rehabilitation counselors, psychologists, social workers, nurses, and physicians.

Marriage and family therapists are trained to understand and work, even with individuals, from the perspective of families as systems, where all the parts and pieces of families, even across generations, impact on and are impacted by the system as a whole. Since I have been trained as a family therapist and train others, I would hope that my understanding of family systems theory and its more practical implications will emerge more clearly throughout this book.

OTHER KINDS OF COUNSELORS

Beyond those I have mentioned, other mental health professionals would include clinical counselors, school counselors, and occupational, rehabilitation, and recreational therapists. Such folk usually have master's degrees and are normally credentialed in their specialties. Some may be licensed also as marriage and family therapists, or in another specialty, such as addictions counseling, sex counseling, or geriatrics.

As I have indicated, I prefer to think of counseling in broader, rather than in more narrow terms. Therefore, I would also want to include lay-therapists, many of whom are quite skilled and effective. This is certainly true in the addictions field and the important work of Alcoholics Anonymous and other Twelve-Step programs. I have had a number of colleagues over the years who developed themselves professionally after first being volunteers at a "Hotline" phone counseling service, at "People Against Rape," in a prison or hospital visitation program. One woman went on to social work school; another completed a doctorate in clinical psychology; others have pursued master's degrees and subsequent licensure as clinical counselors and/or marriage and family therapists.

Also, my sense of what is involved in working with addicted people has heightened in recent years. I think it is important for counselors who work with addicts to be highly sensitized to the inherent problems of addiction. For example, most alcoholics and other drug-addicted people I know are quite willing to participate in any form of counseling, as long as the therapist never confronts them about their addiction. That is why AA, as a fellowship of recovering alcoholics, has such a proven track record of confronting addiction in a powerfully loving and effective way. It takes one to know one, and certainly to understand how addicted people tend to be so winsomely dishonest and artfully manipulative.

As I teach graduate students in clinical counseling and supervise post-graduates for licensure as such, as well as in marriage and family therapy, I encourage students to consider developing a specialty, according to their gifts, interests, and experience. For some, it may be geriatrics; for others, addiction; for someone else, it may involve developing a high level of skill in working with persons who have been sexually abused. Some years ago, I supervised a school counselor for a license in clinical counseling. To qualify for this license, she was required to take additional course work in clinical counseling and to pass the appropriate exam. Her specialized area of interest and expertise is in eating disorders. She has studied the subject for a number of years, has done extensive research on the problem, and has become quite an expert in this specialty.

THEORIES OF COUNSELING AND PSYCHOTHERAPY

One of my family therapy supervisors, Dr. A.C. Holler, emphasizes an important distinction between counseling theory and technique. He likens theory to a crescent wrench, which adjusts to various sized bolts. Technique, he says, is like a half-inch wrench that fits only bolts of that particular size.

I would press this analogy even further and apply it to theory as well, which is why I encourage my students to develop a repertoire of therapeutic theory. By this, I don't mean superficial knowledge, a smattering of this and that, knowing just enough to be other than helpful. My concern is that when any therapist gets locked in too tightly to any particular way of trying to understand and work with people, when she is too rigid in terms of theoretical orientation, then she runs the risk of practicing what I call the "Procrustean Bed" approach to counseling. This is when a therapist tries to fit people to her theory, rather than drawing upon and adapting theoretical perspective to fit the particular needs and characteristics of different individuals and families, even organizations. I think it was Mark Twain who said, "When the only tool you own is a hammer, pretty soon the whole world starts looking like a nail!"

Theory of any kind, and certainly in the social sciences, tends, of course, to generalize. If it is based upon scientific method, it will be developed inductively, from observing details to generalizing about such details, about patterns and themes, about relatively and reasonably predictable outcomes. However, I'm afraid counseling theory is too often applied deductively, from general to specific, in ways that hinder the work, when therapists try to fit clients who are ill-fitted to even the best of theories. I believe the clinical practice of psychotherapy needs to be reciprocal, in that it needs to be flexible enough to go both ways, to operate both deductively and inductively. I am, of course, speaking here to practitioners, since those who write books and articles on counseling theory are often so associated with a particular theoretical approach that such theory might even be named for a particular person.

In this respect, anyone who has read much theory in the counseling field may have noted how theoretical approaches often tend to emerge dialectically. That is, a particular theory of psychotherapy will tend to represent a somewhat defined position, and others may come along and refine such a position to an even greater extent. Then someone else, who may see things quite differently, carves out some theoretical territory in a different, perhaps opposite direction, and others may take this approach to even more of an extreme. This seems to be the pattern of how theory evolves, and certainly how books get written or at least seem to appeal to readers, in a dialectical fashion; one might say, as the pendulum swings, always in reaction to whatever has gone before. In fact, more extreme theoretical positions often attract more attention, at least initially. Effective and responsible counseling practitioners consistently synthesize theory in ways that tend to become less doctrinaire, so that the theory is always better fitted to a particular client, rather than trying to get all of one's clients to fit any particular theory.

Here's an interesting illustration. For several years, I have used an excellent textbook for a graduate course I teach in family systems theory. When this book discusses a particular "school" of systems theory and offers an introduction to several such approaches, with different emphases, it also provides a discussion of that "school's" theoretical consistency or, as the book puts it, "systemic consistency." When you're writing a textbook in family systems theory, when such a significant theoretical orientation is what you're trying to teach, then surely, from that perspective, a consideration of theoretical consistency is important. In fact, more important,

I believe, than when trying to interpret whatever appropriate counseling theory might be more or less helpful in understanding and working with any particular client or family.[7]

Some years ago, I was apparently rather helpful to a client. After seeing me for several months, his symptoms were reduced. He had changed both some of his thinking and some of his behavior, and likely some of his beliefs as well. This was observable, and he claimed it was good for him, as well as for others in his life. In thanking me for my help, he added, "If I had known you practiced Transactional Analysis, I wouldn't have come to you."

I replied, "I didn't know that's what I was doing."

He responded, "Well, this woman at work said you were an expert in Transactional Analysis."

Now, of course, if I did have a high level of expertise in whatever the counseling theory—my clients would not likely know it, or at least my theoretical orientation would not get in the way. That is what I mean by having a repertoire of theory available in practice that is well integrated, that serves the work of the therapist, and certainly the needs of the client, in ways that are not intrusive or distracting, that is best suited to a particular patient, as against trying to fit the client to the theory.

There are almost as many theories of counseling as there are psychotherapists. That's a bit of a hyperbole, but you get the idea. Therapeutic theory abounds. It often becomes institutionalized, and adherents to this or that "school" can be somewhat rigid in their adherence, if not just as harsh in their denunciation of other counselors whose approach to people-helping may not be the same as theirs. All recognized graduate programs in counseling will offer courses in comparative psychotherapies, as well as specialized courses in this or that particular theoretical approach. Still, no one learns to be a counselor in school, as much you learn "about" therapy. The real work of developing one's skills, and certainly one's style as a therapist, begins after graduate or professional school, and the process continues over many years. In fact, I have discovered that the best counselors aren't necessarily the best students, academically speaking—certainly among those who seem to have some "need to be the best"—since so much of being a skilled therapist has to do with certain intuitive qualities of personality and character. Commonly, the best coun-

7. D. S. Becvar and R. J. Becvar, *Family Therapy: A Systemic Integration*, 3rd ed. (Needham Heights: Allyn and Bacon, 1988).

selors are those who have had to figure out, perhaps sooner than later, how to survive in this world in some fairly healthy ways, often in the face of some rather difficult circumstances. Such folk the late Henri Nouwen called "wounded healers."

One of my pastoral-counseling supervisors, Archie Reed, claims that most therapists tend to follow in the theoretical orientation of their clinical supervisors. That may be so. However, in the case of Dr. Reed and myself, our style and approach to therapy would seem so different. The grace of our relationship has always been, nonetheless, in the value we have been able to see in each other's differences. However, that is not always the case among counselors. Others might likely be drawn to the theoretical orientation of a particular therapist whom they experienced as effective or helpful. Someone else might be attracted, perhaps with a kind of intellectual curiosity, to some other kind of counseling theory. What I am now going to do is to briefly compare a variety of counseling theories in terms of some different therapeutic dimensions that they represent.

The oldest and most time-honored of approaches to modern psychotherapy, and likely the most controversial, depending on whom you ask, would be psychoanalysis and its various derivatives. Therapies of this type tend to emphasize the significance of one's past and the power of the unconscious. In this approach, the therapist seems to hold most of the power and the client very little. While it is often referred to as psychodynamic, the interaction between client and counselor tends to be pretty passive. While some would disagree, I think it hard to underestimate the influence of psychoanalytic theory on much contemporary counseling. Modern pastoral counseling is certainly rooted in this tradition and continues to reflect its influence. Those who pioneered in the development of a systemic approach to family therapy were similarly trained.

As a pastoral theologian, I am especially interested in Jungian analysis, since it seems to have been rather thoroughly "baptized" into many quarters of Christendom.[8] Ironically, Carl Jung, whose father was a Swiss Reformed Christian pastor, appears to have been very much the polytheist. He apparently had, throughout his life, quite a rich, childlike fascination with the mythology of gods and goddesses, of fairies and ogres, with

---

8. There are so many books on this interest/subject. The one I have read most recently is R. L. Moore and D. J. Meckel, eds. *Jung and Christianity in Dialogue* (Mahwah: Paulist Press, 1990). This is but one of some seven different titles in a projected series of books on Jung and some dimension of religion or spirituality, offered by the same publisher.

the light and the darkness of life. In contrast, Sigmund Freud, the atheistic Jew, seems forever caricatured in his contempt of religion as something rather childish.

In his *Theology of Culture*, Paul Tillich claims that, in the history of religions, the appearance of ethical monotheism represents what we today would consider a dramatic shift in paradigms, from a mere projection of psychic fragmentation (polytheism) to a more integrated sense of whole-ness of self (monotheism).[9] Given much of the apparent contemporary Christian fascination with Jung, as well as the current popular enthusi-asm for what many would call "spirituality," even among many ostensibly secular people, it makes me wonder: is it easier for God to "die," in one's experience, from a monotheistic framework, such as that of Freud, than from a more polytheistic worldview, as in that of Carl Jung?

Be that as it may, the opposite end from psychoanalytic theory on the therapeutic spectrum would likely be that of the behaviorists. Here the emphasis is hardly on insight or understanding—and certainly not on matters of ecstasy or despair—but instead on how to extinguish, re-inforce, and/or change human behavior. In this respect, the therapeutic emphasis is on the present, certainly the future, and hardly the past. The therapist is not likely to ask many, if any, "why" questions. The concern is rather exclusively with "how." Similarly, one might also understand vari-ous learning theories and more cognitive approaches to counseling. It is this theoretical emphasis that seems to be reflected in the current man-aged care milieu, with its priority of observable and measurable goals for change.

Another grouping of counseling theories would surely include what I call personal, or humanistic and/or existential approaches, as in Carl Rogers' "client-centered" therapy. Here, more emphasis is put on the cli-ent than the therapist, even though the engagement between client and counselor is more interactive and certainly more vital to the therapeutic process. Again, the emphasis is on the present, not the past. From this theoretical perspective, clients have power and autonomy. They are free and responsible to make choices and decisions. The therapeutic concerns include such issues as respect and empowerment. In this approach, the counselor is more "available" to the client, is not as hidden, and is more responsive than passive. The listening and attending is "active." Personal

9. Paul Tillich, *Theology of Culture* (Oxford: Oxford University Press, 1959).

characteristics of the therapist are important, especially in terms of congruence and integrity, as well as a counselor's capacity to engage clients in empathic and more unconditional ways.

"Family systems" is another important theoretical approach to counseling that has developed over the past 60-plus years. Indeed, anyone credentialed and licensed as a marriage and family therapist is trained in and tested on such theory and required to know it well. Systems theory, as applied to families, understands the individual always in a reciprocal relationship with her larger system, across multiple generations, and extending quite beyond her nuclear family of origin. From a systems perspective, function, process, and reciprocity are key concepts. This is commonly called cybernetics.

A rather vivid example of systemic thinking might be as follows: you don't prescribe medication for a patient, but instead introduce medication into the system. If you have ever observed any over-functioning family members working excessively to "make sure" another identified, if not passive-aggressive patient in the system has taken his medicine, then you can perhaps appreciate the perspective of systems theory. In systems theory, the "presenting problem" is more often interpreted as merely symptomatic of dysfunction somewhere else in the system—often a level of dysfunction that tends to promote homeostasis, or balance in the system. Differing systemic approaches may pay more or less attention to how families appear to be organized, and what are the "rules" and/or expectations, particularly those that would seem to be even more implicit than explicit. The same is true concerning the significance of the past.

Also, in different systemic approaches, the counselor may be more or less actively engaged in the therapeutic process. Some would claim that systems theory represents a radical paradigm shift from other approaches to counseling, and it likely does, in that it sees any individual always in a larger or systemic context. I discuss systems theory in greater detail in Chapter III, "Balanced Families."

In recent years, counseling theory has tended to express an increased concern for the social, cultural, and political matrix of psychotherapy, what one might consider the ecology of counseling. This would include a heightened sensitivity to matters of gender, race, culture, ethnicity, sexual orientation, and any number of issues related to power. Such theoretical concerns reflect something of a deconstructionist critique, in challenging some of the time-honored assumptions about the counseling relationship, particularly regarding matters of perspective, power, authority, and the role of the therapist. At a conference I attended a few years ago, one presenter challenged the assumption that male therapists had any business counseling women. The roots of such theoretical concerns, as regards psychotherapy from the perspective of a larger social and political context, can be found in the work of Erich Fromm in the 1940s.

The business mentality on the part of managed care, which currently reflects the interests of third-party providers of health care coverage, has certainly influenced recent counseling theory. For example, insurance for psychotherapy in managed care programs may only provide for a limited number of sessions. Hence, solution-focused, short-term methods of counseling have emerged. Traditional psychoanalytic theory assumes both an intensive and long-term approach to the therapeutic process. In classical psychoanalysis, patients may see their analyst multiple times a week, often over many years. If much subsequent counseling theory has, for some time now, challenged the more psychoanalytic approaches to therapy on theoretical grounds, the emergence of managed care may have well sounded their demise, except, of course, for those committed to such a process, including those who are affluent enough to pay for it themselves. At the same time, I am aware of a few analytically oriented therapists who have refused to acquiesce to the parameters of managed care. These therapists claim that their practices have actually flourished since they made this decision. As one said to me, "There is a difference between income and spendable income." It's interesting how people differ with regard to what is important in their lives and on what it is they are willing to spend their money.

In the latter stages of my career as a counselor, I developed some interest in what is referred to as narrative therapy, both in terms of theological perspective and also with regard to certain personality types. Narrative therapy challenges some of the so-called "scientific" assumptions inherent in traditional counseling theory. In this sense, it is somewhat deconstructionist, in that it recognizes and values the subjective over the presumption of what some would consider more objective forms of counseling. This approach to therapy certainly has its theological analogues, particularly in terms of the biblical narrative, where "truth" is always more important than "fact." It also reflects something of an intuitive priority, in terms of personality type.

I attended a Jungian workshop some years ago. The leader had previously taught pastoral counseling at a seminary in Switzerland. He said he always found it interesting how the more eastern Europeans, such as the Russians, tended to answer even "yes" or "no" questions by way of telling stories. In his book *Story As a Way of Knowing*, the Jesuit priest Kevin Bradt explains how this also tends to be true in his Irish cultural heritage.[10] Such cultural examples would hardly seem exclusive, at least where a more intuitive way of "knowing" is valued. Narrative therapy seems particularly valuable in moving the therapist out of what has often tended to be too authoritarian a role.[11]

Having sketched something of the breadth and diversity of counseling theory that has developed during the past century, I turn now to a matter that has become a kind of over-arching principle in my work as a therapist over the years. It is a concern with balance as a key to health—mental, emotional, social, moral, spiritual, or otherwise. When something is out of balance, eventual dysfunction or disease is likely to be the result. I will explore this metaphor, this image of balance, throughout most of the remainder of this book.

10. Kevin Bradt, *Story as a Way of Knowing* (New York: Sheed and Ward, 1997).

11. cf. Michael White and David Epston, *Narrative Means to Therapeutic Ends* (New York: W. W. Norton and Co., 1990).

2

Balanced Living

"Mr. Penick is the most balanced person I have ever known ... just knowing him has been a life lesson for all of us."

—Ben Crenshaw[1]

BEING MENTALLY HEALTHY IS A MATTER OF BALANCE. CONVERSELY, when we are not well, it means that something is out of balance. Sometime during the past year, I read a feature story about a premier distance runner in our local newspaper. "My life was out of balance." That is how she described her life, referring to her past, over several years, when she wasn't functioning well.

Anyone who has ever developed much skill at playing a sport knows the value of balance, be it in running, throwing, hitting, guarding, shooting, blocking, tackling, skating, putting, or what have you. It is true of governments. Those that have better balance have greater stability and function better. If you have ever taken medicine, if you've been ill or injured, then you know the importance of balance: when there is a problem anywhere in the body, it is likely to produce a problem somewhere else. Many medicines, for example, have side effects. In fact, additional medicine is sometimes prescribed just to counteract the side effects of some medications. Even though the medicine's purpose is to effect healing in one part of the body, it becomes the source of illness in another part. I limped badly for many years from a serious knee injury and subsequent multiple surgeries. I overcompensated, and in trying to protect my bad knee I wore out the other one, my good knee. The orthopedic surgeons and physical therapists used to tell me it would happen. I didn't believe

1. Don Wade, ed., "*And Then Jack Said to Arnie ...*" (Raleigh: Contemporary Books, 1991) 144.

them. I couldn't imagine that ever being the case. After all, I knew which was my bad knee. It only took about thirty years for their prognosis to come true. Because I walked with a limp over all those years, my body was out of balance.

My theory of balance is based on several observations. One is that mental health, or a lack thereof, is never absolute. It is always relative. That is, one is more or less mentally healthy, relative to any number of factors in one's circumstances. My teacher, the late Wayne Oates, used to say, "Even a broken clock tells the right time twice a day!" Experienced counselors know this is true. There are many folk who do a resourceful job in coping with such unreasonable stresses in their lives, just as there are others whose emotional survival skills would seem to be rather limited.

Over the years, I claim to have seen more of the former than the latter. That is, people who were doing a much better job of handling whatever the problems in their lives than they or perhaps anyone else in their world was giving them credit for doing. I recall a rather stylish older woman who presented to me some years ago. I would describe her as attractive, stately, fiercely proud, intelligent, strong, capable, and highly responsible. You get the picture. Her first statement to me was in three parts. It is vivid in my memory, for it was remarkably revealing. Here is what she said: "What is wrong with me? I'm so depressed. I know I shouldn't feel this way." The middle statement was, of course, a fact. It was bracketed by two highly value-laden statements, both of which had to do with how she saw herself. She then proceeded to describe her situation, the highly stressful circumstances of caring for her aged and quite ill husband in their home.

In my judgment, there wasn't anything "wrong" with her. To the contrary, she was doing an exceptional job of coping with an extremely difficult situation. However, she didn't see it that way. She seemed to see herself as something of a failure, as somehow weak and incapable. She was hardly measuring up to her own expectations or perhaps the expectations of others, including her husband, her children, other family members, and friends? Then again, given her high expectations of herself, she may have been projecting this outward onto others and seeing them seeing her as she saw herself. One's own perspective is often reinforced by others, and vice versa.

As true as that may be, if there was anything "wrong" with her, I think it had to do with her assessment of herself in that situation, an assessment, I might add, in which she seemed rather highly invested. Over the years, I believe I have seen more people like this woman, who were doing a better job of handling the stress in their lives than they seemed capable or willing to give themselves credit for doing. There wasn't nearly as much "wrong" with them as they or even others may have thought.

Throughout most of my professional life, I have been privileged to work with many less-privileged people, folk who were certainly economically disadvantaged, who have had to face significant physical, emotional, and social problems in their lives. It is easy to patronize such people. After all, that is how others often see them, and that is how such folk often tend to see themselves. One senior colleague used to chronically observe, "Bless her heart," in reference to patients we would see at the public mental health clinic where we worked. It sounded like something of a euphemism for, "Isn't he sad," or "She's pathetic." If my colleague's comment was meant to sound compassionate, it always seemed rather patronizing to me. Indeed, I have come to see many such folk as quite resourceful, often insightful, sometimes rather heroic, even in the context of usually quite limited and difficult circumstances. Good mental health is relative, not absolute.

Another observation on which my theory of balance is based is that the difference between being fairly healthy and getting pretty sick is not great, but is instead rather slight. If I were demonstrating this visually, it would be the difference between holding my arms and hands a span apart, as against holding my thumb and forefinger an eighth or a sixteenth of an inch apart. This comes from the observation that extremes reinforce their opposite. What's that cliché about how opposites make good bedfellows? At their extremes, they're not nearly as far apart as they might appear, since the pattern of such polarities tends to be cyclical. When extrapolated, they turn back toward each other. That is why skillful therapists will often ask clients to change their "buts" to "ands," as a way of emphasizing that what may seem like contradictions in our lives are usually more complementary than we realize. As in, "I'd like to try out for the team, but I'm scared I won't make it." Are you willing to change that "but" to an "and"? Given that reframe, here's what you get: "I'm scared, and I'm going to try out for the team." How about, "I love my husband, but I hate it when he interrupts me." Or again, "I believe in God, but sometimes I have my doubts." Are you willing to change the "buts" to "ands"?

We are empowered when we embrace the polarities, the dualities in our lives. This applies to any number of apparent opposites that tend to be mutually reinforcing. For example, what is the distance between how generous I can be and how resentful I can get, between my gentleness and my rage, between self-sacrifice and bitterness, between blessing and condemning? How far is it from my need for control to being out of control, between my passivity and my aggression, my humility and my self-righteousness, between prudery and profanity, between being compliant or rebellious, between being independent or dependent?

What's that old saw? "Neurotic people build sand castles in the sky; psychotic people move into them." I would merely add: and it's not that far to go. After all, they're kinfolk—or at least next-door neighbors! I always ask the counseling students I teach or supervise to pay attention to opposites, when someone seems so nice or so angry, so happy or so sad, so helpful or so resentful, so passive or so aggressive, so rational, so rigid, so sensitive, so whatever. What would the opposite of that adaptation, if that is what it is? What would its opposite look like? Remember, they're not that far apart.

The notion that mental health or illness are relative concepts, that extremes reinforce their opposite, and that the difference between being reasonably healthy and pretty sick is slight, not great: this is based on the Hebrew-Christian concept of sin and the classical Greek view of tragedy. In Hebrew-Christian thought, sin is, among other things, "missing the mark," however near or far. This comes from the biblical view of good as absolute and evil as always relative. In the Bible, nothing is absolutely bad in a world God has created. This view is quite different from dualism, where good and evil are seen as equal and opposite forces waging an endless battle with one another. That is how my dad used to explain it to me when I was a youngster. He would say that there was a good little boy and a bad little boy who lived on opposite sides of me, and they were constantly at war with one another. He could have just as easily said a healthy little boy and a sick little boy. There is a sense in which this may seem to be the case. For example, St. Paul in his Letter to the Romans, chapter 7: "The things I do, I would not, and the things I would not, those I do."

I can understand how well-meaning and quite devoted Christian folk, like my father, could certainly see the world as dualistic, not unlike the Zoroastrians of ancient Persia, or the Manichaeism so attractive to the young Augustine. Still, in orthodox Hebrew-Christian thought, as powerful as evil may seem, be it expressed either as natural or as moral, any sense of what is bad is always relative to the absolute goodness of creation.

For those of us reared in a puritanical tradition, sex is typically seen as the worst of all sins. Where I grew up, that message was even more implicit than explicit, which gave it even greater power. However, that is hardly the case in the Bible. Human sexuality is something good. It only becomes something bad when it is distorted, when it is perverted, when it is exploited, when it diminishes what is good and right and healthy about being human. This same ethic applies to many other aspects of our living. For example, pride can be something quite good, something honorable, a healthy kind of self-respect, just as it can become twisted and destructive. Ambition can serve oneself and others well, or it can be the source of extreme moral blindness and brutality. What is it C.S. Lewis said of evil? He called it "spoiled goodness," and he added, "We err when we pay evil too much attention, just as we err when we don't pay it attention enough." [2]

The Hebrew-Christian concept of sin also has to do with subtlety. As any good theologian would observe: in the Bible, Satan, the personification of evil, of distortion, of broken-ness, of what is inherently good being bent out of shape, perhaps even beyond recognition; indeed, Satan is a fallen angel. In the words of Pascal: "Men never do evil more boldly than when they do it in the name of the Lord." In an interview in *Christianity Today*, the Presbyterian minister Eugene Peterson is quoted as saying: "This culture is evil . . . through the media, through friends, through conversations, we are constantly fed lies, and like most lies, they are 90 percent truth." As much as I believe the first part of what he says is overstated, I couldn't agree more with the latter part, that 90 percent of most lies is the truth. [3]

In *The Screwtape Letters*, C.S. Lewis has Screwtape say to his nephew, Wormwood, whom he is teaching how to be a good devil: "Get people to be proud of their humility." If one does not understand such irony, it

2. C. S. Lewis, *The Screwtape Letters* (New York: Collier Books, 1961). I may have also read this somewhere in *Mere Christianity* (Macmillan Paperback Edition, 1960). I've read so much Lewis over the years, I can't remember where I read what; much less what is his idea and/or how it may have become my own.

3. "The Subversive Shepherd," *Christianity Today*, July 14, 1997, 48. Reverend Peterson is the preacher who said he "never wanted to pastor a church any larger than the number of names I can remember." Now there's a radical statement! See Eugene Peterson, *The Contemplative Pastor* (Grand Rapids: William B. Eerdmans, 1989).

is nigh impossible to appreciate that whatever its power, evil is always the perversion of something good, just as sickness, to use a different image, is a distortion of health. At its most powerful, evil will always be its most subtle. As the Reverend Peterson puts it, "90 percent truth," or well-meaning or considerate or thoughtful or sensitive or caring or what have you. So then, from a Hebrew-Christian perspective, you don't have to look all that far if you want to see the difference between what is healthy, good, and right about most of us and what can be pretty broken, twisted, distorted, and ill-purposed.

If balance as a key to health is rooted in a Hebrew-Christian doctrine of sin, it is also rooted in the Greek concept of tragedy. Yes, I know, these days tragedy is an overworked word. I hear it used to refer to almost anything bad: a flood, a fire, a child hit by a car, a young mother dying of cancer. As awful as these things are, they aren't tragic, at least in the classical sense of what the word means.

The Greek philosopher Aristotle defined tragedy over 2400 years ago. In its simplest form, tragedy is a strength taken too far, so as to be turned into a weakness or, as Aristotle saw it, a flaw in one's character. For the Greeks, such character flaws were fated. However, that is hardly a Hebrew-Christian idea. Jews and Christians, at least, understand weakness, even twisted-ness, broken-ness, or fallen-ness in a somewhat different way. As opposed to the classical view of the Greeks, Jews and Christians see the flaws in anyone's character, however tragic, as somehow more ambiguous. That is, if we can do something about the problem, unfortunately, whatever it is we try to do to make things better often only tends to make them worse. Still, the Hebrew-Christian view of humankind is never quite as dark as that of the Greeks. For Jews and Christians, there always remains a dimension of hope, as against mere grim resignation, some sense of vision, as against utter, blind fate. Be that as it may, in the ancient Greek theatre Oedipus is the prototype of the tragic figure. His drive, his competitiveness, his ambition are his strengths. When taken too far, however, they also become his weakness. They reflect a tragic flaw in his character, the source of his undoing.

It is true for the rest of us as well. We learn early on how to adapt in ways that help us survive, perhaps even excel. Our emotional and social survival skills then become our strengths. Except that, as we get older, we usually discover that such strengths can also be liabilities. When taken too far, it is as though our strengths tend to cross over a line somewhere, in something of a cyclical fashion, and begin to turn back on us in ways that prove to be our undoing, that keep us from the very goals we seek. The ancient Greeks called this tragic.

Here is a rather simple formula. By the time you are at least 30 years old, you ought to know what your predominant strengths are, be they your verbal-logical skills, your sensitivity or compassion, your shy-ness, your seductiveness, your salesmanship, the structure and discipline of your life, your organized way of living or your spontaneity, your creativity or the way you can stick with things, your affability, or perhaps a certain distant quality about yourself, your tendency to be aggressive and competitive, or the fact that you may be pretty laid back. If your life isn't working, if you can't seem to accomplish your goals, if you keep shooting yourself in the foot, then more than likely the problem has to do with how your strength has become your weakness. The place to pay attention and devote your energy is in the opposite direction of your strength. In other words, if it is a matter of choosing which direction to go, even to err, move away from what you would normally tend to do. For most of us, that isn't easy, especially the ambiguous part about what direction in which to err. How is it Martin Luther put it? "Trust God and sin bravely!" Most of us would prefer less ambiguous choices in life. Perhaps you've heard this definition of crazy: doing the same thing over and over again, likely even trying harder, and expecting the outcome to be different.

Here's an interesting illustration. I have done counseling with folk who, it would seem, have sold their souls to the Amway dream. As one friend put it, "I don't want the dream, I just want to buy some soap!" I have actually known couples who have brought financial ruin upon themselves trying to live up to some Amway image of success. They have mortgaged their homes, sold off wedding presents, and hocked the wife's engagement ring trying to maintain such an image, while spending an inordinate amount of time and money traveling here and there to this religious-patriotic rally and that motivational meeting. Such folk appear to have something of a character disorder, in which their image of themselves, perhaps their fantasy world, is rather out of touch with the reality of their circumstances, with who they are and are always likely to be.

However, perhaps dreaming such dreams may not be all that bad for some people. For example, I have a friend who got into Amway. He was about as anal as anyone I've ever known. Now you might say that Amway appealed to his alter ego. Jungians would likely call this his "shadow," that somewhere inside this fairly obsessive-compulsive perfectionist was a pretty slick, even risky entrepreneur just dying to get out and take on the world, to dream some really big dreams. I think I saw Amway as, in some ways, good for him, in that it provided a greater sense of balance in his life. Perhaps that was because, unlike too many other Amway people I have known, I trusted him, in the sense that it seemed pretty clear to me that he would never jeopardize the reality of his life for the sake of his fantasies. He was just too controlled and too controlling to ever go that far. He would never allow himself to live on the brink of financial disaster in order to try to sustain some successful Amway image of himself. Nor would I see him as being very good at exploiting others. In that sense, then, if the Amway ethos was appealing or inspiring or perhaps titillating to him, it seemed like something good—at least for my friend, even though I never let him "get me into the business."

Harry Hollis was the first person I can ever recall talking to me about balance in my life. Actually, he was teaching a course in Christian ethics. I was a young adult, a seminary student at the time. That was 40 years ago. Dr. Hollis used to talk about balance in our lives, between work and worship, as in the ancient Hebrew concept of sabbath. Most of us, I suppose, might more likely think of a need for balance between work and play, or perhaps between work and rest. I doubt there are many of us, who would disagree with the need for such balance in our lives. I have observed several other such needs over the years, as well, and I offer them here.

TO LIGHTEN UP OR TIGHTEN UP

Some people need to lighten up. Others need to tighten up. However, most counselors make their living off those who need to lighten up. In a culture that promotes and rewards competition and consumption at any cost, folk who are wrapped real tight, the hard chargers of this world, what we commonly call Type A people are something of a caricature, like the counselor who took his vacation to write a book on relaxation therapy—just the therapist for anyone willing to "work hard at relaxing!"

Of course, it isn't all that easy to lighten up when you've been conditioned and rewarded over a lifetime in such opposite ways, when your epitaph is inscribed to read: "I only wish I could have spent more time at the office." Is it any wonder that books like *Don't Sweat the Small Stuff— and it's all small stuff* or *Chicken Soup For the Soul* have been best-sellers?

Such catchy titles surely speak to a rather desperate need on the part of too many, when we measure our worth by busyness, when doing for others is a strength and caring for ourselves, a weakness. Most people I know need to lighten up. At least others in our lives likely wish we would. As one woman put it, "My husband doesn't just have ulcers, he gives them!" Those of us who need to lighten up are often blinded by our own importance, and we may not be quite as helpful or as necessary as we think.

For most people, to lighten up is even more of a qualitative than a quantitative task. That is, it has to do with an attitude adjustment, as in letting go of some beliefs about how things "ought" to be, the lowering of some expectations toward others, and certainly toward oneself. Therapists see a lot of people with deeply held beliefs about what they "should" be able to do for others, as well as what they have a "right" to "expect" in return. This is a common complaint counselors hear from clients, stated or implied: "I can't get (whomever) to do what I want them to do." People who need to lighten up tend to have some pretty grandiose beliefs about what or who it is they think they "ought" to be able to "control."

People who need to lighten up usually face a dilemma: the harder they try to "fix" things or "make" things happen, the more they seem to be contributing to just the opposite. For those used to being successful at "fixing" and "doing for," this dilemma can feel crazy. I am quite certain that most of the time when I have failed in my life, it has not been for a lack of effort or concern. It has, rather, come from trying too hard.

Some years ago, I watched a video presentation involving a group of Army officers who had been selected for Command and Staff, whose military careers were to be extended with the likelihood of their being promoted to Colonel or higher. To a man (these were all males), they were hard-charging, achievement-driven, Type-A guys whom the Army had discovered needed to be re-trained in the opposite direction of their obvious strengths. In other words, they needed to learn how to "lighten up," lest the intensity of their driven-ness lead to predictable health problems further down the road, given their being middle-aged men. The Army also had a considerable financial investment in their career development. Consequently, following a regimen of classes and exercises in relaxation therapy, one of the officer's family members commented: "He's become a lot easier to be around at home. At least he no longer goes through the house giving the various tables a white-glove test, to see if they've been properly dusted."

In a similar interview in *People* magazine, Harvard psychiatrist George Vaillant discussed the findings of an extensive longitudinal study of nearly 100 college men, from their student days in the early 1940s into their mature adult years, published in 1977 as *Adaptation to Life*.[4] The interviewer asked Dr. Vaillant, "The men who did best—what were they like?" He replied: "They had energy, warmth . . . a basic [sense of] trust . . . a capacity for unambivalent enthusiasm for both friends and work. They had not won success at the cost of poor marriages and neglected children. They also could take good vacations and knew how to play."

Meanwhile, some people need to tighten up their lives, since, despite their denial, they are strangling on a life full of too many loose ends, missed deadlines, tasks not quite completed, promises unkept, and all the excuses that go with such a way of living. Therapists don't tend to see as many of these loose-ended kind of people in counseling, and when we do, it is usually because "So-and-so said I should come"—you know, the family court judge. "You mean you're behind on your child support payments?"

"Well, yes . . . but . . . it's like this, Doc . . . ." And so the story goes . . .

In a clever spoof of the success of Stephen Covey, Bill McClellan has written a tongue-in-cheek piece on "The Seven Habits of Highly Ineffective People." First, "We drink a bit." Second, "We watch a lot of television." Third, "We don't choose good role models." Fourth, "We complain a lot. In fact, we enjoy complaining. We think of it as a hobby." Fifth, "We set unrealistic goals. Our fantasy isn't about running twenty minutes a day, three days a week, it's about winning the Boston Marathon." Sixth, "We let things go, we do everything at the last minute. Actually, for most of us that would be an improvement, for the truth is we wait until after the last minute." McClellan says that's why you always find a lot of "highly unsuccessful people milling around traffic court: We put off getting our driver's license renewed on time, and then when the cop stopped us we discovered all those parking tickets that hadn't been paid."

But, Number Seven is surely the prize. "Because we put things off until the last minute, we often find ourselves in a bind. Here's an example. Let's say a highly ineffective person were to sit down at the last minute to

---

4. George Vaillant, *Adaptation to Life* (Boston: Little Brown, 1977).

write a column. He might say he intended to write about the seven habits of highly ineffective people, but then he could only think of six." [5]

Some people need to tighten up their lives. It would do them a world of good. Come to think of it, it might even do the world some good.

TO SPEAK UP OR SHUT UP

I read somewhere that Billy Graham, in the twilight years of his life, had said that if he had his life to live over he would talk less and listen more. Others of us might likely say the same. Some folk need to speak up. Others need to shut up.

When I'm driving around town, getting from this hospital to that nursing home, I often listen to talk radio, and in particular, sports-talk radio. Your average parish pastor spends a lot of time in the car, getting from here to there. The inventor of talk radio is likely the person who created Richard Nixon's "silent majority" strategy, someone who knew for sure just how desperately most of us want to be heard, how we are just dying to "say our piece" to anyone who will listen, not that most talk radio hosts are particularly good listeners. Conversely, I have developed a close friendship over the years with the brothers of Mepkin Abbey, a nearby Cistercian monastery, where I have retreated from time to time because it is a quiet, reflective place, a place where listening is valued above speaking. To learn to listen, one has to learn to wait on more than just his turn to talk. At the same time, however, just because one isn't speaking doesn't mean she is listening.

Most marriage counselors are familiar with people who need to shut up, those for whom the reasoning seems: if I tell her one more time, she'll surely agree with me, or get it right; he'll start or stop doing whatever it is I want or don't want him to do. This appears to be at least one common caricature of marriage and family life, a pattern of not listening, of tuning the other person out, because I've heard it all before, and I still don't agree, or I'm not willing to comply or concede. There seems to be some chronic need to keep saying the same things over and over again, thinking that surely the next time it will make a difference. There is also usually some mutuality in trying to talk over or above or around one another. However, what is most apparent is that all the parties involved, be they spouses, par-

5. Bill McClellan, *The Seven Habits of Highly Ineffective People, St. Louis Post-Dispatch,* June 10, 2002.

ents, or children, are merely reinforcing each other's posture. This same caricature applies to others systems as well, such as work groups, churches, civic or interest groups, and surely the political process, wherever people are awfully invested in their point of view, in how they want things to be, when it would be helpful if at least someone would shut up.

Another caricature, at least of marriage and family life, is when people need to speak up. In this scenario, the belief seems to be, "If I have to ask for what I want, then it doesn't count. Can't he read my mind? Doesn't she know what I need? I shouldn't have to tell him." Some counselors are pretty good at pointing out how fighting in such passive or passive-aggressive ways is fighting nonetheless, even though the surface may appear relatively calm.

"What's the matter?"

"Oh, nothing."

"You seem as if you're upset about something."

"Who, me?"

Therapists who offer assertiveness training teach folk how the distance between being passive and being aggressive isn't quite as far as they may have thought. Being assertive is asking for what you need or want in powerfully appropriate ways. If some people need to shut up, others need to speak up.

WHO'S RESPONSIBLE FOR WHOM?

Some people tend to internalize too much, just as there are others who externalize almost everything. If you were to put this in terms of the DSM-IVR (the *Diagnostic and Statistical Manual of Mental Disorders*), the internalizers might be termed the neurotic people of this world, while the externalizers would be those who have some kind of character or personality disorder, or perhaps a thinking disorder. After all, that is what paranoid people do: they largely project outward, onto others.

Internalizers are sometimes referred to as co-dependent, which involves quite grandiose beliefs, as in, "If there is a problem here, it must be my fault," and/or, "I ought to be able to somehow make things better." In our culture, this is a common sex-role stereotype for many wives, mothers, and perhaps even sisters and aunts or grandmothers, in which too many women hold themselves responsible for the success or the happiness of the other people in their families.

Conversely, the externalizers of the world are people who seem so masterfully capable at shifting the responsibility for their lives to someone else. It's always the other person's fault. Interestingly enough, this kind of dependency is often expressed rather aggressively, if not passively-aggressively. Externalizers are adept at shifting their feelings to others, at least to others who are willing to accept such responsibility.

I was leading a workshop one time. We were playing some group game. I don't recall the details, except that one woman in the group got stuck on the task at hand. It was her turn to perform, but she seemed paralyzed in her fear of failing, or was it of succeeding? At any rate, she managed to fairly hysterically escalate her sense of helplessness, and before long, she had succeeded in shifting her discomfort to nearly everyone else involved. It was as though her peers were so uncomfortable with her discomfort that they would have done almost anything to try to relieve the stress—hers and theirs.

The main problem with internalizers, as well as externalizers, is that when they collude, one with the other, neither learns much about taking appropriate responsibility for the only person in this world any of us can ever, ultimately, be responsible for—ourselves.

HOW SERIOUSLY DO YOU TAKE YOURSELF?

Most of us take ourselves too seriously. Then again, some folk don't take themselves seriously enough. The latter group has, in my experience, been much smaller than the first group.

When we take ourselves too seriously, we often get our feelings hurt quite easily, or we get bent out of shape when we don't get our way or things don't go our way, when we don't get the approval we seek from whomever, when whoever discounts us in some way or other. Throughout my life, I have surely gotten too upset too often over too little, only to ask myself, more often later than sooner, "Who do you think you are?"

In the classic movie *The Sting*, Robert Redford is a novice con man. His mentor, Paul Newman, is the old pro. Out of revenge for the murder of their grifter-colleague, they set about to swindle a wealthy gangster boss. As the boss is responsible for their friend's death, Redford and Newman hatch a clever scheme to con this rich and powerful character out of a fortune. The "big con" is about to be played, and Redford's character is nervous. He asks his mentor if he thinks it will work, and Newman, as

Henry Gondorf, replies: "Why sure, kid. We had him the day he decided to be somebody important."[6]

When our sense of worth is defined more extrinsically than intrinsically, we are more vulnerable to be seduced, swindled, or exploited. It is here, it would seem, that taking ourselves too seriously hardly serves us well. For theists, and certainly those of Hebrew-Christian faith, God confers anyone's ultimate worth through a personal love that is forever creating rather than seeking value. To this way of believing, then, the worth of persons comes not as much from doing as in being. Such status is never achieved. It is, rather, but received, and gratefully so, as the precious gift it is. Who was it that said, "Take yourself lightly, so that, like the angels, you may fly?" An inflated sense of self-importance can weigh any of us down. It can be too heavy a burden to bear.

There are others who seem not to take themselves seriously enough. I have known few such folk along the way. But those I have known possessed or were possessed of a manner that seemed almost frightening to me. To a person, they were charming and affable, yet they somehow managed to devalue anything significant about themselves, for good or ill, in the glibbest sort of way, usually with a smile, or some form of self-deprecating humor. It has caused me to wonder if not taking oneself seriously enough isn't, in some strange way or other, quite as grandiose as taking oneself too seriously? It makes me think that surely one of life's most important balancing acts has to be that of taking yourself seriously, but not too seriously.

TO HANG ON OR LET GO

This is a sticky one, or as the song goes, "You got to know when to hold 'em and know when to fold 'em." Perseverance is surely a time-honored virtue for many of us. It can also be our blind spot, our *bete noire*, our demon's demon, when we don't know "when to fold 'em," when letting go and giving up and moving on with our lives is a worse failure than the mess we are in, for whatever the reasons. Then there are others who deal with life on far too casual, too careless a basis. Such folk are apt to split at the first little bump in the road, the first sign that things might not be going so well.

---

6. *The Sting*, directed by George Roy Hill, Zanuck/Brown Productions, 1973.

Many would conclude that the latter is a caricature of marriage in America, with roughly a 50 percent divorce rate on first marriages. While driving around town, I also sometimes listen to a "Christian radio station," syndicated in our local market out of California. It is, as with most such media, quite conservative in its religion, and certainly in its social commentary and politics. That is their pitch, and it is consistent: if you want a successful marriage, you have to work at it, you have to be deeply committed, and you have to persevere. And, of course, they are right.

However, anyone who has ever done much marriage counseling has seen the other side of this dilemma, where what one might call the co-dependent spouse is over-functioning, working overtime at trying to make his or her marriage work, except the harder he or she works at it, the more he or she is contributing to the dysfunction in the relationship. Perseverance, resolve, a sense of direction, and focus are obvious and necessary ingredients in anyone's success, be it in a marriage or a career, in parenting, in creative pursuits, certainly in management and supervision tasks, in developing much skill or joy at doing much of anything. It can also become, when taken too far, the often subtle and painful source of one's undoing—and tragically so.

I, for example, consider among my rather limited repertoire of virtues my deep sense of loyalty to be rather prominent. I attribute this to values taught in my family of origin, as well as the small town in which I grew up. There, everyone knew everyone and almost everything about everyone. No one was going anywhere—at least no one in my family and among our friends, nor even our enemies. We were stuck with each other, for good or for ill. Therefore, working things out and the dynamics of staying together were paramount. My father, for example, had incurred enormous debts from the 1930s, during a time when my older sister, as a youngster, was seriously ill. It took my dad many years to pay off his indebtedness—to the local grocer, who had extended him credit during the hard times; to the family that ran the service station, who had done the same, who had sold him gasoline on credit. I grew up in a milieu where loyalty and perseverance were obvious virtues. You just didn't run out on your family or your friends, no matter how bad things got.

Throughout my life, however, this has cost me dearly. I can think of few serious errors in judgment on my part, personally or professionally, that haven't been the result of my stubbornness, my unwillingness to admit having made a mistake, my need to "hang in there" with someone or for someone, lest I face what I have perceived as an even worse sense of failure.

In the Gospel of Luke, Jesus admonishes those who would follow him, "No one who puts his hand to the plow and looks back is fit for the Kingdom.[7] While in each of the first three Gospels, he instructs his disciples to "shake the dust from your feet" and move on, when faced with unacceptable circumstances. In the goal of balanced living, "You got to know when to hold 'em, and know when to fold 'em." And that isn't always easy.

WHAT TIME IS IT IN YOUR LIFE?

As opposed to the ancient Greeks, or the a-historical Eastern religions, in a Hebrew-Christian worldview time is not only real, it is important. In a world that had a beginning and that will have an end, even as do each of our lives, time has a claim upon us. Living in time implies some sense of balance between past, present, and future. As the Book of Ecclesiastes puts it: "To everything there is a season, and a time for every purpose under heaven."[8]

Some people spend too much time trying to live in the past. For such folk, it is as though they are stuck "back there" somewhere, for whatever reasons. My dad used to say, "What good ol' days?" He was not one to romanticize his past. Others seem to have little or no sense of history, perhaps because they are so desperately trying to run from it, or at least from theirs. For some folk, the present is all that would seem to count. Others would appear to be living largely in or for the future, for that day when their ship comes in. Reasonably healthy people seem to live with some sense of appropriate balance between their past, their present, and their future.

Over many years as a therapist, this would seem to be where I have spent a lot of time with clients. I call it "living in the meantime," somewhere between the way things are and the way we might wish them to be. Living too much in any direction can be illusory, be it past, present, or future. Biblical religion seems to offer a balance of all three, between remembering the past, acting decisively in the present, and planning re-

7. Luke 9:62.
8. Eccl 3:1.

sponsibly for one's future. Here, for example, are three relative proof-texts for such balanced living:

> "Remember the days of old,
> consider the years of many generations;
> ask your father, and he will show you;
> your elders, and they will tell you.
> When the Most High gave to the nations their inheritance . . . ."[9]

> "Therefore do not be anxious about tomorrow, for tomorrow will be anxious for itself. Let the day's own trouble be sufficient for the day."[10]

> "Thus says the Lord:
> 'Keep your voice from weeping,
> and your eyes from tears;
> for your work shall be rewarded,'
> says the Lord,
> 'and they shall come back from the land of the enemy.
> There is hope for your future,'
> says the Lord . . . ."[11]

A friend recently passed along this sage piece of advice off the Internet: "To appreciate the value of a YEAR, ask a student who failed a grade; a MONTH, ask a mother who gave birth to a premature baby; a WEEK, ask a parish pastor, for whom the time between Sundays often seems shorter than seven days; a DAY, ask a patient waiting for a lab report; an HOUR, ask two lovers longing to meet; a MINUTE, ask someone who missed the plane; a SECOND, ask a person who just avoided an accident; a MILLISECOND, ask anyone who ever won a silver medal in the Olympics." The piece concludes: "Yesterday is history; tomorrow is mystery; today is a gift. That's why it's called the present!"

ACCEPTANCE AND CHANGE

Surely a major task at some point in most people's lives is finding a balance between accepting ourselves and the integrity of our living, while also being open and willing to change. I suggest that the former requires

9. Deut 32:7–8.
10. Matt 6:34–35.
11. Jer 31:16–17a.

a spirit of gratitude, while the latter depends upon one's flexibility and a dose of humility. There's nothing quite as tragic as an endless searching for oneself. In Arthur Miller's play *Death of a Salesman*, Willie Loman's son speaks his father's epitaph with the haunting words: "He never knew who he was."[12] Balanced living requires an acceptance of who we are and aren't, what we can and can't do, where we have been, or are, as well as where we will likely never go.

I remember once reading a sermon by the late William Sloane Coffin. One passage, in particular, has stayed with me over the years. As Coffin put it: "When we are young we dream big. We're going to sing like Luciano Pavarotti, dance like Patricia McBride, write like Maya Angelou, have the courtroom career of a Louis Nizer, and the lash-like left of pitcher Ron Guidry. But then, say, at about age thirty, comes the cold shower. It is the often painful but liberating realization that we are never going to sing or dance or write or orate or pitch like anyone else but ourselves."[13] It is here, Coffin claims, that if we are willing we can make peace with our lives in a way that is fulfilling. As one might say, "This is what it means to know and to do the will of God." It happens when we stop trying to be someone other than ourselves, certainly when we stop trying to be something more, lest we end up as someone less. Too often, that is what happens. Have you heard of Rabbi Lieberman? He said, "When I meet God in the judgment, he is not going to ask, 'Why weren't you Moses or David or Elijah?' No, he's going to say, 'Why weren't you Lieberman?'"

The late Baptist preacher, Carlyle Marney, claimed that the gift of accepting oneself involves "going through home." We can't go home again, he explained, quoting Thomas Wolfe. None of us can, ever again. We can't go home. What we must do, Marney insisted, is to "go through home, by saying to those who shaped and mis-shaped us, 'thank you for the best, and I forgive you for the worst.'"[14] Self-acceptance is an expression of gratitude. It is embracing our lives, all of who we are and aren't, for good and for ill.

Balanced living also requires us to adapt, to change, and to grow. I suspect the former leads to the latter. That is, the more we are gracefully at peace with ourselves, the less guarded and defensive we will tend to be

---

12. Arthur Miller, *Death of a Salesman* (New York: Penguin Books, 1996).

13. William Sloane Coffin, *The Courage to Love* (New York: Harper and Row, 1982).

14. Carlyle Marney, *The Coming Faith* (York-Nashville: Abingdon Press, 1970).

in the face of circumstances in our lives that require—even demand—change on our part. Surely the more we accept ourselves, with a thankful rather than a begrudging spirit, a spirit of resentment and bitterness, the more open and willing are we likely to face and even embrace change. My experience, at least, tells me the two somehow go together.

SUCCESS AND FAILURE

It's not that most of us don't try to succeed, or that we somehow seek to fail, although you could get a pretty good argument about this from many counselors, since most of us have had plenty of experience working with folk who seemed to be rather committed and often quite as successful at sabotaging themselves. Be that as it may, success and failure would seem to be two of the necessary ingredients of balanced living—at least in proper dosage.

For some people, failure seems to be a syndrome. They appear to have had such little success in their lives that losing has become a way of life. It is how they have come to define themselves. Everyone needs enough success in life to be balanced. Sometimes folk are more successful than they realize or are willing to acknowledge. This is often camouflaged as humility. It can be a powerful cultural message. "Don't think too highly of yourself. Don't be haughty. Don't put on airs." Such humility can often be rather pseudo, for I know many such people who are likely the most arrogant folk in the world. They trade on their failures, their losses, and their disappointments in life as if this were a badge of honor, as though it were the most important thing that ever happened to them. What I am describing is hardly some rare disease. Therapists confront it all the time. Far too many people present this as essentially their life's story.

On the other hand, some people have enjoyed so much success in their lives that they have become rather ill equipped to face even the least terminal forms of failure. I once knew a graduate student who failed a language exam. He was so devastated, he dropped out of school and never returned. I mean, come on. Everyone fails French or German or whatever (the language exam in grad school) the first time. That's like failing some part of the CPA exam. Well, maybe not everyone, but it's certainly not something from which one can never recover. This fellow, however, was used to making straight A's. It was as though he had no sense of himself apart from the unparalleled success he had enjoyed throughout his young life. For others, the price attached to failure may be even higher, as in a failed marriage, a lost job or career, a loss of health, not making the team or winning a championship, or a failed love relationship. Sometimes it involves the cost of one's life, or the life of another.

Over the years, I have learned to pay attention to both how people handle their successes and to how they handle their failures, losses, and disappointments. I see this as the primary measure of one's character. In the words of St. Paul, "I know how to be abased, and I know how to abound . . . ."[15] A balanced way of living is a reasonably healthy way of living, and if we are to live this way, we are called to face both the successes and the failures in our lives with genuine humility, with courage and self-respect, as well as some grace.

15. Phil 4:12.

3

Balanced Families

"My wife said, 'You're so crazy about golf, I bet you
don't even remember our wedding anniversary.' And
I said, 'Margaret, that's not so. I remember it well.
It was the first day I ever broke 90!'"

—Bill Collins

F AMILIES SEEK BALANCE, FOR GOOD OR FOR ILL. FAMILY THERAPISTS
call this homeostasis. When one thinks of balanced families, a mobile is an image that comes to mind. When one part of a mobile shifts
or moves, all the other parts are affected as well. They move, too. Indeed,
movement or change in any part affects all the other parts. In this sense,
then, families are systems, like mobiles. Change in any part impacts on
the system as a whole. This movement proceeds across generations and
extends quite beyond the nuclear family unit.

Alternatively, families, as systems, are like an inter-connected series
of pulleys and levers. When one part moves, the other parts move in the
service of homeostasis, of balance in the system. To press this analogy, a
long enough pole can move quite a load if the leverage is right. That is
how it tends to work in families.

Systemically, families also operate on a principle of reciprocal feedback, or reinforcement. This promotes balance. The image of a thermostat
may serve here as a helpful analogy. A thermostat functions in the service of heating or cooling the air in a room or building. When the air in
that space reaches the right temperature, the thermostat, if it is working
properly, receives the appropriate feedback and shuts off. Until it receives
another message that it is now time to tell the furnace or air conditioner
to start heating or cooling the air again . . . and so on . . . and so forth.

This is not unlike the pattern of how many couples often argue in fairly chronic ways or how they may inspire one another rather positively: they provide a mutual and reciprocal pattern of reinforcement, of feedback for each other.

Here's another human example. My friend, a pediatrician, once described interviewing a mother and her young daughter. The mother described the child's behavior to the doctor, and the doctor asked, "And then what do you do?" The mother described her usual behavior in response to the child, and the doctor asked again, "And then what does she do?" Again, the mother described a predictable pattern of response on her daughter's part, to which she would predictably react . . . and on . . . and on again this mutual and reciprocal pattern of reinforcement seemed to continue, primarily in the service of promoting balance in their system, or if in a larger family, their sub-system.

The study of families as systems began roughly sixty years ago. Among the pioneers in the development of family systems theory were psychoanalytically trained and veteran mental health practitioners such as Nathan Ackerman, Carl Whitaker, Virginia Satir, Lyman Wynne, Murray Bowen and Don Jackson, as well as notable figures in other fields of scientific inquiry, including Ludwig von Bertlanaffy, Gregory Bateson, John Weakland, Werner Heisenburg and Jay Haley. If the more theoretical roots of family systems are to be found in an understanding of cybernetics, including theories of mathematics and physics and studies in anthropology and communications theory, a more applied, clinical basis surely came from work with schizophrenic and alcoholic families.

For example, any mental health professional who has had much experience working with patients diagnosed as schizophrenic, as well as with their families, has observed something of a revolving door syndrome, and a rather chronic one at that. Typically, the patient becomes psychotic and is hospitalized, primarily to protect him or her from hurting or killing him or herself or someone else, as well as to provide the kind of intensive psychiatric treatment hospitalization can offer. The patient then becomes stabilized, at least enough to be discharged from the hospital and return to his community, often to her family. Then, over a period of time, such a dreadful syndrome may begin again, usually when the patient stops taking his medicine. He or she starts to decompensate and become psychotic, requiring additional hospitalization . . . and on . . . and on it goes.

In our society, we generally try to look the other way when it comes to people with this illness. Until a John Hinkley or a Rusty Westin shows up in our nation's capital in the midst of a psychosis and starts shooting at people, even a President. Then this awful illness that affects too many people becomes front page news. Schizophrenia is sometimes termed a "college student's" disease, since the onset of its symptoms often initially occur in young adulthood. At present, there is no known cure for schizophrenia. It can only be controlled or managed, as with many other common, though less stigmatic illnesses. I have worked with many such patients, as well as their families, who have had fifteen or twenty hospitalizations between, say, age 20 into their forties.

The early development of family systems theory drew significantly from this pattern, the revolving door syndrome, involving patients diagnosed and treated as schizophrenic, living always in the meantime, it would seem, between hospital and home. The consequent surmise was reasonable: do "crazy" families, for whatever reasons, produce symptoms of their system's craziness that manifest in certain identifiable "patients"? Some early transgenerational theorists even predicted how many generations of certain kinds of family pathology it would take to produce schizophrenia.

Today the pendulum seems to have swung in an opposite direction. The psychiatric community presently interprets schizophrenia almost exclusively in terms of genetics and/or biochemistry, which is more likely inherited than developed in any particular social matrix. This understanding of such illness stands in rather stark contrast to that of traditional systems theory. Indeed, popular grassroots advocacy movements on behalf of the chronically mentally ill these days take a rather firm posture in distancing families from such illness. From this perspective, then, schizophrenia is not interpreted as a family illness.

However, that would not seem to be the case with the disease of alcoholism, which is largely understood as systemic in nature. Not only does current research suggest inherited tendencies to alcoholism, from a genetic and/or biochemical perspective, the most successful approaches to the treatment of this addiction posit factors of culture and family system dynamics as major contributing factors to such illness. While textbooks in family therapy do not tend to tell the story this way, or at least this part of the story, I suspect that there were any number of astute family physicians or parish pastors before 1940, whose work with alcoholics and their families was insightful enough for them to have likely predicted that if

John ever does get sober, his wife, Mary, will surely be out of a job as the martyred partner of such a pathetic alcoholic. Consequently, she may then need to get sick in some way or other herself. It would be many years later that the term "co-dependency" would come into common currency. The genius of such awareness is surely reflected, however, in the development of Al-Anon. If the powerful program of Alcoholics Anonymous offered (and continues to offer) hope for the alcoholic to attain sobriety, those who first envisioned such an approach to, treatment clearly understood the disease of alcoholism from a systemic perspective. Families inherently seek balance around all sorts of issues, not the least of which involve matters of health and power.

The need and tendency to maintain balance in families can promote good or ill. For example, covert messages can serve either purpose. The point here, to which any well-trained family therapist is highly sensitized, is that the most powerful messages in families, in organizations, in any system, even in cultures tend to be more covert than overt, more non-verbal than verbal. This is especially true when nothing explicit is said, or when what is promoted overtly is contradicted by more powerful ulterior messages.

Here's an example. In his autobiography, the late William Sloane Coffin describes teaching many years ago in a prestigious New England prep school for boys. In this context, wealth as power was simply bred into the culture. It was assumed so much so that the public rhetoric, perhaps even the private rhetoric, regarding the school was anything but about money as power. Indeed, it generally tended to be about such abstractions as altruism and service, courage and honor. As Coffin said, "Values, I began to understand, are more caught than taught. They are experienced concretely more than they are taught abstractly. No classroom, for example, consciously promoted wealth as a value; in fact, quite the contrary. Yet living in surroundings that only wealth could provide tended inevitably to enhance its value, and to such a degree that I found a few scholarship students who could forgive their fathers anything except their inability to make money."[1] I think of Coffin's illustration, in even more glaring terms, every time I hear the popular television preachers declaring how important "spiritual riches" are, compared to anything "material," while at the same time soliciting contributions to sustain the opulence of their particular image of success – "in the name of the Lord,"

1. William Sloane Coffin, *Once to Every Man* (New York: Atheneum, 1977) 128.

of course, as if material prosperity has much of anything to do with what it means to be a Christian, at least according to Jesus.

The same is true in families. What is promoted overtly may stand in rather stark contrast to or is subtly and powerfully subverted by much stronger ulterior messages. For example, if I am always preaching to my children about the virtues of a strong work ethic, yet I hate my job, or if I tell my kids how important it is to have good self-esteem yet chronically discount and devalue myself in any number of ways. How about this one: if I teach my children the importance of gratitude, but am, myself, quite incapable of accepting much of any gift with grace, if I am somehow always trying to pay back what others may wish to do for me or give to me. These are almost trite examples of powerfully incongruent covert messages common in many families. And it doesn't even take into account the blatant "do as I say, not as I do" hypocrisy on the part of too many parents concerning the use of tobacco, alcohol, and other drugs.

Conversely, covert messages in families can also be positive. The father, Atticus Finch, in Harper Lee's lovely novel, *To Kill a Mockingbird*, is surely the prototype of such strong, positive non-verbal communication in a family, in the way he relates to his children. In organizations, this is commonly referred to as a particular "corporate culture," values which tend to get promoted at a far deeper level than anything circulated in memos, or in a host of rules and regulations. My father was something of an Atticus Finch. The integrity in how he lived and the way he related to others of us in his family was congruent and powerful, it engendered respect and cooperation on our part, beyond anything he may have ever said. Some organizations even function like that—even some churches. Not many, but some. They tend to promote a similar management style.

In the development of Transactional Analysis, Bob and Mary Goulding observed ten different generic injunctions, essentially negative ulterior messages not uncommon in families: 1. Don't Be; 2. Don't Be You; 3. Don't Be a Child; 4. Don't Grow Up; 5. Don't Be Close; 6. Don't—that's right, just Don't; 7. Don't Make It; 8. Don't Be Sane (or Well); 9. Don't Be Important; 10. Don't Belong.[2] Then a psychologist named Taibi Kahler came along with something called "mini-script" theory, in which he identified five different, somewhat similar generic messages, or counter-injunctions, of an ostensibly positive nature. However, Kahler claims that

2. C. J. Sayer and H.S. Kaplan, eds. *Progress* in *Group and Family Therapy* (New York: Brunner/Mazel, 1972) 107.

these messages, in that they are overt, often and ironically reinforce such negative injunctions as the Gouldings identified. Kahler's five "drivers" are: 1. Be Strong; 2. Be Perfect; 3. Try Hard; 4. Hurry Up; 5. Please Me. [3]

To illustrate, "trying hard" is part and parcel of almost anyone's work ethic, except sometimes trying too hard is the subtlest and most socially sanctioned way of sabotaging even the best effort or the most worthy goal. A chronic pattern of "not making it" is often accompanied by quite as chronic a pattern of "But look how hard I tried." Some who have come to identify such a theme in their lives have learned to see just how subtle a way of sabotaging themselves this can be, and how socially sanctioned it can be. I always pay attention to anyone's "trys," and I teach my students and clients to do so as well. People who take greater responsibility for their choices in life, for both their successes and certainly for their failures, don't tend to "try" as hard as those who seem to spend more of their life losing and always wondering "why?" while never seeming to see the connection between the why and the try.

Consider how subtly a "Be Strong" message tends to reinforce a "Don't Be a Child" injunction—in essence, "don't feel." How about a "Please Me" message that in too many families means, "Don't Grow Up." In other words, "I want you to stay dependent on me. We'll call it love, but what we're really learning is to resent each other," since that is what such dependency typically tends to produce. What is significant about such mixed messages in families is how they can collude to promote pathology in a system, how what is not said, or the backside of what is said, how whatever is "spoken" covertly is so much more powerful than anything overt.

Here's another illustration. It comes from my own *Life's Little Instruction Book*. I have always said to my children, "Take care of yourself." This is a different message from "Be careful." The latter implies the possibility of danger. The former adds to it a message about capability and responsibility. Others may care about you, but they can't take care of you. Only you can do that. Such capability and responsibility is yours. I also say this to clients I counsel, to friends, to folk in the church I pastor, to anyone I care about. Take care of yourself.

When pathology is present in a system, covert messages are often extended to what therapists commonly call "the family secret." This is what

---

3. Graham Barnes, ed. *Transactional Analysis After Eric Berne* (New York: Harper's College Press, 1977) 224.

everyone knows, but doesn't know, or isn't supposed to know. It is fear-based. There is a simple principle of mental health that goes something like this: anything we are afraid of will end up controlling and perhaps even ruining our lives. What is important to understand, if one is to be reasonably mentally healthy, is that more often than not our fear is worse than whatever we fear. As ambiguous as truth may often be, such fear still tends to distort it, usually making it worse. Any experienced counselor has encountered this. A client presents. He tells you that he "needs to talk to someone" about "something I have never told anyone." You listen. As hard as it may be for the client to tell you what is troubling him or her, as long as it may take for him or her to finally say what it may be, or as much as people may reveal this or that more indirectly or symbolically, whatever is involved in the process, when the truth is finally told, people begin to heal and to change for the better. If the family secret is usually fear-based, it may also be shame-based: what we are afraid of, or ashamed to face ourselves, and so are afraid for others to know. However, they likely know already, or because of the nature of family secrets, what they think they know may be even worse than whatever there is to know.

Adult children of alcoholics, for example, often describe unspoken agreements and elaborate schemes on the part of their families in an effort to try to hide someone's alcoholism. This is often called "the elephant in the living room." What elephant in the living room? Some families collude in a similar conspiracy of silence with regard to mental illness, or perhaps a suicide. Some families have, at least in the past, had a need to do so around adoptions, or what may have been perceived as the scandal of "having to get married." The same is often true of an abortion.

The family secret also operates in other systems. For example, a minister colleague once described serving a congregation for several years. The church wasn't even 50 years old. It was a relatively young, suburban congregation. Somewhere along the way of his tenure, however, my colleague inadvertently stumbled upon the name of a minister who had apparently served that church sometime in the past, but for whatever reason or whatever scandal, the congregation had "forgotten" this fellow. A conspiracy of silence had grown up, over some years, around this man and his family. As far as that church was concerned, he had never even been there.

Another minister I know, while serving a particular congregation, discovered that the church secretary had embezzled a sizable amount of money from the church. This was a small, country church, full of "family," relatives of this church secretary. They quickly closed ranks, made restitution of the stolen money and, not long afterward, asked this minister to leave. He had become a threat because he had exposed their family secret.

Likely the most scandalous of family secrets involves sexual abuse. I teach a graduate course in family systems theory. In the class I use a film entitled *Nuts*, which stars Barbra Streisand and Richard Dreyfuss.[4] I remember seeing the movie when it first appeared in theatres a number of years ago. Throughout the film, it seemed that most of the people in the theatre were laughing at the antics of Streisand's character. However, the story isn't funny. It's about sexual abuse in an ostensibly "good" family. I use the movie to try to teach two things to my students, who are pursuing a master's degree in clinical counseling. One has to do with being a skilled therapist. Ironically, the psychiatrist in the film is unwittingly in collusion with the pathology in the family presented. It is the court-appointed attorney, played by Dreyfuss, who demonstrates therapeutic savvy. He knows there is something not right about this family, that there is something quite incongruent, that Barbra Streisand's character must be a symptom-bearer of far deeper dysfunction than the public image of her family would suggest. He is observant and intuitive, and he plays his hunch. In the process, he exposes the family secret, scandalous and painful as it is. The other thing I use this film to illustrate, as vividly as it does, is how the family secret serves to promote balance in the system, as pathologic as it may be, and how exposing the secret de-stabilizes the family. In this instance, if the family falls even farther apart, in terms of how the parents have previously seemed to understand, and certainly how they presented themselves, the mother-daughter relationship is re-established in what would appear to be a reasonably healthy way.

As I have worked with families over many years, it strikes me that the function of balance in a system is ambiguous at best. If it can promote strengths and health in a family, as often as not it promotes pathology. In most cases, such pathology is manifest in a particularly symptomatic person in the system, often identified as the "patient." When one understands families in this way, it is ironic, for when the "sick" person starts getting well, the balance in the system is de-stabilized. The family begins to frag-

4. *Nuts*, directed by Martin Ritt, Barwood Films, 1987.

ment. Frequently someone else becomes symptomatic. The caricature of such families is almost as if they hold one another hostage. It is as though they are too connected to one another. Family therapists call this being "enmeshed." I often explain that, in such families, everyone seems to be too busy trying to take care of someone else's emotional business, so no one is doing a very good job taking care of his own. Ironically, such enmeshment tends not to promote much closeness in families. In such families, people often feel quite isolated and alone, quite alienated from one another, even though the ostensible dynamics may appear otherwise.

What is called Bowen natural systems theory speaks of this as a lack of "differentiation" among family members. Bowen traces this across multiple generations. Differentiation involves a healthy and appropriate sense of one's "self." It has to do with where any of us begin and end, what some would call "ego boundaries." In this way of thinking, it is the adequate defining of a "self" that is essential to sharing much intimacy with another. I once heard Scott Peck observe that in healthier families, "children are better able to leave," to separate out from the family, and are thus better equipped to join with another comparably differentiated person in creating a new family. Conversely, in more dysfunctional families, where the people involved seem forever stuck with or to one another, children appear to have a harder time "leaving the nest." Experienced family therapists know how true this is. It is surely what the Bible must mean when it says, "Therefore a man leaves his father and his mother ...."[5] Bowen theory posits that people tend to (unconsciously?) seek out others of comparable differentiation, or a lack thereof, in the mating process. Differentiation is a relative rather than absolute concept. People aren't differentiated or not. They are, rather, more or less differentiated.

When balance serves families for good, not ill, it will always have to do with how power and intimacy are connected, with the important way in which being adequately differentiated as a person and an increased capacity for closeness go together. This is what some might call "interdependence." Power and vulnerability are a paradox: the more truly powerful one is, the more capable he will be at owning and expressing his vulnerability. Differentiation implies an appropriate sense of power. It has to do with how well one is defined as a person. This is essential to the vulnerability necessary in intimacy, in being close.

5. Gen 2:24

When people share an intimate relationship, as spouses, as friends, as parents and children, as brothers and/or sisters, they are more open and revealing with one another. In terms of self-differentiation, this is a characteristic of strength, not weakness. Their capacity for closeness is in direct proportion to how well defined they are as individuals. As Kahlil Gibran says in his meditation on "Marriage": "Two oaks don't stand in each other's shade." [6] This is the function of balance in healthier families, where people are well defined in relation to one another. This is different from families where there seems to be such confusion over where people begin and end, over who is responsible for whom, where such neediness and dependency and presumptuousness tends to drive people away and promote even more ambivalence and resentment, where what is portrayed as power is really rather petty and pseudo at best.

I will now discuss the balance of power in marriage and in parenting.

A BALANCED MARRIAGE

A lot of different factors seem to contribute to good or ill in a marriage. These may include cultural and religious values; personality compatibility; matters of taste and personal interest; health factors; energy level; moral development; intelligence, or perhaps level of education; sexuality; maturity; a sense of humor; depth and degree of commitment; sleep patterns. And on and on it goes. The list may seem endless. Some family counselors might even suggest that for two people to be compatible, the pathology of each needs to somehow "fit" with that of the other, that they need to share some mutuality in this respect. For example, the hysteric and the sociopath, to use fairly pejorative labels, can often get along famously! In contrast, the hysteric and the obsessive-compulsive don't tend to do so well together, since the former is often so out of control, while the latter is generally over-controlled, and likely just as controlling.

Another strange pattern of apparent compatibility one frequently sees in marriages is what is sometimes called that of the "distancer" and the "pursuer." [7] In this marital pattern, one of the spouses tends to chronically over-function emotionally, while the other normally under-functions. In such roles, the spouses may mutually reinforce each other's primary style

6. Kahlil Gibran, *The Prophet* (New York: Knopf, 1952).

7. E. G. Pendagast, ed. *Compendium II: The Best of the Family, 1978–83* (New Rochelle: The Center for Family Learning) 45–50.

of operating, so as to promote, even if in rather chronic ways, at least some sort of balance in their system. I often say that sometimes it seems that there are just two kinds of people in this world: those who fear being smothered, and those who fear being abandoned. And they often marry one another.

Then there is love. It's interesting that we would have but a single word in the English language for what is likely the most ambiguous subject. Is love an emotion? Certainly. Is it a decision, a choice? It is, at least in the Bible. Is it a commitment? Ditto. Is it a priority? Double ditto! From a biblical perspective, love is goodwill, not wishing another harm. The King James Bible calls this "charity." It has an unconditional quality to it. Love can also mean liking another person, as in friendship. This tends to be more conditional. We don't "like" everyone or necessarily everything about anyone. Love can also mean sexual attraction, although this Greek word never appears in the New Testament. Erotic love tends to be more conditional, and sometimes those conditions can seem rather strange. From this perspective, all three kinds of love seem important in a marriage. Most people who have been very successfully married for many years would insist that these first two kinds of love, a less conditional goodwill and genuine friendship, are essential to growing and sustaining a marriage over the long haul, certainly when people get old or sick.

It may seem strange to some that most people in the world, even today, don't choose whom they will marry. Their families do the choosing. The idea is that you both learn, as well as learn how to love your spouse. As strange as this may seem to many of us for whom romantic love, or "falling in love," is the criterion for marriage, most of the rest of the people in this world look at our divorce rates (they get even higher after the first try!) and likely conclude that maybe "love," in the way it is romanticized, isn't the primary criterion for marriage after all. Most family therapists have had ample opportunity to see people loving another in some of the most unlovable of ways, especially when loving seems to be understood almost exclusively as getting, or perhaps even as a way of giving in order to try to get. Jesus defined the highest good as loving another in proportion to one's own love of self, even as this is rooted in God's way of loving any of us, indeed a love that evokes our love for God.

Some years ago in my counseling practice, I saw a young man who had immigrated to America. He came from a culture and a religion quite different from mine. He was "in love," he said, with a woman he worked with, a woman whose culture and religion were just as different from his. The conflict in this man's life involved whether he was going to tell his parents, since his parents had arranged some years before, with another family of their religion and culture, for him to marry a daughter from that family. He was suffering emotionally from his conflict over what to do. What choice should he make? I listened to him over a couple of counseling sessions. Like most therapists, I was not willing to tell him what I thought he ought to do. That was his business, his decision to make, not mine. He seemed to accept, and even appreciate my respect for him in this regard. He left, and I never saw him again. A year or so later, I asked the colleague who had referred this young man to me if he knew what had happened. She told me that this fellow had broken off the relationship with the woman he worked with and had married according to his family's wishes. From listening to him, as he told me his story, that is not what I would have predicted. Most of us modern Americans prioritize our individuality, the value of "self," what many of us call "our own personal happiness," to a far greater extent than do many other people in this world.

Given all the criteria that may contribute to the success of a marriage, when I counsel with couples or interview people who ask me, as a minister, to perform their wedding, I pay the most attention to the balance of power in their relationship. My experience is that power in such a relationship can often be expressed quite subtly. For example, I know couples where the woman might have more education or make more money than the man does, or vice versa, yet they are comparably powerful. I know couples who would seem to be rather well suited to one another in any number of ways, such as physical appearance, health, wealth, talents, strengths, compatibility of religion, culture, or what have you. However, there is a significant power differential in their relationship that is likely to contribute to some level of dysfunction. So the circumstances of power in a marriage aren't always that easy to put your finger on, at least according to lots of generally accepted criteria.

One source of power seems to be an adequate and comparable level of self-differentiation. When neither person in a relationship is adequately differentiated, there tends to be an excess of blaming or scape-goating of one another, a variety of styles of manipulation, be they passive or aggressive, and certainly a mutual tendency to escalate pseudo-power-plays, often seen as attacking, withdrawing, or defending. Others might see an important connection between self esteem and power in a marriage.

I sometimes speak of power as leverage. For example, I teach a principle called "Monty's Law." Monty's Law states that, in any relationship, the person who needs the least controls the most. This is not always understood at face value. Sometimes it may appear that the needier person, what some might call the more recalcitrant person in a relationship, is controlling. This is not, however, likely to happen if the other person's need to accommodate, to placate, even to patronize isn't pretty high. I suspect that, more often than not, such a need has at least something to do with wanting approval, with some fairly high need to be thought well of or to at least reinforce some image of oneself as "the good guy."

It is clear to me that when married partners can't or won't or don't deal with one another out of some sense of strength, out of a perspective of genuine power and respect, the mutual respect of oneself and of the other, their capacity for intimacy is limited, and an increased level of dysfunction in their relationship is likely. As a rule of thumb, dependency, however well disguised to oneself, or even to others, tends to produce resentment. As for Monty's Law, in its simplest form, think of it like this: if I want whatever for you or from you more than you want it for yourself, or want to give it to me, then I will be giving you the power to control my life, to jerk me around, as it were. The "whatever" may be anything, from success, self-esteem, good grades, good health or good sex, patience, kindness, approval, or affection, all the way to sobriety, fidelity, loyalty, confidence, courage, or faith.

I once heard George Orvin say, "We don't need more parent effectiveness training; what we need is more spouse effectiveness training." At the time, Dr. Orvin was a prominent child psychiatrist at the Medical University of South Carolina. His point was that children learn most and best from what they see modeled before them. When they see men and women relating to one another in weak, manipulative, passive or aggressive or passive-aggressive ways, that is what they are learning. They are learning that this is who men are and who women are, that this is how they are supposed to relate to one another. Conversely, when children see emotionally strong men and women inter-relating in powerful and appropriate, and certainly in intimate ways, what is being modeled before them is a very different understanding of what it means to be male or female, and likely what it means to be married in some reasonably healthy ways.

Here's a rather vivid case study. I once saw a couple in my counseling practice. Once. They never came back. I must have listened to them—I

mean, him—for at least 45 minutes without saying a word, except to inter-
rupt one time. That is when I asked the husband if he always talked for his
wife. Whenever she tried to talk, he would finish her sentences, or correct
her. Neither seemed dismayed by my question. They both seemed to agree
that this was normative in their relationship. It was just how it was. The
same dynamic applies, as well, to gay and lesbian partners.

Her complaint was that she didn't trust her husband and that she was
jealous and threatened by the way she said he "looks at other women."
He, of course, defended himself by saying that she was making too much
out of something quite inconsequential, that she was insecure at best and
likely paranoid at worst.

I noticed that the man wore glasses. I asked him how well he could
see without them. He explained that his sight was very poor, that he had
worn glasses since he was a youngster and that he never took them off
except to go to bed or take a shower. That is when I suggested to his wife
that whenever she thought her husband was looking at another woman
in a way she didn't like, to just go over and take off his glasses. That is all
I said.

Both of them looked at me like I was crazy. They didn't say anything.
They just started laughing, a kind of nervous giggle. Then they stood up
and walked out of my office holding hands. That was the first sign of affection between the two of them that I had observed. As they left my office
that day, they were smiling in what seemed to be a fairly lighthearted way,
a demeanor very different from how they looked when they arrived and
appeared throughout the hour we were together. The next day, the wife
called my office and told the secretary to cancel their next appointment. I
never saw them again.

What I have just described is an example, a fairly rigorous form of
what is commonly called "strategic therapy." There was no counseling relationship developed, no joining or bonding, not much apparent goodwill
expressed between this couple and me. They were in distress. I listened
attentively and then intervened by what strategic therapy would term
"prescribing the symptom." Indeed, I prescribed something that seemed
as crazy to them as the way they were dysfunctioning in their relationship.
The former they could see; the latter, not likely to see. However, maybe
they did see it, and maybe they talked about it on the way home, or perhaps didn't or couldn't, maybe they were too embarrassed or ashamed.
Perhaps that is why they didn't want to see me again. It appeared to me

that they were in some collusion, one with the other, as painful as it may have been for both of them. However, I doubt either would have seen it that way. I expect each felt rather estranged and powerless in their marriage, each wanting the other to change his/her point of view and behavior. The harder they tried to get the other person to change, however, the more resistance they encountered.

Therefore, maybe they felt empowered, in the sense of being joined together in some sort of newfound alliance against "that crazy therapist." That might have actually been an improvement over their chronic alienation, their distrust and resentment toward each other, over how they seemed to be so consistently reinforcing one another in ways designed to produce just the opposite of what they wanted, as though it were, in fact, a well-choreographed dance.

Perhaps they left my office thinking, "Maybe we're not as crazy (as sick or as bad?) as we thought. I mean, after all, that guy was looney tunes!" My intervention was, of course, designed to redress the imbalance of power in their relationship. I just didn't spend any time talking "about" their problem, which most counselors would likely do. In fact, more often than not, I would tend to do so. Some would consider what I did with this couple as something other than helpful. If I was not unethical, I at least appeared uncaring and seemed to trivialize the distress they were experiencing. Not that this isn't an example of how people can take themselves either not seriously enough, or far too seriously, such that trivializing is relative, and likely ambiguous at best. Frankly, I don't know if I helped this couple or not. I can certainly see where I might not have, that they were so defended, that the way I worked with them tended to reinforce some fairly deep feelings of self-recrimination, that they needed much more apparent tenderness, gentleness, and kindness. At some level, though, I suspect I may have done them some good. Perhaps another counselor might be able to build upon any good I may have done, before this couple fled. I had surely exposed a fairly toxic "game" they seemed to be playing, if unwittingly, together. At least I didn't get seduced into trying to protect or "rescue" this "poor, powerless woman," or in trying to "fix her philandering husband." Just as I think it worth remembering in this context, as a general principle, that chronic jealousy in a marriage is quite as damaging as unfaithfulness. Neither posture serves to move a marriage in a good direction.

A more conventional paradoxical intervention with this couple would have more likely been one of suggesting to the woman: "Did you ever think of becoming your husband's talent scout? Instead of being threatened and offended by his ogling of other women, how about pointing this or that one out, with a 'There's a real babe. She's worth looking at, don't you think?'" The rule of thumb is that negative behavior we pay less attention to often gets extinguished. Otherwise, there's not much we can do, short of giving the very behavior we don't like more attention than it deserves, thus making a bad situation even worse.

BALANCED PARENTING

Effective parenting may be as hard as it is simple. To be a good parent, you have to keep at least two things balanced. You have to be fair, and you have to be firm.

Another way of understanding firmness in parenting is that it means being consistent. My experience is that parents who aren't fair usually aren't very consistent either. They are often too rigid or too harsh, too demanding, and their expectations for their children may be too high. In contrast, if their kids raise enough of a fuss, if they escalate the kind of power-plays most children seem to be pretty good at doing, the same kind of parent will too often cave in and back down and let the kid off the hook. This style of parenting does not tend to promote stability of character in children.

All research concerning children and self-esteem seems to indicate the value of structure, not to mention how children deal with fear, how they develop some sense of success, how they learn to handle failure, or relate to others in appropriate ways. Children need firm guidelines. They need to know where the parameters of life tend to fall, just as they need nurturing and warmth, affection and acceptance, encouragement and challenge.

As I see it, these dimensions are not only compatible. In more functional families, they tend to work together, and one promotes the other. Fairness is reasonableness. It takes into account where a child is developmentally and what is reasonable, as a parent, to expect. Firmness is letting a child know where the lines are drawn, and it is certainly teaching a child that if she crosses that line, you, as a parent, are not going to give in. I have always thought it important to be even more than fair with kids. It is important to be generous. And when they push for even more, as most children do, it is necessary for parents to be strong, to not be intimidated by or to be in a popularity contest with their kids. Otherwise, how do children develop any sense of limits, boundaries, appropriateness, fairness, reasonableness, or generosity?

What I am speaking to here, family therapists often understand as family structure, with how families tend to be organized—or for that matter, dis-organized. This emphasis in family counseling comes from the pioneering work of Salvador Minuchin. From such a perspective, a stereotype of family dysfunction is when the lines between the role of a parent and child are not clear enough. Unfortunately, this is not uncommon in many families, where there seems to be considerable confusion over just who is supposed to be the parent and who is the kid. In this scenario, children often tend to "run the show." This is an example of weak parenting, which may be an even more common and serious problem in our culture than when the structure between parents and children in families is too rigid.

A variation on this theme commonly occurs when there is a breakdown in the marital relationship, for whatever reasons, such that one parent isn't available to the other physically or emotionally. Consequently, the other parent becomes enmeshed with a child. In such circumstances, children tend to become confused as to their appropriate role and usually suffer significant developmental problems. For example, if you listen to most adult children of alcoholics reflecting on the structure and dynamics of their families, the caricature is somewhat stereotypical. In this scenario, if daddy was the drunk and mom tended to be the enabler, the story often goes something like this: When dad was drunk, you had better watch out, or you might get hurt. Conversely, when he was sober, he was a nice guy and would give you anything. Or vice versa, when he was drunk he was a soft touch. Otherwise, he was pretty irascible; don't expect him to be very available or to cut you much slack. Likewise, such marriages tend not to have been made in heaven. In such a scenario, mom is often trying to parent dad, fighting with him, placating him, letting him off the hook, making excuses for him, or bailing him out. It is also not uncommon, in such circumstances, for mom to turn to her children, or perhaps one of her children, to try to meet some of her needs for companionship, closeness, understanding, support, comfort, protection—what some refer to as "emotional incest." Most experienced counselors have heard such a story more than enough times, from people who describe growing up in the kind of family dysfunction where they were chronically caught between and just as confused about the roles of parent and child. Who is the parent here, and who is the child? How do I, as a child, try to take care of my parent (s)? What happens to me when I am not cared for by my parent(s) in necessary and important ways? Do I, then, learn how to try to take care of others, while not learning much about how to take care of myself? As hard as they may be "trying," people who grow up in such circumstances usually learn fairly soon and often how to be rather grand failures in terms of care-taking and care-receiving.

If children, most of all, need to learn something about reasonableness and consistency from parents, it is in families that children also learn subtler things, like taste and manners, propriety and sensitivity, even priorities, if, indeed, they learn much about any of this at all. Meanwhile, I doubt there is a family counselor anywhere who hasn't been asked about spanking. Some would say that spanking merely teaches children how to express physical violence. I make a distinction between hitting a child, as in lashing out, and the "ritual" of spanking, which, of course, is time-limited. For example, how old should a child be when you stop spanking? Most would not find this surprising. When my children were little, I would often give them a choice of discipline between receiving a spanking and losing a privilege. When given such an option, my kids would take the spanking every time! What's a little physical pain compared to not getting to do something you wanted so very much to do? Spankings tend to be over and done with a lot sooner than the loss of a privilege. Therefore, spanking is not such a good thing if it is the only tool of discipline in your repertoire. My father seldom spanked me, and when he did, it was ritualized, not spontaneous. My dad didn't need to spank much. He dealt with me from such a position of legitimate power. He was quite a good model of fairness, even generosity, of firmness and consistency.

In contrast, my mother was always trying to be more powerful than she surely saw herself being. I call this "pseudo-power." That was not my dad's fault. It was her problem. And I would say he was pretty adept at staying out of being triangulated, either with me, or with my mother, for or against one of us. As a result, my mother ended up abusing me fairly chronically, in some ways physically, but more often emotionally. Of all the techniques to try to manipulate or "control" a kid, "shaming" was the one my mother had learned best where she grew up, and seemed to have mastered by the time I came along. That was my mother's primary approach to parenting: shaming, along with "worrying." It seemed to be her rationale, at least with me, that if I felt bad enough about myself, and she worried about me enough, that should keep me in line.

My observation, from most of the people I have interviewed over the years, is that my family of origin was not the cultural stereotype concerning male and female sex-roles in families. More often, it seems, their mother was the stronger, the more powerfully nurturing presence, and it was dad who was the bully or the blowhard, who was always making pronouncements and trying to control through intimidation, through a fear-based style of parenting. Some would say that neither was a particularly negative caricature in their family.

Perhaps the most critical balancing act for parents comes somewhere between over-parenting and under-parenting children, between doing too much and not doing enough for your kids. When parents under-parent children, they at least neglect if not abuse their kids. They don't or aren't able to provide adequately for a child's needs. Such parents are care-less. They are usually pre-occupied with other matters, such as their own problems, their loneliness or neediness, their addiction, the demons that they may be fighting in their own lives, their pride or ambition or aspirations, their career goals, their ego or health or work problems, perhaps conflicts still unresolved with their parents, whomever that may have been, the fact that they are merely immature, or may be primarily invested in fighting overtly or covertly with their child's other parent.

Parents who tend to under-parent their children don't provide good role models. They often don't know how to take care of themselves, much less a child, or they may be quite selfish. When parents under-parent children, they are often unavailable. More often than not, this is more emotional or physical than financial. They may buy the kid plenty, but they don't prioritize the time to spend with the child. And even if they are present, they aren't available emotionally. They are too guarded or defended or pre-occupied to let their child get very close to them. Some parents are too insecure with regard to their children. They are so worried that their children won't like them, they tend to be in some kind of popularity contest with their kids, so they do not set good limits and boundaries. They are weak parents. They give in and back down too easily whenever their child tries to push them around, when the child pouts and withdraws or tries to intimidate and threaten them. These are all examples of under-parenting.

Over-parenting is being too involved in your kid's life. It is doing too much for children. It is having grandiose expectations. It may be living too much through your children, wanting them to have or to do whatever you did or didn't have, whatever it was you did or didn't do. Most kids aren't going to be in the Olympics or sing in Carnegie Hall. Some small children shouldn't even be expected to sit still in church or in the doctor's office. Most kids aren't even going to live perfect, mistake-free, success-assured lives. Those who tend to over-parent would do well to remember at least two things: 1) my child is not in this world to meet my needs or to make me look good; 2) I am not in this world to make my child look good, to be a slave to my child's every need. One of my minister-colleagues claims that this is the curse of "good" families in our society: over-functioning parents, especially mothers, who think that if they are anxious enough about their children, if they do for and give their kids even more of everything, their children will then become happy and successful enough to make their parent(s) look good. Then, when everyone is living happily ever after, such children will surely thank their parent(s) for making all of this possible, for making this the way the world is supposed to be.

My parents were rather underprivileged people who had not gotten the opportunity to realize nearly as much of who they were as they might have become. Their gifts certainly exceeded their opportunities in life, so they set upon a course of making sure that their children got the chances they didn't get. And the truth of it is, we all did pretty well according to this way of living. However, I do believe my parents lived too much through their children, which is understandable, given some of the deprivation they had experienced in their lives, especially my mother. Such expectations for children to succeed and excel can seem burdensome.

I once tried to talk with my parents about this. I was a junior in college. I think it is worth noting that I was obviously so over-adapted and far too compliant ever to consider rebelling. When my parents said, "Jump," I asked, "How high?" Fortunately, the thing about compliant kids is that they usually get in less trouble than more rebellious ones, unless, of course, the compliance is with such toxic, even lethal pathology in some families. For example, I had a friend in seminary who said that he had "rebelled" against his family by going to church, by making it his life, by being there every time the door was open. Who ever heard of such rebellion? It is hardly the norm. In his case, the church, without exploiting him, was able to affirm him, to appreciate his particular kind of sensitivity and gifts in a way his family could not and did not. At least that is how he interpreted his circumstances to me.

Be that as it may, on the one occasion I ever tried to confront my parents, I broke down, crying, saying: "Your expectations are too high. I can't live up to what you expect of me." Of course, they were threatened by this and became rather defensive. That is when they sent me their bill, which had by that time accrued over twenty years of interest! "How can you say that to us, after all we've done for you?" That is how they put it to me. In this instance, my mom and dad were in collusion, quite clearly aligned, one with the other. I, of course, at that time in my life didn't have a clue about what to do with what they were saying to me. I didn't know how to take care of myself, emotionally, with my parents, nor did they know how to take care of themselves, emotionally, with me. I had tried to shift my discomfort, my understanding of how things were, and how I felt about it, to my parents. It was uncomfortable and threatening enough to them, such that they shifted it right back to me. I didn't know anything else to do but to take it and feel guilty, even ashamed, for what I thought and felt, as they surely expected me to.

No one runs a guilt trip on any of us, no one shames us when we won't let them, be they parents or children. It would be some years later, with the help of a capable and effective counselor, that I would begin to differentiate somewhat, primarily in relation to my parents, to define my life in ways other than merely on their terms, to what they thought and felt about me, to whatever their expectations of or for me may have been. My unspoken job description began to change, from that of being in this world to make my parents look good and to meet their needs, to one of beginning to take care of my own emotional business. I no longer had to try to live up to their expectations anymore than I had a right to expect them to live up to mine. It was no longer my job to try to "take care" of my parents' feelings, anymore than it was any longer their job to try to "take care" of me in any way. In fact, in the process of doing this, I began to see that my perception of their expectations had likely been distorted from my childish perspective.

It often works that way. When we are little, we don't always see things the way they really are. We are often rather mystified. As my mentor, the late John Claypool, put it: "Children are good observers, but poor interpreters." Often it is many years later, when we are a lot bigger and supposedly a lot smarter, when we discover that we are still operating under some very childish perceptions, early decisions that may have been quite clever, and likely helped us survive, the kind of introjected beliefs that have tended to form and shape how we live.

I have a sense that I internalized expectations of myself that were far greater than even those of my parents, even though I may have gotten my cues from them and what they seemed to have wanted and needed for and from me. Thus began a process of healing, of growth and change in my life that I would describe as rather profound. I found myself better able to enjoy my parents, certainly my mother. In fact, I began to accept them for who they were, in proportion to my acceptance of myself. I no longer held them responsible for how I would see myself, nor for what or how I would feel. Because I was no longer willing to give them that kind of power in my life, whatever their approval or dis-approval of me might have been, it didn't seem so great, and I became better able to thank them and to bless them for their many good and important gifts to me.

I have worked with many such clients over the years, folk going through a similar crisis, whom I have helped as they went through the process of changing their perceptions and reactions significantly with regard to the seminal people in their lives. When they report a later en-counter, and it seems so different, so much less reactive or conflicted from how it may have been in the past, I often ask: "So what did you do?" Or I may ask, "What did you say?" To a person, they all report the same: "I don't know?" When we do the inner work of changing our own percep-tions, much less our mis-perceptions, the need to try to change others is no longer as great. Even as we discover how some people do not have near the power in our lives we may have once given them.

I wish the same for my children. I have consciously sought to see their lives less connected to mine than my parents may have seen my life connected to theirs. Still, childish perceptions persist, for most of us, and it generally takes some time to gain a better perspective. People often compliment me on my kids, just as I'm sure they also compliment their mother. My children are winsome and capable and have some genuine strengths and gifts. However, that is not something for which I need or wish to take credit. I live my life, and they live theirs. I try to live with some integrity. Not everyone may see me as I might wish. The same is true for my children. I happen to admire them, and I am thankful for them. I like them as much as I love them. Still, when someone tells me I have neat kids, I don't say, "Thanks." Such credit is due them, not me. I am not responsible for my children's lives, anymore than they are responsible for mine, for good or for ill. Therefore, I just say, "I'm glad you like my kids. I do too."

I recently came upon a remarkable book by Jeannette Walls entitled *The Glass Castle*.[8] I have also had the privilege of hearing her speak. She and other of her siblings represent an unusual example of children figuring out how to survive and land on their feet in the absence of much of any structure and stability on the part of their parents. However, as Ms. Walls tells her story, her parents appear to have provided an abundance of intellectual stimulation for their children and, apparently, at least some level of emotional warmth.

A CASE STUDY

A friend called recently and asked if he could have lunch with me. He said he needed to talk with me about something. Usually, when someone says that to me, I expect it to have to do with some personal problem. He's in his thirties, a husband and a father. He has also been trained as a mental health professional, so he knows a lot about counseling. We met for lunch. Here is pretty much a verbatim account of our conversation. It is illustrative. I asked him if I could share our conversation in this book. He agreed.

Him: I need to talk to you about something.

Me: ...

Him: I got this letter from my brother. He was telling me, essentially, what a bad person I am, trying to run a bunch of guilt on me, about never coming home. Ever since I went to college, I've been alienated from my family. It really pissed me off. I don't know what to do.

Me: ...

Him: What do you think I should do? How do I respond to that?

Me: How are you?

Him: What do you mean? It's the same thing my mother does. She's always trying to run guilt on me, like I'm her little boy. Like I'm supposed to take care of her. I just want to tell them all to go to hell. I think I know what's going on. I just don't know how to handle it.

8. Jeannette Walls, *The Glass Castle: A Memoir* (New York: Scribner 2006).

Me: What is going on?

Him: I told you the last time we talked. It's my mother. She wants to control my life. And when I won't do what she wants, she tries to make me feel guilty. My brother, he's still stuck there. Like he said to me in the letter: "I don't care where you've been, or who you think you are. This is still your home!" Who does he think he is?

Me: It sounds to me like you're grieving.

Him: What do you mean?

Me: Like you're caught. It sounds like, emotionally, you're still pretty hooked in there with your mom . . . What about your dad? You've never mentioned him.

Him: He's been withdrawn from her for years, ever since I left to go to college. He stays out in his workshop most of the time. My mom was pretty young when she had me. She's about your age. Sometimes I feel like I'm the parent and she's the child. I think I understand what the problem is. I just don't know what to do.

Me: There's a woman therapist over here on (I give him the street and the name of a counselor). If you go see her, she'll hold you, not physically. Just tell her what we've been talking about. She'll understand what's going on. I think you need a safe place to grieve, a safe space, where you can be held, emotionally.

Him: I don't know that I've ever seen a woman therapist.

Me: . . .

Him: I think I understand the problem, it's just that . . . that letter really ticked me off.

Me: Yeah, I think you do understand. My sense is that your primary defenses are . . . intellectualizing and . . . it's like you know how to understand things. Except that's also a way to try to avoid . . . a way to try to walk around your pain, instead of touching it. You know, to own it and bless it. That's how I think of it. As a kind of blessing, where we may feel the most hurt, or perhaps the most misunderstood. Where we may feel wounded. Like maybe we didn't get something we needed. That can be a lonely place, perhaps a frightening place?

Him: Yeah, like I got cheated somewhere. You know, my mom, it's like I'm supposed to take care of her. It's like she can't appreciate me . . . I think she's proud of me, in what I've accomplished, how that reflects on her ... She's just so needy.

Me: That's pretty common. I hear it a lot, how it is in many families. Like that was your job. How most of the energy in your family got spent on ... you know, trying to keep your mom from getting upset. How you were working real hard, trying to take care of her, trying to please her. Not that she would have seen it that way.

Him: Yeah, that makes sense. It's like the messages are confused. She's supposed to be your mom. She's supposed to take care of you. But I've always felt like it was my job, you know, to try to please her. And it's like I never could.

Me: So ...

Him: I don't know. What'd you say that lady's name was? I can see what you're saying. I really don't want to face it. I just want to get away. What's the difference between what you're saying and just cutting myself off from them?

Me: That's Murray Bowen's language: "cut-off." That's when you move to California to try to get away from your family. Except they move with you, in your own head or your heart. Or you find yourself having to deal with someone who wires you up just like your mom, or your brother, or whomever? I remember the first time I ever asked my therapist: "What do I say to her when she starts ... ?" And he said: "It's not what you say to her. It's what you say to the her in your head." The part of her that's in you, when you treat yourself the same way, when you get hooked.

Him: Why can't I get over this? I feel stuck ....

Me: You're right on task, developmentally.

Him: What do you mean?

Me: I don't think most people get to this point until ... How old did you say you were? That's about right. It's a thirties thing, I think, at least in our culture. You know, particularly with professional people, who stay in school so long. It's like school becomes the authority figure in your life. You're always trying to figure out how to survive in school. Like you. When you were a little kid, I think you figured out how to survive by being smart.

Him: Yeah, and by being nice, being a good little boy. I have this image of myself, with my hands turned up, reaching out, like, "Take care of me." But I'm so depressed. I think that's what it is. I think I'm depressed a lot.

Me: I think that's how it works, when you intellectualize about your pain, about whatever is so troubling. You still end up carrying it around, often in a low-grade depression. If you go see (the therapist's name), tell her what we've been talking about, and tell her that's what you want her to do. That you want her to hold you, that you're grieving. She'll have you talk to your mom, in a gestalt. You could do it yourself, but I think you probably need someone to provide some protection for you. You seem to have a fair amount of anger . . . and a lot of sadness.

Him: Like I'm grieving. I think you're right. What did you mean by that?

Me: I think that's what it is, when you feel caught--how would you say it? "Between two worlds?" Between where you grew up, and where you are today. It's kind of like being a cultural anthropologist. I think there's a kind of grieving to that. When you get enough distance, emotionally, to look at your family. It's like, where do you belong? Where is home? I've noticed with young adults, when they start calling "home" where they live, instead of where they grew up, or where their parents live. It's like they're starting to . . . Bowen would say, "differentiate." I think you're right on task.

Him: Do you ever get past this point?

Me: I don't know. Some of the deepest issues in our lives . . . I call it spotting it quicker, stopping it sooner and not getting into it as deeply. I think that's important, when you get hooked, that you have some clues about what's happening and how to take care of yourself . . . emotionally. Even then, sometimes it seems like hard work, the energy it takes to take care of ourselves with some people. They tend to make us feel crazy if we let them.

~

There's a pattern most therapists have noticed, I think. To use Bowen's language, the better differentiated a person is the less painful their grieving process tends to be when, say, a loved one dies. Grieving is generally harder the more ambivalent our feelings for whomever we have lost. It is like we are still trying, as it were, to get that person to be more of what we wanted or needed them to be for us. The grieving process seems to be not quite as painful when we can get such conflict worked out before they die.

Of course, many folk are grieving other kinds of losses. For sexually abused people, it is typically a loss of innocence, a loss of childhood, because, developmentally, they were exploited. Adult children of alcoholics often report grieving the loss of their childhood, where they had to grow up too soon, in order to try to take care of an alcoholic parent who couldn't or didn't know how to take care of him or herself, much less his or her child. Some people are grieving the kind of loss reflected in the case study I have just shared, the loss of some previously held perceptions, the kind which may have served one well in childhood and adolescence, but which usually do not serve one well when it comes to maturing as an adult. Some people are grieving the loss of some image of themselves or their family or their career, when it would appear that things aren't now and likely aren't ever going to be as they may have thought or wished.

Some years ago, another friend shared a rather seminal dream with me. He said that, in his dream, he had arrived at church. His family was sitting together in the same pew. When he tried to sit with them, they wouldn't let him in. They told him there was no room, no place left among them for him to sit. One would not have to be a psychoanalyst, nor even know very much about my friend, to figure that one out. His grieving wasn't all that different from the young man in the case study I have shared.

4

Balance and Personality Type

"I often think people are strange.
Except for me and thee. And sometimes
I have my doubts about thee!"

—Quaker saying

MOST PEOPLE I ENCOUNTER SEEM RATHER FASCINATED WITH VARIous methods and approaches to trying to define or to at least understand various character and/or temperament types. The ancient Greeks spoke of such different personality traits as the sanguine, the melancholic, the phlegmatic, and so forth. Some counselors use those terms even today. In her book, *Footprints on the Heart*, Muriel O'Tuel devotes a chapter to the Peformax Personal Profile System and its clever acronym, DISC, for "dominating, interacting, steady, and cautious."[1] Dr. O'Tuel, a popular motivational speaker, retired as the school psychologist in our community. We worked together for many years.

My buddy from college days, Pat Conway, owns a franchise for the Predictive Index, which is a rather tightly controlled instrument. He markets this primarily to industry, as a tool for personnel work and organizational development. The Predictive Index measures such personality characteristics as dominance, extroversion, patience, and formality. The last of these has to do with the degree to which people may differ over the importance of structure, protocol, rules, regulations, policy, the kind of guidelines some people value highly as a way of knowing how or where they stand in relation to others. This instrument claims to be able to quantify the amount of emotional energy someone may be spending in

1. Mariel O'Tuel, *Footprints On the Heart* (Folsom: Executive Press, 1992).

trying to negotiate the difference between how she sees herself and how she perceives others may see her.

Some years ago, I ran across a newspaper article about an "inter-personal skills trainer" in Nashville, Tennessee, who had come up with a personality profile based on the four main characters from the "Seinfeld" television show. She calls these the "Kramers" (optimistic extroverts), the "Elaines" (dominating, director types), the "Jerrys" (introverted, low-key and supportive) and the "Newmans" (analyzers, somewhat more pessimistic doers).[2] What is notable, I think, at least in this context, is that no attempt to characterize different personality types would seem to suggest that any one type is better than another. They're just different, and some types seem better suited for certain roles or jobs or tasks than do others.

I am most familiar with the Myers-Briggs Type Indicator (MBTI), which seems to have become rather mainstreamed in our culture. Over the years, I have often consulted with students in a Clinical Pastoral Education (CPE) program at a local hospital to discuss their Myers-Briggs profiles. CPE is a training program particularly for chaplains, and in its broader context it is a hands-on, clinical training program in pastoral ministry for clergy in general. In the hospital where I have consulted, various Roman Catholic religious, many of them nurses, and other lay folk from a variety of religious traditions and helping professions are also included. A number of the participants are often seminary students. Some denominations require or encourage CPE for ordination. Some sense of who you are and how you tend to operate is, obviously, essential for those engaged in sensitive pastoral work, such as that of chaplains, pastoral counselors, and parish clergy.

The Myers-Briggs is also used fairly broadly in business and industry, in both the private and public sector, as a tool in personnel work and in interpreting various organizational problems, or in predicting the possibility of such problems. I have been involved over the years in a fair amount of consulting with various organizations that wanted training for their personnel in the MBTI. One large local industry employed consultants some years ago to train all of their management and labor force in the Myers-Briggs. Subsequently, in their staff directory, each person in the organization is identified by her Myers-Briggs profile. Their rationale is that, when you are meeting with or talking on the phone with someone

2. *The Post and Courier,* April 27, 1998.

86

you're trying to do business with, or preparing for such an engagement, it is helpful to know such salient traits as the MBTI reveals. Many marriage and family counselors find the Myers-Briggs helpful in their work. Some clergy use it in pre-marital counseling.

I once worked with a family where most of the over-functioning involved the concerns of a natural mother and a step-father over the under-functioning of her teenaged son. This kid was about as recalcitrant as they come. He was pretty much holding their family hostage in the sort of passive-aggressive ways that many teenagers seem to have mastered. I had seen this boy and his family in therapy for over a year, and I could not see where I was connecting with him at all. I was hardly as frustrated with him as were his parents. Still, he had pretty much defeated me as well. He remained fairly inert. We scheduled a meeting on a weekend when his natural father, who lived quite a distance away, was in town. The natural father presented as one of the most skilled intellectualizers I have ever seen. He was a master at keeping others, and certainly his son, at a distance, with lots of verbiage, with an abundance of fairly abstract thinking and speculating, as well as lots of colorful details, anecdotes, and observations about the world in general and himself in particular.

Sometime during our rather extended meeting, this father mentioned something about his Myers-Briggs profile. It's amazing how many people have been exposed to this instrument. That is when his son's face lit up, his eyes brightened, and his energy level rose a bit. "That's what I am," he said to his dad. Somewhere along the way of quite a battery of psychologists and social workers and family counselors who had tried, without much success, to connect with this boy, someone had given him the MBTI. His profile was the same as his dad's. And from what I could tell, that may have been the best news the kid had ever heard, even though his dad remained just as persistent in his manner of distancing himself from his son.

The MBTI measures tendencies along four different continua of temperament traits, based on Jungian archetypes. It is not concerned with pathology. It is not concerned with etiology, with why people tend to be as they are, nor with claiming that any of these tendencies are better or worse. They just are. The goal is that of understanding and accommodating people's differences accordingly. Indeed, one of the most popular of the Myers-Briggs books, which is available in almost any bookstore, is titled *Please Understand Me.*[3] In this sense, then, the Myers-Briggs represents another instance among us humanfolk where the relative nature of how people tend to be and behave would seem significant, where balance may be a key to personal and/or vocational effectiveness.

EXTROVERT/INTROVERT

Garrison Keillor has made a career for himself on "A Prairie Home Companion" on National Public Radio, caricaturing the nature of "shy people" and of the transforming qualities of "Powder Milk Biscuits—they make shy people get up and do what needs to be done!" Whether introverts are shy people, less assertive, less talkative, less sociable than their more extroverted counterparts, is debatable. It appears to be so. Introverts do seem a bit more selective about when and how and to whom they may have much of anything to say. I often tease the monks out at the monastery that they are a bunch of repressed extroverts. Some of those guys are like Garrison Keillor. They can do some serious talking. Most extroverts report being able to "work a room" better in unstructured social situations, like a cocktail party, where they seem to find such a level of socializing not nearly as uncomfortable as it is for the more introverted. After all, isn't that why there's a bar, to help the introvert loosen her tongue?

What is pretty clear, between extroverts and introverts, is how they process and energize differently. Extroverts tend to externalize, and introverts tend to internalize, with regard to both processing and energizing. For example, extroverts tend to energize off external stimulation. For introverts, such stimulation may be rather exhausting. A rule of thumb is that if you're married to an introvert, don't try to talk to him when he gets home from work. He's emotionally exhausted and needs some time to recover. I often say that extroverts are like windmills, and introverts are like microwaves. Extroverts energize from the outside inward, whereas introverts energize from the inside outward. To an extrovert, an introvert may seem guarded, not as open and revealing of herself. In relationships, introverts often appear to be conserving rather than expending energy.

I'm an extrovert. As a counselor, most of my supervisors have been introverts. Introverts, in my opinion, make better therapists, since their process tends not to get in the way of clients, especially introverted cli-

3. David Keirsey and Marilyn Bates, *Please Understand Me* (Del Mar: Prometheus Nemesis Books Company, 1984).

ents. Introverts may or may not be less verbal than extroverts, but they generally appear to be less so, because their process is more internalized. Extroverts are more inclined to "think out loud," both verbally and non-verbally. Someone has said that introverts practice an 80 percent rule; that is, they have to have about 80 per cent of what they want to say figured out before they say it, what one might call the "ready, aim, fire" method. Whereas extroverts tend to practice more of a 20 percent rule. They only need to have figured out about 20 percent of what they want to say before speaking, what might be considered the "ready, fire, aim" method! Introverts are usually seen as better listeners. Extroverts sometimes appear as if they are just waiting for their turn to talk. Earlier in this book, I mentioned one of my pastoral counseling supervisors, Archie Reed, a Presbyterian minister, who is a serious introvert. I used to accuse him of being passive, perhaps even passive-aggressive. He would say, "I'm not passive. I'm assertive, even quite competitive. I'm an introvert, but I'm not passive." It would, of course, take Dr. Reed longer to say that than it would someone like me, because he'd have to think about what he wanted to say and how he wanted to say it for a while. Sometimes introverts enjoy the energy we extroverts tend to produce when we're around almost anyone. At other times, we may wear out people, especially introverts. As I've gotten older, I think I have become a bit more introverted. For example, the over-stimulation of a Sunday morning at church sometimes feels draining. As a result, I tend to distance myself from it in some ways. I think there are many ministers who are introverts, yet they are required to function in an extroverted role, and they find it wearisome, even as congregants may perceive them as "cold" or "distant" or even "unapproachable." One physician I know claims that patients want three things from their doctor: "affability, availability, and ability—in that order!" In case you haven't guessed, he's an introvert.

In this respect, research suggests that in America at least 75 percent of all people are extroverts.[4] Since there are far more extroverted roles and jobs in our society, many introverts are required to function much of the time as extroverts. As a result, introverts can play an extroverted role easier than extroverts can play introverted roles. The demands of an introverted role can be quite frustrating to an extrovert. If, for example, the extrovert's job is that of auditing the books in the back of the bank,

4. Ibid., 25–26.

she may in fact spend even more time up at the water cooler looking for someone with whom to socialize. Conversely, an introvert in an extrovert's job may find such work emotionally draining, perhaps even threatening or tyrannous. I have an artist friend for whom just going to church is pretty painful, given the fairly intense level of socialization that usually goes on there, not that he doesn't love God as much as anyone else who likes to go to church. He would just rather stay home and design bulletin covers and other graphic designs for his church. That is his preferred way of contributing, of being there. And even when he does go to church, he arrives late and leaves early to avoid the crowd. He prefers his interactions to be more selective, what some would consider deeper and more narrow, as against a pattern of socialization that tends to be fairly broad, perhaps even shallow.

For readers unfamiliar with the Myers-Briggs, the book I have mentioned, *Please Understand Me*, includes an MBTI self-test, which anyone can take and score herself. Almost every community has someone available as a resource person—a psychologist, an educator, a management consultant, or a minister—qualified and skilled at interpreting this instrument. Remember, it's not really a test, as such, at least in the way one thinks of taking a test in school. The MBTI is more of a mirror, an instrument for measuring something of what most people find interesting and helpful to know about themselves.

Are any of the Myers-Briggs profiles better or worse? Absolutely not. Does each dimension on this scale have its inherent strengths as well as weaknesses, relative to different circumstances and situations? Of course. For example, for an extrovert to be a good counselor, she has to watch getting in the way of a client's process, even if the client isn't an introvert, and certainly if he is. Conversely, even if you are an introvert, even if you're not talking, you still might not be listening. For a therapist, it's important to be a good listener.

According to Jungian theory, opposites tend to attract, as we unconsciously seek to complete ourselves. Therefore, it is not uncommon in counseling, or anywhere else for that matter, to see an introvert married to an extrovert. In my experience, the extrovert is more often the female, though this is not always the case. Couples can become quite resistant and resentful to something of a caricature of their partner, over enough time, if they don't understand and make allowances for such differences. For example, an extrovert may tend to have a loose tongue and often appear to go on the attack verbally, whereas a common fighting style for an introvert is to withdraw or avoid verbal confrontation, even disagreement. Even then, the introvert, whose process is more deliberate, may feel somewhat overpowered, like he can't get a word in edgewise.

A fairly hysterical female client once said to me of her husband: "If you cut him open, all you will find is wires!" She was in pretty much a rage at the time. He was sitting there. An electrical engineer, he was quite the introvert. You could tell that her caricature of him—the imagery was pretty graphic—was hurtful to him. It was hurtful that his wife would see him in such a way. People often marry perfect frustrators. She had obviously absorbed a fair amount of emotional damage from him as well. It's just that their ways of trying to survive, and certainly their fighting styles, were so different.

SENSER/INTUITIVE

These differences in type can be rather subtle, unless one understands the dynamics involved. The differences between a senser and an intuitive can often be quite bothersome, even conflictual. I was once training some management consultants; I was teaching some sort of human relations theory. Following one of my presentations, one of the students approached me and said, "You and I have a problem communicating."

"How so?" I asked.

He replied, "Well, you see, I'm a senser, and you're an intuitive." He knew Myers-Briggs-ese, and he was right. My way of teaching tended to be a bit abstract for him, not as graphic or as clearly organized as he would have preferred. He needed me to present the material in a manner more compatible with his predominant learning style. Indeed, sensers often seem to be more visual learners. Most sensers seem to like "tests" like the MBTI, instruments that attempt to quantify or objectify various human characteristics. When I later observed this man teaching the same material to a group of industrial supervisors, he had all sorts of graphs and charts and overhead projections to illustrate and make clear what he was talking about. It more clearly reflected his learning style, and likely theirs as well. He needed the material organized and presented in a fashion that made the connections more obvious. Today, he would likely make a PowerPoint presentation. Whereas an intuitive person, such as myself, might likely find such a teaching style rather pedantic.

Sensers operate more inductively, from specific to general. They pay close attention to details and put details together in a logical fashion to form conclusions. When a senser is trying to put a complex toy together for Santa Claus on Christmas Eve, for instance, she will tend to follow the directions quite carefully. That is not always the case for the intuitive, who may then end up with all sorts of strange parts and pieces he can't quite figure out what to do with!

Was it Winston Churchill who replied to a woman who had criticized him for ending a sentence with a preposition by saying, "Madam, that is the sort of nonsense up with which I will not put?"

Intuitives are more deductive thinkers. They tend to move from general to specific, and they are often better at seeing the big picture. Intuitive people are inherently poetic. They think in terms of metaphors and images and make connections between things that may, for a senser, seem quite unrelated. If sensers think logically, intuitives think more analogically. For example, I have a friend, a theologian, who claims that poetry is concrete. Kathleen Norris would agree. I respond, "Only an intuitive person would think of a poem as something concrete." Most sensers, if they ever read poetry, the poetry of Auden, Eliot, or Hopkins, for instance, anything other than something in a birthday card, they usually look bewildered and ask, "Huh? What's it talking about?"

Because the strength of the intuitive involves more analogical rather than logical thinking, the intuitive often makes connections between disparities that may seem quite un-connected to a senser, as in television ads, where the right car and the pretty girl don't necessarily go together logically. However, that is the implication in the ad: that to get the girl you need the car. In fact, David Shields, a distinguished English professor at the University of South Carolina, once said to me that he thinks the use of modern advertising offers the best way to help the senser develop more of the intuitive's abstract thinking. In case you hadn't noticed, most sensers don't work in the "imaginative world" (what some would call the "right brain world") of advertising. Similarly, most intuitives don't typically work in the more precise world (the "left brain world") of engineering.

There is a rather dramatic illustration in the Bible of an intuitive and a senser trying to communicate with one another. In the third chapter of the Gospel of John, in the New Testament, Jesus says to the Pharisee, Nicodemus: "You must be born again."

Nicodemus asks, "How can a man, when he is old, enter his mother's womb and be born a second time?"[5]

Jesus replies: "It's a metaphor, stupid!" Oh, I know, that is not what Jesus says in that story. That's Dick Hamm's great line. He used to be the General Minister and President of the Christian Church (Disciples of Christ). Nicodemus isn't stupid. He's a senser, so he thinks in more concrete, literal terms than would an intuitive person, such as Jesus or Dick Hamm. Intuitives think more figuratively, perhaps even imaginatively.

You can see where people get into conflict in all sorts of ways, somewhere between these rather different ways of thinking, or perhaps perceiving, as in the case of religion, over which there seems to be no shortage of conflict. If a Christian fundamentalist, for instance, makes the statement, "The Bible is the word of God," because she is a senser, it is not necessarily because she believes in God or the Bible any more than her intuitive Christian counterpart who is apt to reply, "That's a metaphor, stupid!" The senser isn't stupid. He just thinks in more concrete, literal ways about such things. Sensers and intuitives seem to fight about religion as much as anything, except their fighting isn't as much about religion as about how sensers and intuitives see almost everything so differently. It is like when the preacher spoke of Jesus "sitting on God's right hand." In response, a little boy sitting in church exclaimed, "Ouch! I bet that hurt!" It strikes me that the senser/intuitive paradigm is perhaps the least pejorative way of describing the seemingly endless conflict between so many Christians over how to read the Bible.

In terms of ethics and decision-making, intuitives seem a bit better than sensers at appreciating irony, ambiguity, and paradox, examples of a more abstract, less concrete way of thinking. For example, consider the logic that if you want better results, you need to try harder. An intuitive would be more apt to point out the irony that things aren't always as they might appear, and sometimes the harder you're trying, the more you're defeating yourself or perhaps contributing to your problem. Sensers often want to know what is the "right" thing to do, while an intuitive may be better able to make peace with "the lesser of evils," or perhaps even "the better of goods" in a given situation. Sensers sometimes have a harder time seeing how the truth in any number of circumstances may, in fact, have more than one side to it.

5. John 3:4.

Indeed, many of the hot-button social and political issues, which have become so polarizing among so many here in America, might better be understood in terms of the differences, as subtle or dramatic as they may be, between sensers and intuitives, between more concrete and more abstract thinking. For example, if one is running for President, he apparently needs to identify himself as either "pro life" or "pro choice" in order to appeal to a majority of concrete, either/or thinkers. More abstract, both/and thinkers would likely observe that being "pro-choice" doesn't necessarily mean one can't also be "pro-life." One can also find irony in the growing tendency on the part of certain Presidential candidates, and even others running for office, who claim to be the "most Christian." Eventhough Jesus himself seems to have suggested just the opposite: that the more authentic one's faith, the less one needs to trade on it.[6]

I have a rather prodigious step-granddaughter named Elliott Thomas. Elliott has seemed to understand irony from the time she learned to talk. Even when she was a just pre-schooler, and I would be teasing her, she would look at me as if to say, "Who do you think you're dealing with here, bud!" Elliott is not one to "suffer fools gladly." When asked what she wanted to be when she grew up, Elliott said, "An entrepreneur." She was about five years old at the time, which was when she also declared: "If the guy gives you a cold-fish handshake, the deal probably isn't going to go through." I have always thought her pretty remarkable, particularly when I consider how many adults appear to deal with the world so totally at face value.

According to the research, 75 percent of Americans are sensers.[7] "Success" in our culture has largely to do with how things are quantified, with how they are measured, weighed, packaged, produced, priced, marketed, and consumed. Therefore, when Jesus says such things as, "If you want to save your life, then lose it for my sake," that tends to sound pretty crazy to a lot of us. Moral and spiritual growth and depth are not always so easily quantified. Many other things are. The genius, for example, of "Habitat for Humanity" is that it combines the two, the "losing" and the "saving," about as concretely as possible. That's no accident. Millard Fuller was a lawyer. How better, if you want to feel good about yourself for giving something of yourself away, than to take a couple of weeks' vacation

6. Matt 6.

7. Keirsey and Bates, *Please Understand Me.*

and help build a house for someone who doesn't have a decent house to live in? Who knows, you might even save "your life!" That is how I would say it, which is, of course, a metaphor. It's a figurative statement, not a literal statement. That is, at least, how Jesus says it. Except some would say your "soul," which most people seem to understand in quite literal terms, even though the Bible doesn't. As if one has a "soul" in the way we have a liver or a spleen. In fact, in the Bible, even such an essential human organ as the heart is spoken of metaphorically.

Be that as it may, in participating in "Habitat for Humanity," you would at least be doing something good for someone else. Then, when the house was built, you could see that the task was completed. That isn't quite as easy when you teach Sunday School or lead a Scout troop, and week after week, year after year, you wonder if you're doing any good. For some children, if they ever do grow up and might want to thank you for making much of a difference in their lives, you may not even be around by then. In our culture, we like our success sure and certain, and we want to be able to see it, to somehow measure and evaluate it. And for most of us, the sooner we see our success, the better.

Economic reward in our culture tends to favor the strengths of a senser. For example, your average dentist makes more money than do most ministers. Accountants are usually paid better than the majority of "starving artists." Sensers seem to stay with tasks longer and better. If intuitives appear to be more creative thinkers, they often become bored more easily than sensers do, certainly with the more tedious and ordinary chores of living and working. Sensers seem to pay more attention to details. This is surely what we expect from our doctors and lawyers, those who build our roads and bridges, our houses and office buildings. We want them to read the fine print. If the plumber is blessed with some intuition, it may help him better understand his wife and kids, but to install my water heater, he really needs the skills of a senser. The same is true for a secretary, although today he is apt to be called an administrative assistant. Most secretaries are likely still to be women, however, and even though they make less than whomever they work for, it is their attention to the details in any office or organization that is meant to make the boss look good. In this respect, and it's something of an aside, involving, as it were, the sexual politics of the work world, I ask people in management training workshops I often conduct, "Would you rather work for a man or a woman?" More men typically indicate at least a willingness to work for a woman, whereas more women tell me they would rather work for a man.

The details are important for those who manage our money, depending, of course, upon who is paying or earning the interest. As one of my professors used to say: "I'm a conservative when I'm giving and a liberal when I'm taking!" Such is the thinking of an intuitive.

A minister-friend recently offered this rather vivid illustration. Since he is fluent in Myers-Briggs-ese, here's how he said it. It seems a committee in the church he serves was discussing the pros and cons of buying and installing some playground equipment on the church's property. "The intuitives," he said, "all the brainstormers in the group, they thought it was a great idea. All they seemed to be able to see were the plusses. They kept talking about how this would attract young families with children to the church, how it would make a positive, welcoming statement to the neighborhood, things like that. Whereas the sensers on the committee seemed to be the ones playing devil's advocate. They kept raising questions about liability, about how much this might increase the church's insurance premium, about all sorts of problems they could foresee."

Most of what we consider "scholarly" work involves the strengths of the senser, which, of course, eliminates this book! Or as someone has observed, "Scholars are given to learning more and more about less and less". What we know as "the scientific method" is an often tedious process of inductive reasoning which proceeds from close attention to detail, moving quite methodically from specific to general. Sensers sometimes seem to have some fairly narrow constructs, some rather fixed categories in which they tend to place people, in order to fit folk into their particular scheme of the world. To illustrate, I have always appreciated Transactional Analysis as a social psychology because of the value it places on balance as a key to emotional health. However, in the mind of a senser, all those constructs and all that jargon can be pretty dangerous. Such people, who tend to label others, are sometimes called "psychopests."

In most organizations, it is the intuitives who are more apt to think, as we say, "outside the box." For the sensers, it is "the box" that's important. What are the rules, the regulations, what does the policy document say, the company handbook, where are the lines of authority? Throughout my career, my critics have always accused me of appearing to "not have a boss." Such folk are, of course, sensers who are usually pretty anxious to ensure who "the boss" is, if not wanting to be at least someone's "boss" themselves. I've never had much of a need to try to "boss" anyone, preferring instead to teach and train and even lead. Consequently, the sensers who have supposedly "worked *for* me" have been provoked by my less micro-managing style. While the intutitives have found it just as empowering and affirming, as supportive and encouraging. In personnel work, for example, an intuitive manager, when interviewing someone for a job, will often attach more value to the interviewing process itself, to how the person comes across in the interview. The senser, by contrast, will generally be more interested in the applicant's resumé, where the applicant has worked and what he can do. For a senser, what a person can do depends a lot on what she has done and how it is documented, how that person seems to fit into the senser's preconceived categories. Being more intuitive, I often say at this point: "Willie Mays could play left field." At which most people usually respond with a rather blank stare, as if to say, "What are you talking about?" It's a metaphor, stupid! If you don't understand, it may have even less to do with being a senser than with not knowing much about baseball.

It is in this sense that the work of a counselor might be better seen as more of an intuitive task, certainly when a therapist tends to get caught up in too much detail, in too much of an either/or way of thinking, or cause-effect reasoning. I often explain to students that being a good counselor is like reading a novel. You have a setting, characters, a plot, and a theme or themes. Sensors often have a tendency to become so preoccupied with the first three of these considerations, the characters, the setting, and the plot, that they miss the fourth, the theme or themes that run through anyone's life. According to the cliché, they are "missing the forest for the trees." This is especially true when working with obsessive clients, with worriers and perfectionists, with us everyday garden variety neurotics, folk who are so afraid that either they or someone else, such as the counselor, isn't going to know or is going to forget some minute detail concerning whom or whatever, their unabridged life story. In other words, when you ask some people what time it is, they tell you how the watch was made. It is this kind of over-detailing that makes some people crazy. When a therapist tends to collude with such pathology, she is merely reinforcing the problem. Sensers, in particular, have to watch such a tendency, because sensers like details.

Here's an apt illustration. I saw a patient at the mental health clinic years ago. I thought he was schizophrenic, that he had a major thinking disorder. His verbiage was so loosely constructed. Like pieces in a puzzle, each of the parts made sense as a distinct unit, but the way he seemed to have them connected didn't make sense. His thinking seemed confused, if not confusing. The psychiatrist who consulted with me regarding this patient suggested that he wasn't schizophrenic. She saw him as overly obsessive and somewhat pressured in his speech and manner. There was an urgency, an intensity about this fellow that seemed fairly explainable to that psychiatrist. As she put it, "It's like he's trying to pour a gallon into a quart. You get a lot of spillage." What a vivid analogy. Indeed, my work with that patient over some years proved the psychiatrist right.

In terms of Bowen theory, involving counselors who tend to get too caught up in details, who often don't seem to see the theme or themes in a person's life, in a marriage, in a family, this is often a form of what Bowen would call getting "triangulated" in the system. Eventhough a more common understanding of triangulation involves getting caught, somewhere between the needs of different people in a family, or any other system, in such a way as to appear to be siding with someone or other. Of course, any competent therapist is going to do this in the face of more extreme forms of family violence, by way of trying to protect, in whatever way is necessary, anyone who is being victimized, sexually or physically, and sometimes even emotionally, especially involving children and the elderly. However, the last of these factors requires some clinical savvy. Competent therapists don't "rescue" the kinds of "victims" who need to learn how to "take care of themselves" with the "crazymakers" in their lives. As the late Rabbi Friedman said, "You can't eliminate pathogens in an environment; you have to strengthen the resiliency of the host."[8] That's another metaphor. This is a kind of therapy that tends not to patronize people, even in the guise of being caring, a kind of counseling that leads to a person's strength, not her weakness.

Any experienced family counselor is familiar with this common scenario, at least if she knows systems theory. As I often put it, no one comes to therapy by himself. She always brings someone with her, sometimes the entire family, often several generations. Again, I'm speaking figuratively, not literally. The most common and quite literal caricature, however, would involve spouses who "bring each other" to counseling so that the therapist can "fix him," or "her," as the case may be. Another ex-

8. Edwin Friedman "Getting Unstuck," AAMFT Master Series videotape.

ample involves parents who call and ask you to "fix" their kid. When the teenager comes in, her story is: "If you could just fix my mom (or dad), then everything would be OK." Capable counselors know how to stay out of such triangulating. It is, however, the details in anyone's story that can often be even more seductive, when they serve to obscure what is really going on, as when facts get in the way of truth, or perhaps reasons in the way of feeling or need, not to mention motive. Over-detailing is usually the culprit. Therapists who don't understand this often become triangulated with such a process in a system and end up reinforcing the pathology. As trite as it may seem, this is "missing the forest for the trees."

Given the data that a significant majority of people tend to be sensers, in terms of Myers-Briggs typology, I have begun to pay more attention to the work of counseling from this perspective. For example, I notice that many of my students seem to gravitate to a more "structural" approach to family therapy. Looking at how families tend to be organized seems easier, for a majority of students, than grasping the principles of, say "strategic" therapy. This is likely because there are more sensers than intuitives, even in a graduate program in clinical counseling. Structural therapy is more objective, while strategic therapy is more subjective. Structural therapy has a certain logic to it, while strategic therapy involves more of a paradoxical approach. Even Murray Bowen's genogram, which provides a kind of logical, methodical mapping or plotting of patterns in families, is a visual tool that many therapists, as well as their clients, seem to find helpful and revealing, and likely less threatening than some other interventions.

Here's a common illustration of the senser and the intuitive in therapy. I don't know how many couples over the years have said to me: "That other counselor we saw, the one before we came to you, she said we ought to get a divorce." Now, of course, any reputable marriage counselor is likely never going to ever say such a thing to anyone, short of a concern over explicit family violence. What I suspect the previous therapist may have said was something like this, in the form of a paradoxical intervention. He may have conjectured, "Hmm. I wonder why you two stay married? I wonder what you're getting out of this?" Highly intuitive therapists tend to think and to intervene paradoxically. If the client or clients tend to be sensers, they are likely to hear such a question as an assertion: you should get a divorce. This is especially true if such a way of understanding, of hearing or seeing things, is compounded by even the least bit of defensiveness, not to mention paranoia.

Students often call my counseling courses "Paradox 101." That is because I am forever trying to impress upon them the importance of looking for opposites. Opposites reinforce each other, and they are never as far apart as they may seem. Most psychotherapy involves reframing; it concerns how people perceive their lives in the face of the more "objective" circumstances. This, then, is essentially a paradox. For example, healthier and more effective people are not usually the way they are because their world is so understanding, so nice and sweet, so fair and gentle and kind. Rather, it is because of how they choose to see their world and act upon it because of how they see themselves. Consider yet another cliché: "Is the glass half empty or half full?" The paradox is that it is both. Effective counseling helps people to reframe their lives in ways that emphasize, not what is wrong, but what is right; not what won't work, but what will; not what they can't do, but what they can. It is embracing both your strengths and your weaknesses and seeing a connection between the two. Things aren't always as they appear. If solving people's problems were a logical task, then we wouldn't need therapists. All we would need is teachers. Just explain the problem, and people would change. However, it isn't that easy. Given all the twists and turns in most of our lives, logic, as a tool for problem-solving, often tends to break down.

Here's a fairly generic and nearly as benign example. By definition, at least in my way of thinking, what we call being neurotic is an often unconscious, frequently learned, and just as socially sanctioned, perhaps even normative way of trying to avoid or defend ourselves against some sort of perceived threat. However, in the very process of doing so, we often hurt ourselves even worse than whatever we fear would. Isn't that what those of us who tend to be perfectionists do? When we fear making a mistake or being criticized, we usually end up borrowing more trouble in our lives than what we are apt to face in the first place, be it the sternest of criticism or perhaps even the worst of mistakes. As a result, counselors commonly see neurotic clients who are trying to be "perfectly not-perfect." Did you catch that? Any therapist who doesn't understand irony, who can't seem to think paradoxically, is likely to reinforce such pathology. In fact, someone may be paying big bucks for all that help!

Too often our neurotic defenses, as good as they may look, become our hedge against the truth of our lives. Consider, for example, to what extent we will often go to try to deny, to run from, to not face, much less embrace and bless, the truth of our lives. In the end, as ironic and even painful as it may be, what we are doing to ourselves is often worse than whatever we're trying so hard to avoid. How did Jesus put it? That only "the truth" will ever set us free, even if, at first, it may scare us or make us mad. Most of us pay too high a price for our denial. The late Clarence Jordan was a highly educated and a sophisticated Greek scholar and theologian, as well as a country Baptist preacher and peanut farmer. In his inimitable style, Dr. Jordan used to tell a story about the traveling evangelist who caught syphilis but wouldn't go to the doctor. Or as a fellow once said of his wife: "I call her Cleopatra, the queen of denial!"

A friend once confessed to me that he had gotten his feelings hurt. Someone he was close to had offended him by something he had said. My friend disclosed, "I didn't speak to that guy for over a year. But then I began to feel guilty that I was acting this way. So I went to the fellow and apologized. That is when he said to me, 'Oh, that's OK. I hadn't noticed.'" That reminds me of a sign I once saw hanging in a hamburger joint, back in southern Illinois, where I grew up. It said: "When I was 18 I didn't care what people thought of me. When I was 30 I worried too much about what people thought of me. And when I turned 50 I began to realize that people weren't thinking all that much about me after all!"

Since a majority of people, according to the research, would seem to be sensers, I have taken a more inductive approach to teaching even graduate students in counseling. Traditionally, theory, which tends to be more abstract, is taught first. Students are then expected to be able to apply such theory to more concrete or clinical situations. The movement here is from general to specific. However, for a number of years, I have approached this task from a different direction. I begin with films, and later I introduce novels and plays, which dramatize concrete human situations. From this perspective, students observe, in at least one course I teach, particular dynamics and characteristics of families that we then discuss in terms of various theoretical constructs and approaches to family therapy. Thus, whenever we are trying to understand the theory, we have a variety of concrete examples that provide rather vivid frames of reference. This seems to work better, at least for sensers, whose process tends to be more inductive, who sometimes find it harder than their more intuitive peers to move from the abstractness of theory to the concreteness of clinical situations. Sensers have a harder time making connections between apparent differences that may seem quite unrelated. Intuitives think more analogically and recognize the more symbolic, interconnected, and sometimes ironic nature of patterns and themes in most families.

Films I use include *Mr. and Mrs. Bridge* and *Ordinary People. Mr. and Mrs. Bridge*[9], which stars Paul Newman and Joanne Woodward, dramatically illustrates much of what structural family therapy is concerned with. In this instance, it is almost stereotypical. The husband is emotionally unavailable to his wife, and in most such cases, women in these circumstances tend to become emotionally dependent upon one or more of their children. In Mrs. Bridge's case, however, the children distance themselves from her, even in disdainful ways, not unlike her husband. It is a painful film. It also tends to have certain characteristics of a home movie. Many students complain that *Mr. and Mrs. Bridge* is "dull" or "boring," which suggests that such students aren't apt to be very good therapists, since much of the important work of a counselor involves paying attention to what might not seem all that interesting or important. Also, there is in this film a suggestion of some sort of alliance, even emotional incest in the system, involving the father and the older daughter. *Mr. and Mrs. Bridge* is characterized by its subtlety, so it provides something of an aptitude test for graduate students in counseling, since the best therapists have a knack for appreciating subtleties.

Ordinary People[10] is a masterful film for the purpose of teaching marriage and family counseling. For one thing, the therapist in the story is credible, even though he and the work he does is dramatized. Unfortunatly, most shrinks or preachers in the movies are not credible; they are frequently caricatured as incompetent, if not worse. In particular, the therapist in *Ordinary People* avoids getting triangulated in the family presented. This film, from a family systems perspective, vividly portrays an adolescent boy's process of differentiation in an ostensibly "good" family, a family that is, nonetheless, toxic, if not lethal, for this boy. The film portrays the dysfunction surrounding triangulation in a system: the father seems caught, and painfully so, between his wife and his son. Also, as the homeostasis in the family is disrupted—the kid gets well and is no longer a symptom-bearer in the system—the balance of power in the family shifts, and the family appears to disintegrate. *Ordinary People* is credibly realistic enough for anyone watching the film to learn a lot about how

9. *Mr. and Mrs. Bridge*, directed by James Ivory, Cineplex-Odeon Films, 1990.

10. *Ordinary People*, directed by Robert Redford, Paramount Pictures, 1980.

families often operate, even to their detriment. The most important rules and expectations in the family, particularly as they concern the mother's needs, are implicit, assumed, primarily unspoken.

In addition, I will mention two different novels. *Father Melancholy's Daughter*, by Gail Godwin, provides something of a variation on the more common stereotype. In this instance, the mother is the parent who isn't available. She leaves, and despite the conspiracy between the father and young daughter that her absence isn't permanent, she dies. This puts the little girl in what is called a double-bind. What do you when you're a kid, with a mother who leaves you and then dies on you? In fact, a mother you never really knew, and are therefore then driven to spend much of the rest of your young life trying to get to know. In the case of Margaret Gower, in *Father Melancholy's Daughter*[11], her spousified relationship with her father isn't any more unusual in many families than it is hardly good for either parent or child.

Clyde Edgerton's *Raney*[12] is another remarkably realistic novel about the kind of extended family Murray Bowen would describe as an "undifferentiated ego mass." Set here in the Bible Belt, in the rural South where I and most of the students I teach live and work, *Raney* is a hopeful story of a young woman beginning, with considerable struggle, to differentiate in some appropriate ways in relation to her family of origin and her new husband. Such that she and he can likely create a more functional family than what they might have otherwise either been stuck with or tried to run away from.

More intuitive people tend to be better therapists in the ways I have described. A more effective kind of counseling involves certain intuitive strengths, particularly as it has to do with not letting theoretical constructs or circumstantial over-detailing get in the way of what is really going on with and between clients and counselors, of obscuring the more important symbols, patterns, and themes that characterize our lives. Some might reason that since most people seem to be sensers, doesn't it make more sense to approach counseling from such a framework? I can certainly understand this rationale, unless the kinds of problems most people face are compounded by such a way of thinking: when being too concrete or literal is blinding; when it serves to obscure the truth of

11. Godwin, Gail. *Father Melancholy's Daughter* (New York: Avon Books, 1997).
12. Clyde Edgerton, *Raney* (New York: Random House, 1985).

anyone's life; when a person or a family is being strangled by all the details or the kinds of constructs or categories in which some folk seem to need others always to fit; by the way that fact often betrays truth.

It's interesting that the original work of the late Eric Berne, a psychiatrist who first developed Transactional Analysis, a system of social psychiatry, had to do with intuition, what he would later call "the little professor." His concern was with the function of intuition in problem-solving, with how figuring things out often involves a child-like quality, as in the story of "The Emperor's New Clothes." All the big people and all the smart people admire the emperor's new clothes. However, it is a little kid who can see and tell the truth. He isn't blinded by too many other "important" concerns. He knows the guy is naked.

It is just such an image of a gifted counselor that reminds me of Columbo, the little lieutenant on the Los Angeles police force who solves the most difficult crimes in the most disarming of ways. That's what I tell my students: if you want to learn how to be a good therapist, watch *Columbo*. He can still be seen on some cable television channels. Both his inductive and his deductive process are more reciprocal and flexible than exclusive and rigid. He doesn't miss anything, and he still plays his hunches. Details only count as a means, not as an end. He is hardly concerned with how he comes across, even as others in his world are far too invested in some less than authentic image of themselves. In Bowen's terms, Columbo's "self" is "solid"; he is anything but "pseudo." He is not unlike the lawyer in *Nuts* or the therapist in *Ordinary People*. Columbo's theoretical apparatus and his clinical savvy don't get in each other's way. Rather, they work together. He is provocative, even annoying, but he is also winsome and disarming. He has a knack for getting behind others' often well-crafted defenses. To borrow another image from Clarence Jordan, Columbo uses a "Trojan horse" style of sleuthing. Most counselors would do well to learn from him.[13]

Eric Berne's interest in intuition grew out of his own clinical experience as an Army psychiatrist, where he was tasked with interviewing new recruits. However, there were too many for him to evaluate adequately in the allotted time. Thus, he began to question how much of traditional theoretical and clinical apparatus in counseling often tends to get in the way and hinder the process. Berne's father was a country doctor in Canada,

13. Clarence Jordan's reference was to the story of the prophet, Nathan, in the Bible, to his disarming encounter with King David, II Samuel 12.

and Berne often said that doing counseling is like delivering a baby in a one-room cabin with a wood stove in the dead of winter. You have to be pretty resourceful. All of what you need isn't necessarily available, and the circumstances aren't always optimal. This is certainly true when it comes to making connections and seeing meaning in what may seem so unimportant, insignificant, or unconnected in the ways that people tell their stories and how anyone's life is revealed. I often tell my students that good therapists aren't always looking for more information. Good therapists do more with the information they have, and that involves playing some hunches.

If the intuitively gifted seem to be better counselors, in this era of managed care they may not be able to stay in business, unless they do a better job of taking care of certain details and learning how to translate even the most creative forms of therapy in terms compatible with the framework of a senser. These days, some of the best therapists can be heard muttering: "I went to the wrong school. I should have majored in accounting!" Surely the sensers will survive, because they are the majority and the quantifiers of the world. In most organizations, even of the caregiving sort, the sensers usually end up running things. After all, sensers, even among counselors, are more apt to have their insurance forms filled out correctly, or to at least get their license renewed on time!

THINKER/FEELER

These character and temperament differences seem fairly obvious. They can, however, be quite subtle. Thinkers tend to take a predominantly rational approach to living, while that of a feeler is more emotional, or at least tends to be more sensitive to the emotional content of human interaction. This may be particularly noticeable in the ways people make decisions and/or how they handle stress. It also seems characteristic of what we generally think of as someone's personality. For example, words that we use to describe feelers might include "friendly, sensitive, considerate, warm," or perhaps "touchy, irritable, hyper-sensitive." Whereas we might describe a thinker as "cool," or perhaps "calculating," "unflappable," or "cold." The point here is that each of these predominant styles has an upside and a downside. What can be a strength can also be a weakness. At their extremes, thinkers have to watch being perceived as cold or uncaring, as distant or aloof, as unsympathetic or inconsiderate, as perhaps harsh or blunt. On the other hand, feelers have to watch out for being too reactive, not defining themselves firmly enough, being perhaps too emotionally available, too accommodating, or too placating.

At a subtler level, thinkers seem to value matters of principle, justice, or truth. A higher value for feelers seems to be a concern for harmony and cooperation, for making sure people get along and aren't offended. Feelers seem to be awfully good at greasing the wheels of social intercourse, whereas thinkers are more apt to stick their neck out for the underdog or challenge perceived injustice. One friend describes his two daughters as quite different in this respect. The feeler goes along more easily when things aren't always fair, and the thinker seems much more concerned, not just with her "rights," but with those of others as well. When he asks the feeler if she likes his new sport coat, she is likely to say something like: "Yes, it's very pretty. I think you might like it with that other tie, though. You know, the one mom gave you for your birthday. You might want to see how that would look." The thinker, however, would be more apt to say something like: "It's a pretty coat, but don't you know it doesn't go with that tie?" End of conversation. That may be a bit of a caricature, but you get the idea. In fact, when thinkers and feelers clash, it normally involves such caricaturing of one another. The Myers-Briggs Type Indicator isn't concerned with pathology. Still, there are some feelers who can be pretty histrionic, as any experienced counselor knows. Consider the fellow who told his wife one time in my office: "Calm down, you're being too historical!"(sic) Similarly, there are thinkers whose intellectualizing of their feelings can keep others at a distance, even as they can maintain themselves in a fairly chronic state of depression.

Keirsey and Bates claim that there is an even distribution of thinkers and feelers in our society.[14] That is not, however, my experience. In some groups I have worked with, particularly in the military, the overwhelming majority, all of whom were men, were almost all introverted sensers, who were also thinkers. This is something of a strong, silent, macho stereotype. Among all other groups, however, I have found the distribution of thinkers and feelers to be quite the opposite, including both males and females. The majority of people who disclose their Myers-Briggs profile to me are feelers. If I were spending all of my time with counselors or ministers, this might be explainable, since they might be expected to be more "sensitive," more feeling-oriented. However, I have found this to be true even

14. Keirsey and Bates, *Please Understand Me*, 25.

among industrial work groups, with which I have, over the years, done a lot of consulting. It makes me wonder if the stereotype of the feeler is that he tends to be more sensitive or accommodating, perhaps even at times hyper-sensitive. In contrast, if feelers deal with the world on more emotional terms, does that mean that even one thinker at her bluntest and harshest can inflict all sorts of emotional distress on a whole host of feelers? This is a common pattern in many organizations, where the majority of the work force may "feel" discounted or devalued by their company's policies and procedures and management style. I've found it somewhat stereotypical of the organizations I'm familiar with, where a majority of employees "feel" there is a kind of institutional lack of consideration for their "feelings."

At the same time, however, I have also noticed a common pattern among managers and supervisors in workplace settings, a pattern of trying to "please everyone." However, such a management style just as often backfires, where no one ends up being "pleased" or at least "pleased" enough. Hence, books like this one about "balance," even in the workplace; balance somewhere between the "firmness (toughness?)" of the "thinker" boss and the "softness (niceness?)" of the "feeler" boss. Or as one supervisor told me she said, recently, to a supervisee: "Don't confuse my niceness with weakness."

A predominance of apparent feelers has also been my experience with respect to church life, where I have spent so much of my life. Indeed, every time someone has expressed to me, in my role as pastor or not, either appreciation or criticism, compared to expressing it in terms of thinking (involving some rationale, be it information , fact, or reason), more often what has been revealed are feelings (the personal, the subjective, merely the opinion of whomever, however uninformed). Unfortunately, in some churches it seems that whomever it is that "gets their feelings hurt" the easiest is then able to leverage the most control, the proverbial tail that wags the dog. My observation is that if one were to interview most people in most congregations as to why they even "belong" to a particular church, the responses would, overwhelmingly, have less to do with the more objective matters of theology, ethics, or ecclesiology than with family and social relations and interaction, with feelings of closeness to someone or other besides Jesus, Augustine, or Aquinas, Luther, Calvin, or Wesley, Spurgeon, Stone, or the Campbells; some sense of community, of belonging, the currency of feeling. In one of my favorite stories, a Jewish kid asks his uncle:

"Why do you go to synagogue, Uncle Saul? You don't believe in God?" His uncle replies: "My friend, Abe, believes in God. He goes to synagogue. I go to synagogue to be with Abe."

What about parenting, when it comes to the relative strengths and weaknesses inherent in thinking and feeling? Are "thinking" parents more firm, and likely more consistent with their children, perhaps even more reasonably fair? Do "feeling" parents tend to be weaker, less strict or structured in dealing with their kids? Are feelers better nurturers than "thinking" parents tend to be?

It is here that the MBTI is particularly fruitful for the counselor with respect to the functions of feeling and thinking, in that it provides an appropriate context for this important discussion. A common belief, held by too many, it would seem, is that one cannot feel and think at the same time. Otherwise, we wouldn't hear such excuses as, "I was so mad I couldn't help it," or "I was so scared I couldn't think," or "If she knew I felt this way, she would just die!" What seems fairly deeply ingrained for many people, in terms of culture or family history, is that either thinking or feeling has been valued higher. In some families, for example, there appear to be quite strong, even overt and certainly covert messages that say, "Don't feel!" For example, "Big boys don't cry," or "Hush up now, or I'll give you something to cry about." In some families, even in some cultures, one even gets the idea that smiling is frowned upon, that it is considered frivolous and inappropriate. Who, for example, hasn't found themselves amused by Grant Wood's familiar portrait, *American Gothic*? Those who might not be amused are likely among those who would agree that if you were to smile, your face might break.

In other families, and likely in some cultures or at least subcultures, an opposite message is even more implicit than explicit. It is "Don't think!" In such settings, the normative way for people to deal with problems is to emote. The message seems to be that if you escalate your discomfort enough, someone will "rescue" you, or at least consider your emoting par for the course. Many would see such different cultural messages as stereotypical for males (don't feel) and females (don't think). There seem to be some examples in certain families, even in certain cultures, where such messages and sex-role stereotypes appear to be reversed. Experienced therapists are familiar with these stereotypes. Some clients need to learn, more than anything else, that it is OK to feel, that your feelings won't kill you or anyone else. Feelings might hurt, but you can handle the pain. You can survive. You won't die from such discomfort. Some counselors would call this "giving a client permission." Some clients need to learn that they can think, that they have a mind and that it works. They need to learn that they are not dumb or stupid or weak or helpless or incapable. They need to learn that they can solve problems and take better care of themselves than whomever they may have been too dependent upon. Just as, I have observed, many people haven't learned, or don't believe, that they can feel and think at the same time.

My daughter is as smart and strong as she is soft and sensitive. When she was a little girl, she once climbed a relatively small tree in our front yard. It wasn't too dangerous. However, she called to me, with a bit of histrionic flair, "Daddy, daddy, come get me down!"

I went over and stood beneath where she was and calmly said, "Amy, if you got yourself up there, you can get yourself down." I wanted to provide appropriate protection, and certainly support for her, while at the same time letting her know that in our culture at least, anyone as pretty as my daughter can always find someone (at least some man) to get her down "out of a tree," as it were, or any number of other tight spots. Except he will then likely send her a bill! It tends to work that way. When any of us, female or male, expect someone else to do our thinking and problem-solving for us or, for that matter, to do our feeling, we may end up paying an awfully high price for such service.

Years ago, I learned something important from a psychiatrist, the late Gerry Donovan, who was a remarkable psychotherapist. According to Dr. Donovan, there are only four feelings: mad, glad, sad, and scared. All other feeling words are euphemisms for these four basic feelings. Such a strict construction seems particularly helpful when working with the kind of neurotic people who tend to intellectualize their feelings, who tend to live too much in their head and not enough with their heart. Such folk have usually learned to discount their feelings, or perhaps certain feelings that they may fear or have been taught were bad. There is no such thing as a "bad" feeling. Feelings are appropriate or inappropriate, depending upon the circumstances, or what a psychologist would call the "stimuli." That's why feeling and thinking go together. They are not, as too many claim, exclusive of each other, as if you can feel or think, but "never the twain shall meet." When feeling and thinking work together, feeling is then seen as OK, and the function of our thinking becomes one of discernment. For example, "Is my anger here reasonable? Is my fear appropriate?" This is not intellectualizing about feelings. It is feeling and thinking at the same time.

The issue here is one of congruence. Most good therapists pay a lot of attention to congruence or, conversely, to incongruities. An incongruity is when something doesn't fit. The Pittsburgh Steelers, for example, play football these days in a city where there are no longer any steel mills. Likewise, the Utah Jazz play basketball in the home of the Mormon Tabernacle Choir. Those team names are incongruent with those respective cities. They don't fit. The Jazz were named when the team was in New Orleans. That's congruent. When the Steeler football team was born, Pittsburgh's skyline was filled with black smoke from the steel mills. Once upon a time, the name fit. Speaking of incongruity, an ad that appeared in the newspaper asked for help in locating a lost dog. The description said: "Only has three legs, is blind in one eye, and part of his left ear is missing. Answers to the name Lucky!"

The same is true in our lives. Sometimes what we feel doesn't fit with our circumstances, or with a particular situation, despite what someone may have told us in the past, when they may have had some need to tell us what or what not to feel. For example, when we accidentally hit our thumb with a hammer and exclaim, "Praise the Lord!" That is incongruent. When we rant and rave at our teenager because he has a ring in his nose, we appear angry. More than likely, however, we are frightened or threatened. Our anger is incongruent. That ring in her nose may suggest to us that our kid is a lost cause. It may symbolize to us a style of living with which we are awfully uncomfortable. It may cause us to worry about our child's future, not to mention our own self-image. "What will people think of me if my child looks like that?" This process tends to be more spontaneous than reflective, when we are scared and act mad. In case you don't remember, there was a time when parents all over America were threatening either homicide or suicide over the length of their son's hair. Or again, when we are grieving legitimately over a loss and someone discounts the depth and significance of such sadness with a cliché like, "Don't cry now, it'll get better," or "It's not so bad," or even "God knows best." Smiling in such circumstances is incongruent. Some might even call it phony. It is the discounting of feelings that tends to produce such incongruity, and that can make people crazy. As for the "God knows best" claim, have you ever noticed the amount of raging and weeping in the Psalms?

It is with respect to feelings that one can likely best understand the difference between being congruent and incongruent, because feelings are energy. When our feelings are congruent, our energy tends to be creative and effective. Our energy works for us rather than against us and serves us well. When our feelings are incongruent, however, the energy tends to be blocked. The energy is not directed toward a good purpose. In fact, it may often be the source of psychological depression. Such intra-psychic conflict tends to be more destructive than constructive. Energy from congruent feelings helps us to solve problems. A lack of creative energy from incongruent feelings produces or contributes to our problems. Feelings that are congruent become a means to an end. Incongruent feelings become an end in themselves. When our feelings are congruent, sooner than later we get off *of* them. When they are incongruent, we get off *on* them.

Here are some examples of congruity and incongruity with respect to our feelings. I have already mentioned one of the more common examples: when we are scared and act mad. Most intellectualizers would prefer a softer, more euphemistic word like being "upset" or "annoyed." That's why these four basic feeling words are so important. They are the language of a nine year old. For anyone whose primary psychic defense tends to be that of intellectualizing, nine-year-old feeling words keep us more honest. They serve to confront how we often try to deny our anger or sadness or fear, sometimes even our gladness. When we stop denying or rationalizing what we feel, we become healthier, more genuine, and likely even happier people, if in fact happiness is appropriate to our circumstances, if it is congruent. Another example I have also mentioned: when we are mad or sad and act glad. Here in the Bible Belt, where I live and work, this is a common caricature: people who, with a smile on their face, would just love to assault you in Jesus' name!

It is my sense that fear is the most primal of emotions. I don't say that glibly. It is hard for me to think of any form of dysfunction in our lives that isn't somehow connected to perceived fear, such as family secrets, neurotic defenses, the kinds of power plays most of us tend to escalate when we get threatened in some way or other, be it over our turf, our comfort zone, or some image of ourselves in which we are highly invested. At the same time, a healthy sense of fear is important. Anyone who doesn't have an appropriate sense of fear is heading for trouble. What is most important, in the face of fear, is to feel and think. Some folk tend to get mad when they are scared or sad. This is incongruent. It tends to produce fit-throwers and/or chronic complainers. There are far too many people in this world who walk around either grousing or in a rage because they are afraid to face the depth of their fear or sadness. I believe the most congruent reason for anger is when someone discounts us. That's the time to be angry. That anger will tend to promote good problem-solving on our part, and it will help us take care of ourselves in some responsible, appropriate ways. Discounting comes in lots of forms, not the least of which involve patronizing, prejudice, or stereotyping.

Have you ever noticed how often people say they feel something when what they are describing is a thought or a belief? Unless you have been taught to pay attention to this, you might not have noticed. For example, as a counselor, I frequently ask someone what she feels. More often than not, the reply goes something like: "I felt like he wasn't listening to me," or "I felt like she shouldn't have said that." These are common constructions. I often confront such responses with, "I didn't ask you what you thought, I asked you what you felt." When someone isn't listening to you, what do you feel? Do you feel mad? Do you feel scared or perhaps sad? If you feel glad, you may be a bit disoriented! This exercise can be helpful, particularly for folk who seem to have some confusion between feeling and thinking, especially if they believe thinking is more important than feeling.

Most of what we believe, think, or feel about feelings, as well as thinking, is learned. In some families, cultures, organizations, or institutions, the incongruities can be pretty pathologic. I was having lunch one time with two clergy colleagues. They were both of the same denomination, different from mine. I remember the occasion well because it was so crazy. Throughout lunch, these two preachers teased and joked with one another. It seemed amiable enough, but it wasn't. It wasn't cute or funny. It was lacking in goodwill. These two guys were hardly missing a chance to "stick it to" each other. Their posturing with one another, clothed in affability and humor, was about as incongruent as anything I've ever seen. It was pretty sick.

Bowen theory appears to value thinking over feeling. However, I have, over the years, come to frame it differently, since what I have observed is feeling usually having primacy over thinking. Hence, my belief that feeling and thinking need to work together. According to Bowen theory, the better differentiated one is, the more readily and congruently his thinking will interpret the reasonableness and/or appropriateness of his feeling. Put another way, if a person is better differentiated, she will be more behaviorally pro-active rather than merely emotionally re-active in whatever the circumstances. The rule of thumb is that higher levels of differentiation result in lower levels of reactivity, whereas lower levels of differentiation contribute to higher levels of reactivity. In fact, this is what I've come to pay the most attention to with respect to any system—family, workplace, church, civic, social, or fraternal organization. Who is calling the shots, who is setting the agenda: the more reactive persons in the system, or the less so? In more functional systems, it will be the better differentiated, less reactive people, with the converse being the case in more dysfunctional systems.

Effective psychotherapy is balanced. It is both a hug around the neck and a kick in the butt! That's how I often say it. The best counselors know how to affirm and confront. And not that confronting is necessarily harsh or blunt or insensitive. Quite the opposite. The best therapists I've known have never seemed to have any great need to try to make me feel bad, as if in some perverse way they may have been getting their needs met at my expense. Hardly. More often what they have confronted me about, gently and powerfully and congruently, have been the ways I was hurting myself. Take any of the examples I have mentioned: when a counselor has confronted some of the ways I have been most adapted, such as appearing so nice when I was really mad, or getting my feelings hurt when I should be angry. That's the kind of incongruity that can keep you pretty depressed, often in the most socially sanctioned of ways. If one of the oldest definitions of psychological depression is anger turned inward, I submit that it is also anger turned into some other incongruent feeling.

In case you hadn't guessed, where I grew up, in my family, we weren't supposed to get mad. Nice people didn't get angry. We were chronically scared, except we carried this kind of low-grade fear around in the form of worrying a lot. "What will people think?" We might get our feelings hurt, it was OK to be sad, but we weren't supposed to be angry, because when we got mad, it scared us. We didn't know what to do with our anger. It often got us into trouble, which tended to reinforce our fear of such anger. It would be years later that I would learn to embrace and even bless my feelings: fear, anger, sadness, and joy. This can happen when you learn to feel and think at the same time.

I've often confronted clients who have tended to put themselves down. "What's going on? What's your need to put yourself down? Where did you learn to do that?" Such confrontation is considerate and respectful, because power is a paradox. The more any of us are trying to look powerful, the less powerful we are. Powerful counselors are normally as gentle and kind as they are tough and strong, whether a person is acting helpless or intimidating, passive or aggressive. That's why the most potent confronting many good therapists do may not involve their saying anything. This concept is based on a belief that, apart from genetics, biochemistry, or certain characteristics of brain function, people develop in two ways: by what is modeled before them and by how they are reinforced. For example, if I grow up around fit throwers, I might likely learn how to do that myself. If the role models in my life tend to be pretty helpless, I'm apt to emulate that way of trying to survive, even if it may be highly manipulative. If whenever I throw a fit, it scares people and they seem to accommodate me, then I am likely learning that fit-throwing works; or again, if my niceness seems to get me what I want, then I am apt to trade on it to try to make my life work.

Normally, when anyone seeks the services of a counselor, it is because what may have worked so well for them in the past is no longer working. Consequently, such people often become symptomatic. I have read all kinds of research findings concerning what clients claim as being helpful to them in either changing something about themselves or acting on their world in healthier, more responsible, and more effective ways. Two of the more salient qualities mentioned are always: 1) the modeling of the therapist and 2) how congruently the counselor interacts with the patient.

For example, if I start to escalate either incongruent anger or manipulative helplessness, and my therapist isn't threatened by either, something different is beginning to happen in my life, in terms of what has always "worked" for me in the past and how most people would react. Without even saying a word, my therapist has confronted me. She is both modeling a different kind of behavior before me and reinforcing me in some ways dramatically different from what I may be used to. The late Ed Friedman called this a "non-anxious presence." And when it is congruent it is powerful and effective in helping people change. The counselor is attending, if you will, paying attention to some different things in some different ways. As such, people's lives are changed in ways that are good for them and others.

The point here is not about when this doesn't work, because often it doesn't work. It is rather an interpretation of what is happening when powerful, effective counseling does serve to help people change and grow. Just ask anyone who has had this experience. It comes from being with those who model before you and reinforce you in different ways, in some ways that are better for you. I've mentioned the late Reverend William Sloane Coffin. Elsewhere in his autobiography he describes his homiletics professor from when Coffin was a student at Yale Divinity School. Speaking of one Browne Barr, Coffin writes: ". . . if his outer life was uneventful . . . his inner life was wildly adventurous, in fact as exposed as my own was sheltered. Having courageously befriended his most hostile emotions, he seemed unthreatened by any. With no blind sides, he was easily the school's best pastor. In our practice preaching classes he managed to establish such a climate of acceptance that we could be highly critical of one another while at the same time being supportive."[15] This is the quality and character of the effective counselor: having courageously befriended her most hostile emotions! Indeed, this is the only way that any of us can finally ever help anyone else. Remember, if getting angry may seem hostile to one person, being sad or scared or even glad may be quite as "hostile" to someone else.

At least two things are important here. When there is tension in a counseling relationship—and when therapy is effective there will always be tension—the tension will occur when a counselor confronts a client. Again, the scenario often isn't necessarily harsh or scandalous. It may even seem rather benign. For example, this may occur if your therapist won't let you play "stupid." This may seem strange. You might not even like it, particularly if you've been getting lots of secondary gain out of playing "stupid," no matter how much you may have resented others treating you as if you were. You may get mad at your counselor, and that irony is tragic. Because your therapist isn't putting you down, you are. You're putting yourself down, whether you realize it or not. This may be similar to how you may have been discounted or devalued by someone else in your past, or even in the present, except your therapist is now reinforcing you in some different ways.

Some counselors call this your "sweatshirt." You come in the door wearing a sweatshirt. On the front, it says, "Help me." On the back, it says, "But I'm not going to let you." When people may be highly invested in a way of trying to survive in the world that is no longer good for them, if it

15. William Sloane Coffin, *Once to Every Man* (Gateshead: Athenaeum Press, 1977) 117.

ever was, changing that about oneself isn't always as easy as it might seem. Other adaptations besides playing "stupid" might include how you escalate fear to anger and try to intimidate others when you are threatened, or how you may allow others to intimidate you. Perhaps you may have some inordinate need to try to take care of others, or perhaps to expect someone to take care of you. The list of all the ways that people may have learned to live that aren't proving to be very successful or fulfilling is endless. When any good counselor starts to confront such adaptations, this is when the tension in therapy occurs.

That is why therapists are clinically and ethically responsible to be aware of such threatening issues in their own lives and to be able to manage them in ways that aren't part of the problem a client or family may present. Here is the simplest and clearest axiom: a counselor's clinical and ethical responsibility is to not collude with the pathology presented, to not reinforce it. Any good therapist, who has been well trained, knows that whenever such collusion or reinforcement does happen, it has to do with whatever is going on with the counselor himself. That's why you don't usually learn how to be a therapist in school. It is there that you learn "about" counseling. In fact, I know plenty of counselors who made straight A's in school as a way of staying quite unconnected with what is involved in being a good therapist.

I was privileged to know, in his lifetime, the great Baptist preacher-educator Samuel Dewitt Proctor. Dr. Proctor used to describe some people who "went through school, school just didn't go through them!" Even so, formal academic study, at least in the training of counselors, hardly provides the leverage needed for confronting students with some of the most important issues involved in becoming an ethical and competent therapist. This has to be developed in one's own therapy and clinical supervision. Even then, confusion between therapy and supervision can constitute an ethical dilemma, if not a violation. Those students who become the best counselors have to be rather intrinsically motivated to look more deeply and carefully at themselves and whatever the problematic issues in their lives. It has been my experience in supervising post-graduate students for licensure as professional counselors, that those who are better able to make use of the supervisory process have been those most in touch with and aware of their own personal and family issues, who are less threatened by such "problems," who have either worked through more of these issues or have at least been willing to be involved in their own therapy concerning such matters, apart from the supervisor's suggestion or encouragement, if not urging.

The question that arises with regard to the Myers-Briggs thinking and feeling paradigm is, "Are thinkers better confronters than feelers?" Perhaps? To confront pathology potently and effectively, a counselor has to be well defined; Bowenians would say more highly differentiated. This is, indeed, how Bowen speaks of differentiation, as a rational, reflective process, which is different from mere emotional reactivity. In fact, the counselor who is powerful and effective has to be capable of staying out of what is, after all, the client's business. Therapists can't, finally, think or feel or make decisions for people. If they try to do this, they will fail. When any of us believes that we should or could think or feel or make decisions for anyone else, we are not being respectful of them, though it may appear otherwise. We are, at best or worst, patronizing them.

My experience, over many years of teaching and supervising counselors, is that most counselors tend to be feelers, and this strength becomes their most glaring weakness. If they may be good at empathizing with others, empathy being an admirable and important quality, a gift, essential to effective therapy, most therapists still seem to have a harder time confronting clients. When we are good at getting people to like us, to agree with us, or appreciate what we are doing for them, the fact that they may not, can be threatening, even when what we are doing is both clinically and ethically responsible. Except the best counselors know that confronting and affirming aren't that far apart; a hug around the neck and a kick in the butt may have more in common than we might think. Indeed, the softness might be stronger and the toughness even kinder than it would appear.

I have mentioned some subtleties that I frequently confront in clients, because a good counselor pays attention to the subtleties. For example, "Are you willing to change your 'buts' to 'ands'?" This involves owning and claiming the apparent contradictions in our lives, of seeing these polarities as somehow complementary. Our "opposites" aren't quite as far apart as we might think. Another example involves the "trys" that can be so self-defeating for too many folk, when "I'll try," or "But look how hard I'm trying" is either a socially sanctioned way of denying the truth of and to ourselves, or our situation, or of even lying. If that sounds harsh, how many times have you said to someone, "I'll 'try' to come" to something they invited you to, knowing full well that you had no intention of going.

You might have replied in such a way not necessarily because you are such a malicious liar but because you were already over-committed. In our society "I'll try" is one of the most socially acceptable forms of lying, even though most of us would prefer a less pejorative term.

I also often confront the "we's," as in, "What are 'we' going to do?" or, "'We' have a problem here." Such language tends to reflect how people think and what they believe. Those who use the generic "we" are often quite unclear about subject-object relations, about who is whom, including who is responsible for whom. This has to do with how poorly defined some people are, when they see their "self" somehow always connected to someone else. Some therapists call this being "symbiotic," which is a technical word a biologist might use to speak of two organisms living as one. That image is pretty graphic.

Here's an example of a considerate confrontation designed to clarify who is responsible for whom. When you say, "What are we going to do?" who is going to do what? I notice how many therapists I supervise often talk like this. "It looks like 'we' have a problem," they will say to a client. This would seem empathic, and there's nothing wrong with empathy, unless what the client needs is to get clear concerning who has the problem, not to mention who can do much of anything about it. Is he trying to shift his problem to the therapist? Is the counselor willing or trying to take that responsibility? Does she believe she should or could take on such responsibility for anyone else, the responsibility of making another's problem hers? Establishing firm ego boundaries and defining appropriate responsibility is awfully important if people are to function in reasonably healthy ways. Otherwise, things can get awfully confusing, maybe even crazy.

Another bit of jargon I often confront is commonly stated as "working on." A client may say, "I want to work on . . . ," or a therapist I'm supervising may say, "I'm helping this client work on . . . ." What does "working on" mean? How is this different from, "I want to change" whatever? Is "working on" a lot like "trying"? I'm not "trying" to write this book. I'm writing it, for good or for ill. This world is full of people "trying" to do something they will never do, because too much of their energy is invested in the kind of "trying" that can too easily sabotage doing. Many people are always "working on" whatever as a way of never changing anything or reaching any goal. It's not unlike the difference between feeling whatever it is you feel and "talking about" your feelings.

Some might say, "Picky, picky, picky! You're just being picky, Monty." That may be so. But perhaps not. Since such jargon and the fuzzy thinking it represents, much less a lack of will or purpose, of direction and commitment, perhaps even courage, keeps far too many folk chronically stuck in their confusion, their discomfort, their helplessness, their selfishness, their carelessness, or whatever their particular self-defeating believing, thinking, or behaving may be. Confronting this doesn't have to be harsh, nor hardly cruel. Confrontation merely involves pointing out something important. Awareness can be a helpful thing, certainly when one seems rather blind to what he may be doing to himself. I know that I have been helped immeasurably by counselors who were aware and congruent, strong and sensitive, and considerate enough to expose such things to me.

Here, I also want to take a personal point of privilege and acknowledge two important mentors in my life, the Reverend Carroll Owen and the Reverend Dr. Alan Graves, both distinguished Baptist ministers. The Reverend Owen is still living, and vitally so. Dr. Graves died some years ago. Each modeled for me and reinforced me in some different and important ways. Neither was a therapist whose counsel I sought. The Reverend Owen pastored a congregation in which I, as a college student, worked as a summer youth director. He was the first minister of whom I found myself thinking: "Now there's someone I want to be like." Dr. Graves was Dean of the School of Religious Education when I was a seminary student. Like the Reverend Owen, he carried himself in a quiet, even reserved, intelligent and dignified manner, hardly the stereotype of too many ministers I've known. I don't remember either of these gentlemen saying much of anything to me, in terms of instruction, admonishment, or direction. It was merely the strength and integrity of their very presence that spoke in such clear and profound ways. Those guys knew who they were and weren't trying to be anyone else. In those days, I was trying way too hard to impress at least someone. Rather than being put off by my anxiety, they embraced me in the least anxious of ways. In fact, they saw more in me and believed in me more than I was capable of seeing and believing in myself. That's why I was so anxious. They, on the other hand, were capable of understanding, accepting, and encouraging me quite unconditionally. It's called grace. And eventually I became better able to accept such a gift.

JUDGING/PERCEIVING

Some would call judgers the list-makers of the world. Others would say no, it's not the lists, it is crossing completed tasks off their lists that rings the chimes of a judger. Judgers tend to be fairly structured people, in contrast to perceivers, who are generally less structured. Judgers organize their lives in more of a linear, logical fashion. My friend says that when his wife gives him a "to do" list, if he doesn't do each of the tasks listed in that order, she can become rather annoyed with him. Ray Snyder is a management consultant who teaches the Myers-Briggs in industrial and organizational settings. As he puts it, "If you're a perceiver (P), married to a judger (J), and you want to mess with his mind, pee on his list!" I mentioned that to a group of managers one time, and one of the judgers in the back of the room exclaimed, "But I'd have a back-up copy on my hard drive!" So would most judgers.

You can see where judgers and perceivers can get on each other's nerves. If half of the people who come to counseling are there about their personal life—their marriage, their kids, their family of origin—the other half are in therapy over their jobs. In my experience, even more folk seem to feel underemployed than overemployed, and they are usually pretty frustrated about their situation. The most common complaint in the workplace comes at the point of judging and perceiving, as the MBTI would have it. Judgers are commonly interpreted by perceivers as being "micro-managers." They want things done, not only the "right" way, but also in quite the same way they would do them. As something of a carica-ture, judgers commonly consider perceivers to be "dawdlers" or "piddlers." To a judger, a perceiver can seem so unstructured or undisciplined, even non-compliant. Whereas perceivers often see judgers as over-controlling. If perceivers frequently "stop to smell the roses," judgers can often be too compelled by their agendas. The strength of a judger is her organization and structure. A judger's weakness is often in being too rigid. The strength of a perceiver is his spontaneity and flexibility. A perceiver's weakness is likely a lack of discipline and focus.

In terms of decision-making, perceivers tend to be more deliberate. Perceivers are sometimes seen as procrastinators, as though they keep walking around a problem, looking for more information, before they seem to be able to make a decision. Judgers appear to be more decisive. However, sometimes a judger's decision-making can be too hasty, when she needs closure on this before he can move on to that. Judgers like to cross items off their lists, so their pattern of organization tends to be sequential. They don't jump from here to there and back and forth as easily as perceivers do.

When you start putting combinations of personality type together in the Myers-Briggs, certain caricatures commonly appear in individuals. For example, a sensor and a judger (S and J) together are bound to be pretty literal and concrete. They can also be quite organized and structured. Add to that characteristics of a thinker, and this person can be pretty firm, perhaps blunt. She may appear cold or rigid. If he is also an introvert, he will seem even more distant, perhaps aloof. Over many years, I worked with a female nurse who is an ISTJ, hardly the stereotype of most women in our culture. She wasn't one to offer her opinion on much of anything, but if you asked her, you had better be prepared to hear the truth, or at least her version of it, in fairly unvarnished fashion. Some would see her as a snob, aloof and unapproachable. I would see her as shy, perhaps even insecure, highly disciplined, organized, and motivated, even fairly judgmental. Her world is pretty cut and dried. Things are the way they are. If you wanted sympathy, she would not be one to console you in particularly comforting ways. Conversely, with someone like her, you know where you stand. You don't have to factor in for much of anything extraneous, what some might call the b.s. quotient. Her strengths and weaknesses are fairly obvious.

I also worked with a man, over almost as many years, who is an ENFP. He is quite accomplished, one of the most gifted and creative therapists I have known. His strengths and weaknesses are just as obvious. He's the life of the party, an imaginative and creative thinker. He is also the kind of person you would turn to in times of trouble, certainly in emotional distress. His is indeed a nurturing and comforting presence. However, I don't see how he ever gets anything done! He seems so undisciplined and disorganized, so easily distracted by whatever the temporary stimuli, the most immediate of needs (what some might even consider a symptom of Attention Deficit Disorder). He's not glib, much less arrogant about his more casual style. Not at all. For him, it is merely how things are, or at least how he is.

From the perspective of the Myers-Briggs, the strengths of the best counselors tend to be those of the introvert, the intuitive, the feeler, and the perceiver. I have discussed each of these, the first three in greater detail than the last. In Myers-Briggs-ese, judging is not quite the same as we generally think of it in the function of counseling. Judging, according to the MBTI, means getting closure, and often the sooner the better.

The process of the introvert is important in therapy, since the introvert tends to get in the way of the client's process less, which the extrovert can often do, particularly in the way of a more introverted client. This is also often the case with intuition. This quality tends to be more expansive. I worked for many years with a psychiatrist who would become absolutely livid if anyone called him a "shrink." He would insist: "I don't 'shrink' people; I expand their awareness, their options, their possibilities!" Intuition tends to be a less limiting, less confining way of thinking. The weakness of the feeler may be one of being too placating, if not enabling, even though the emotional sensitivity of the feeler is essential to effective counseling. Indeed, all research suggests that empathy, some capacity to connect with others emotionally and experientially, is crucial in the therapeutic process. A non-judgmental, non-condemning attitude is also crucial. That is not to say that being non-judgmental isn't ambiguous at best. None of us are totally non-judgmental, and anyone who thinks she isn't is likely more judgmental than she realizes.

We all make value judgments and consequent choices. This is a delicate issue in counseling. There are certain instances in which no counselor is expected to be non-judgmental, such as when an awareness of sexual or physical abuse is a concern; in particular, involving children, adolescents, and the elderly. Therapists are ethically and legally bound to report such incidents. Still, a primary function of psychotherapy is to help clients come out from behind whatever their defenses may be, in the service of their becoming more emotionally integrated persons. No one is likely to even begin considering such a possibility in the face of condemnation. Rather, they are apt to become defensive. Only in a context of acceptance, even blessing, of our best, and often our worst, can healing begin in anyone's life. This is yet another paradox. When we dare to own, to claim what may be or what may merely seem to be so bad about any of us, it will no longer own us in quite the same way as when we are trying to deny it, to somehow run from it. To say it another way, perhaps negatively, counselors don't help anyone when they collude, wittingly or unwittingly, with a client's attempts at deceit, denial, or not telling the truth. Because only the truth can set us free.

As they say in the Twelve Steps of Alcoholics Anonymous: "Admitted to God, to ourselves, and to another . . . the nature of our wrongs . . . made a fearless moral inventory . . . made a list of all persons we had harmed . . . made direct amends to such people, except when to do so would injure them or others." Therefore, a non-judgmental attitude is essential for the capable counselor, even though living this out isn't always so easy. A wise and seasoned mentor, Dr. Bill Blanton, once offered this axiom to me: "There's a difference between exposing one's values and imposing them," he said. Given the ambiguity of being non-judgmental, this may be about as close as we can get to such a worthy goal. And even then, we sometimes impose our values.

5

Balanced Religion

"We were redecorating Beth Elohim, the oldest
Reform synagogue in America. There was, of course,
considerable discussion, even disagreement, over matters of
taste. Which was when one rather distinguished woman, a senior
member of the congregation, declared: 'We must remember,
this is Chah-ah-ah-lston, and we are not Baptist Jews.
We're Episcopalian Jews!'"

—Rabbi Anthony Holz

SOME YEARS AGO, MY PASTORAL COUNSELING COLLEAGUE, WES EADES, was offering a workshop entitled "Co-Dependency as a Christian Heresy." When I asked him what that meant, Dr. Eades explained that, historically, in the life of the church, a heresy has always been a Christian orthodoxy taken too far. At the heart of the matter, such beliefs and/or practices represent definitive Christian truth, but at the extremes they become distorted and bent rather badly out of shape, sometimes beyond recognition. What's that great line? "Beware of half-truths: you may be believing the wrong half."

As a Christian minister, I am commonly asked about matters of faith and practice. The questions, wherever and whatever, are pretty much the same. I graduated from seminary and was ordained nearly forty years ago. For most of my career, my ministry has been practiced in ostensibly secular settings—a large state university, a private prep school, a public community mental health center, and a private practice group of family physicians. I have taught in a church-related college, in both a private and a public university, and in a couple of different state prisons. I now pastor a church.

My career pattern is a bit different from many. More often, parish ministers seem to burn out and become counselors. I've done the reverse of that. However, I can't say I burned out as a therapist. I miss it, especially the more personal dimension of counseling. A pastor's role is more public, and often fairly superficial. In addition, you meet some people in counseling that you're not likely to ever see in church. Not that I don't like church people, it's just that I miss some of the characters I used to enjoy working with in my counseling practice, the ones who wouldn't be caught dead in church, unless church is the next-to-last place they're likely to end up being caught dead—in a coffin. Come to think of it, Jesus kind of liked those people too! Still, I enjoy my current ministry and am called to be here. As the sign in my office says, "Bloom where you are planted!" I have read those words almost every day for many years now, wherever I have worked. I have had ample opportunity to look at life, and certainly at work, from more than one angle of vision, and I have found there's not a lot of difference. Despite how we may present ourselves in different circumstances, people are people, and are pretty much the same wherever you find them, even at church.

If anything has been confirmed in my experience, it's that when it comes to being a Christian minister, where you work isn't all that important. It's not what you do; it is who you are. I was taught that in seminary. It was called "spiritual formation." During the height of the Viet Nam war, there was considerable concern, certainly among the faculty, that not everyone who was in seminary ought necessarily to be there. Not that going to seminary isn't a valuable way to try to discern a sense of vocation. In those days, it was mostly men who went to seminary upon graduating from college. That is not quite the way it is today, with many women and second-career folk pursuing vocational ministry out of perhaps a more mature awareness of their calling. Still, what I was taught in seminary has proven true: ministry has even more to do with being than with doing. Some people hide behind their role. Others, even among clergy, try to hide from it. All institutions in this world are fallen; they are inherently broken, be it the church, the school, government, business, or what have you. Those you serve can be a pretty sorry lot or the grandest folk in the world. It is true of us all, wherever.

Given Wes Eades' interpretation, I am, in this chapter, discussing a variety of traditional Christian beliefs and practices, any of which, when stretched too far, can be bent out of shape and become the least, if not the worst, of heresies. As such, they are not good for anyone. Or as Jesus says, in a rather harsh way: "Whoever causes one of these little ones to stumble, it would be better for him if a great millstone were hung round his neck and he were thrown into the sea."[1]

Unbalanced religion is unhealthy. Extremism turns on itself. It is sinful, in the Bible's sense of sin as distortion or bent-ness. For even if it would seem that something so good, taken but a bit further, should indeed result in something even better, that is not, however, how it works. That's where the logic breaks down, at least when it comes to Christian faith, because being a Christian is a matter of balance.

Christian theology is essentially paradoxical. All the great truths of our faith are held in tension, one with the other: the transcendence and the immanence of God, the sovereignty of God and humankind's free will, faith and works, law and gospel, the relation of this life to the next. Even though the nature of God is so profoundly abstract, we experience, seek to understand, and certainly speak of God in the most concrete, the most particular and literal of ways. Not to mention the "losing" and the "finding" of oneself along the way of Christian living, the divine and human nature, if you will, the godliness and earthiness of the scriptures, and the temporality of the church as we experience it. This even applies to the law of love. Jesus put it in a context of human relations: that a healthy loving of oneself is always rooted in a response to that transcendent personal love who is God's self-revelation, to each and to all the same; such that we can love others as we should only out of such a grace-full loving of ourselves.[2] A therapist might call this self-respect, or self-esteem, and refer to such a paradigm as one of inter-dependence. Here are some rather common examples of how any of us can take even the best of things too far and turn it into something pretty shabby. As such, it becomes but a bad case of unbalanced religion. The following are some of the essential tensions inherent in a vital Christian faith.

FLESH AND SPIRIT

Christians live with a foot in two worlds. One is spiritual, and the other is material. The spiritual is unseen. That doesn't make the spiritual any less real. In the Bible, these two realities, the spiritual and the material,

1. Mark 9:42.
2. Matt 22:34–40.

are somehow bound together. The created world is both real and good. It is also fallen. This is called sin. That's the language the Bible uses to tell its story. The Bible is not a textbook of theological propositions, nor a law library, much less a scientific treatise. The Bible is a divinely inspired anthology, replete with history, saga, myth, parable, poetry, letters, ecstatic visions, confession, invective, witness, and testimony, compiled and edited in the ancient Near East, Asia Minor, and Europe, in at least some written form, over nearly 1,400 years, from roughly the tenth century before the common era up through likely the first four centuries C.E.

In all its diversity, the Bible is still a passionate story of God creating a world in love; of humankind willfully, selfishly, and rebelliously rejecting God; of God entering into human history in the life of a people called Israel, culminating finally in an utterly unique and personal way to redeem this fallen world and all of us in it. This is at least a Christian understanding of the Bible's story, the fulfillment of which is in the person of Jesus as the Christ, the Son of God. What Christians call incarnation, the personal disclosure and redemptive presence of God, in Christ, is quite unbelievable apart from the conviction that flesh and spirit have more to do with each other than even many Christians often seem to believe. This is because one of the tendencies in Christian piety is to separate the two and value spirit above flesh.

This is, of course, the oldest of heresies. It first appeared near the end of the first century in this common era. It comes from the Greek philosopher Plato's view of the world as dualistic, where spirit is good and flesh is bad. The Gnostic heresy of the late first century, with which early Christians contended, denied the humanity of God (Spirit) in the incarnation of Jesus as the Christ (flesh). This is also called Docetism. Today, we see such a heresy manifest, not only in much traditional Christian piety, but also in the enthusiasm of many so-called secular people for what, in these days, is generically referred to as "spirituality."

In the New Testament, flesh is used in two ways. One is good, the other is bad. When the Gospel of John declares that "the Word was made flesh," that is good.[3] It refers to the incarnation, to God's humanity. That is, of course, anthropomorphic language. Nonetheless, it bears witness to essential Christian truth. In the words of Athanasius, a fourth century

---

3. John 1:14.

church father, in Christ, "God became one with us, that we might become one with God."

However, when St. Paul uses the Greek word *sarx* for flesh, it is not good. Because Paul uses "flesh" to refer to mankind willfully turned away from God.[4] Here flesh does not mean our bodies, our physical nature, that which God has created as good and has redeemed, "in Christ," as Paul would say it. To "live according to the flesh"—again, in Paul's terms—is not normal, healthy, physical, emotional, and social functioning. It is willful, selfish rebellion against God, which is ultimately destructive, indeed self-destructive. "Flesh," as Paul uses the word, is a hyper-sensual/materialistic way of living, an appetite that is never satisfied.

Have you ever heard someone say, "He's so heavenly minded, he does no earthly good"? This is a pejorative statement. It commonly refers to a kind of Gnostic spirituality; as it were, taken too far, so as to have become somehow twisted, distorted, bent out of shape, and tragically so. Conversely, when St. Paul speaks of "living according to the flesh," he is speaking of a rather hedonistic way of living that perverts the goodness for which God has created us. To err in either direction can lead to some serious problems, not the least of which is movement away from God. Ironically, the first Christians had to contend with the heretical denial of God's humanity, as revealed in the personhood of Jesus as the Christ. If this has not been, at least since the eighteenth century, the focus of most modern Christian apologetics, it has likely become a matter of some concern for thoughtful Christians in more recent times. If the Jesus of the Enlightenment was surely a paragon of human wisdom and virtue, though not divine, much of the "spirituality" these days would seem to be decidedly Docetic.

LAW AND GOSPEL

In the congregation I serve, some of the most dedicated and sincere Christian people I have ever known have said to me: "We are New Testament Christians. We don't believe in the Old Testament." Whether stated quite as bluntly or not, this is, nonetheless, a somewhat incipient belief on the part of many Christians. And, of course, this is but another ancient heresy reincarnated in our time. This one is associated with Marcion, in the second century of Christian history. Like the Gnostics, Marcion denied the

4. Rom 8.

created goodness of the material world; he also rejected the divine role of Israel in God's redemptive purpose and the inter-relationship of what one might call law and gospel, between the witness of what we Christians would call the Old and the New Testaments of the Bible.

The caricature of an angry, judgmental God in the Old Testament and a loving, forgiving God in the New Testament is not uncommon in the minds of many Christians. One of our adult Sunday School teachers commented on such a caricature to me recently, and I suggested he read the prophecy of Hosea. In that there, God is hardly hurling lightening bolts at "sinners in the hands of an angry God." To the contrary, in that parable God's heart is breaking over an unfaithful spouse. In the story of Hosea, God's sovereign power is revealed in the sort of vulnerability that would one day lead Jesus to a cross. I might also have referred him to the prophecy of Isaiah, chapters 40 thru 55, to those magnificent "Suffering Servant" poems: "Surely he has borne our griefs and carried our sorrows." I often explain to folk that Jesus wasn't a Christian any more than John Wesley was a Methodist. Indeed, in the witness of the Gospels to Jesus, our Lord is forever reaching back into the rich prophetic tradition of ancient Israel in an attempt to renew a vital faith on the part of his own. Jesus was a Jew. And when we forget this, we truncate Christian faith. We sever our vision and witness from its roots. Our faith is grounded in God's redemptive purpose in and through the faith of Israel, of which Jesus, at least for a Christian, is the ultimate fulfillment.

Even within the New Testament, there is tension between what we might call law and gospel, or perhaps faith and works. If the gospel is God's gift, is not law what God demands? St. Paul struggles with this tension as much as anyone in all of scripture. In his Letter to the Galatians, Paul likens the law of God to a schoolmaster, preparing his students for the gospel.[5] Paul knows that God's saving love is a pure gift, "not of works lest anyone should boast."[6] Still, he knows that the holiness and righteousness of the love who God is evokes a comparable response. Redeemed people don't live shoddy lives, no matter how "spiritual" they may think they are. In his letters to the Corinthians, Paul addresses this problem more than anywhere else.[7] If, on the one hand, Paul denounces legalism,

5. Gal 3:24.
6. Eph 2:9.
7. 1 Cor 13.

he also rejects what is called antinomianism. *Nomos* is the Greek word for law. Law and gospel, faith and works: they function together in a balanced way whenever anyone lives credibly as a Christian. Otherwise, our witness is diminished in one direction or the other, be it by an arrogant, self-righteous legalism, or by a casual, undisciplined lifestyle that is just as arrogant, a "cheap grace," as Dietrich Bonhoeffer called it, a careless way of living that would presume to take God's way of loving for granted. All you have to do is look around, you can see plenty of both in our world.

JOY AND SUFFERING

In contrast to that of the ancient Greeks and that of the a-historical Eastern religions, a Hebrew-Christian worldview posits our material circumstances as real. In the Bible, we human-folk are not on a treadmill, going nowhere, nor are our souls something good, only trapped in our bodies, which are bad. To the contrary, Christians believe in the resurrection of the body, which is a notion radically different from believing in the immortality of the soul. The latter emphasizes the indomitable human spirit; the former bears witness to the sovereign and eternal love of God.

This is troubling to most modern Christians, it would seem, for at least two reasons. One reason is that we are influenced considerably in our culture by the Greeks, so if you go to church, and certainly if you attend a funeral, you are likely to hear some preacher saying that so-and-so's soul has gone to heaven. Such a view is, even with its adaptations, more Platonic Greek philosophy than orthodox Christian theology. A second reason such a belief is so popular, even quite sacred, among many well-meaning Christians, is that it tends to reflect the narcissism of our culture. Most of us are primarily concerned with me and mine. The idea that we have a soul, trapped in our body, which upon death goes immediately to be with God can be quite comforting, against a faith in God which transcends our finitude, the limits of time and space, which can seem rather intimidating. It is, however, just such a faith that declares, that when we die, that we are "asleep in Christ" and will one day be resurrected by the sovereign power of God's love in a manner not all that different from how and why God created any of us in the first place.[8] Any Christian minister who has ever counseled a grieving loved one or conducted a funeral has

8. 1 Cor 15:16.

faced this issue on its most practical terms. Certainly, when a loved one asks, "Is my daddy in heaven?"

In the New Testament, one can discern at least two types of answers. On the cross, Jesus assures a dying thief, "Today shalt thou be with me in Paradise," and St. Paul even speaks of being "absent from the body and present with the Lord."[9] However, it is Paul who develops more fully the Christian belief in the resurrection of the body, such that the oldest of creeds among Christians affirm this understanding.[10] But, didn't Paul anticipate the day of resurrection in his own lifetime? Not that nearly 2,000 or so years is all that long to God. If this is not quite as comforting to our modern sense of immediacy, it calls us as Christians to a deeper and more mature faith in that sovereign, personal love who is God. In such a belief, the greater emphasis is on God, rather than on us, much less our more immediate needs.

Over my more than thirty years of pastoral ministry, I've observed this to be perhaps the most disturbing of all orthodox Christian doctrines to most confessing Christians. It is here that many people seem to feel terribly threatened. "You mean we don't have a soul? Why, I've never heard of such a thing! This can't be." To which any responsible Christian minister might well reply: "From a mature Hebrew-Christian understanding, the spiritual and the physical dimensions of what it means to be human are inexorably bound together." Of course, such an explanation is not all that comforting in the moment to someone who has never even considered such an idea before, much less if she has just asked, "Is my daddy in heaven?"

Though I actually had a beloved woman in the congregation I serve engage me otherwise. "I know that when we die we are 'asleep in Christ,' awaiting the resurrection," she said. Which is not something I've heard many Christians declare. "What bothers me, however," she added, "is the time involved, between when we die and when we will be resurrected."

And then she said, "But my daughter says: 'Mama, when we die, we move from our time into God's time.'" In other words, we move from time into timelessness. As the gospel song says it, "When time shall be no more."[11]

---

9. Luke 23:43; 2 Cor 5:8.

10. 1 Thess 4; 1 Cor 15.

11. Rev 10:6.

From a faithful Hebrew-Christian perspective, suffering in this life is not necessarily something to be avoided or denied. Suffering can be purposeful and redemptive. In the words of the nineteenth century Russian, Nicholai Berdyaev, a decidedly Christian philosopher: "When a good man suffers, those around him are healed." Indeed, it is a cross that stands at the very heart of Christian faith. Paradoxically, the power of love who is God is revealed most fully on that cross. St. Paul, of course, claims that suffering is essential to Christian faithfulness.[12] Such a conviction stands in radical contrast to the a-historical and otherworldly nature of Eastern religions, and certainly to much contemporary "spirituality."

As Jesus implies in the Sermon on the Mount, there is a marked difference between suffering "for righteousness' sake"[13] and suffering for suffering's sake. It is just such a caricature, a kind of suffering that merely serves its own ends, that marks most of the neurotic Christian living in any age, certainly in our own. As if such a way of living isn't something other than how God has created and redeemed us to live. In the way that opposites may be similar, this is not all that different from a kind of Gnostic caricature that floats quite above the troubles and cares of this world and this life.

If you have been paying attention, you have noted, perhaps, that whenever and wherever people live faithfully as Christians, they will be suffering for righteousness' sake, not merely for the sake of suffering. And that in such redemptive suffering, there seems always to be a deep sense of joy. This joy is likely something different from happiness. I used to have a Sister Corita print which translated that Greek word, *makarioi*, from Matthew 5, as "happy." Most translations say "blessed." Whether any sensitive Christian is ever truly happy in this world is debatable, given all that has gone wrong, not the least of which is the most innocent and unjust suffering, that which not only breaks God's heart, but the heart of any sensitive Christian. If faithful Christian living isn't necessarily anyone's key to happiness, there is after all something quite joyful about being a Christian, rooted deeply, as it is, in a divine love human enough to suffer.

For anyone involved in counseling, pastoral or otherwise, this always seems a matter of much concern. Theologians sometimes call it theodicy, or unjust suffering. Most of us seem to be a lot like Job's "friends." As logi-

12. Rom 5.
13. Matt 5.

cal people, we live by the law of cause and effect and are forever trying to explain or understand what seems so bad in our lives. There is nothing really wrong with this, but it has its limits. Therapists spend a lot of time with folk seemingly shattered by life's unfairness. In the face of such unfairness, there are any number of ways to respond: from rage to grim resignation, from a detached stoicism to perhaps a rather passive, even fragile submission. Then there are some who endure and even overcome in the face of gross injustice and some of the worst ways that life can be so unfair. It is as though, for such folk, there is a connection between how passionately they live here and now and how deeply their lives are rooted in something or someone quite beyond this life. Is it a loving, sovereign, personal God? It would seem so. Many such folk are humble and thankful enough to claim the name Christian. And even if this weren't so, they would still seem to bear such a witness. What is so remarkable is the apparent balance between the legitimate suffering and joy in their lives.

For many years now, folk have said to me, "Don't you get tired of hearing people's problems? Doesn't it get to you?" I usually reply, "No." Then sometimes it does. It is all a matter of perspective, of how we frame things. The best people-helpers know how to "take care of themselves," which includes knowing how to receive as well as to give. It includes letting oneself be cared for. I'm remembering some important lines I read years ago from Robert Raines: "Is there a difference between being careless of human misery, and being carefree in the midst of it—caring, but free of care?"[14]

If one would seek to discern such a spirit, here's something to think about. Joyful Christians are not chronic complainers. It is not that their suffering isn't often quite intense, or that they are in denial, or perhaps even disassociating. It is, rather, a way of living that is different from those who seem to trade on their troubles. The New Testament makes a distinction between one's "thorn in the flesh," as St. Paul says it, and the "bearing of one's cross," which is Jesus' call to his followers in the Gospels. Put simply, cross-bearing is a choice, a decision we make. It is will-full. A thorn in the flesh is a condition, something we would hardly choose. It is something bad which appears to have chosen us. In Jesus' day, cross-bearing represented an act of civil disobedience. Today, it may mean that, or any number of other expressions of what Bonhoeffer called "the cost

14. Robert Raines, *Soundings* (New York: Harper and Row, 1970).

of discipleship." Conversely, Paul prayed fervently for God to remove his "thorn in the flesh," whatever it may have been. And though he didn't get the answer to his praying that he wanted, he could yet affirm divine purpose and presence in and through his suffering, even as Paul suffered willingly, if not even joyfully so, for Christ's sake.[15] For Christian people of integrity, it has been so ever since.

CO-DEPENDENCY AS A CHRISTIAN HERESY

What Wes Eades was speaking to is a delicate issue among sensitive, responsible Christians. Because in Christian ethics there is an inherent and genuine concern, compassion, and commitment to others outside oneself. We are, indeed, "our brother's keeper."[16] And our sister's too. "Who is my neighbor?" a lawyer asks Jesus, if indeed we are to love our neighbor even as we love ourselves. And Jesus tells the parable of the good Samaritan. The extending of oneself with regard for our neighbor, even our "enemy," is central to Christian faith and practice.[17]

However, as Dr. Eades suggests, this can be taken too far and turned into a kind of self-giving that may be even more self-serving, a helping which may not be helpful, a selflessness that may, in fact, be quite selfish, the sort of giving which may, after all, be even more concerned with getting. Such a problem has, perhaps, less to do with the extending than with the defining of oneself. That is where too much Christian "charity," unlike what the word means in King James diction, often goes wrong. Giving to others can be patronizing, a kind of giving that does more harm than good.

First, however, I think I need to comment briefly on what is likely most perilous when it comes to the extending of oneself: the "loving of one's enemy." Recently, I saw a second-rate movie, except for its punch line, which was: "The hardest people to love are those who need it the most." Christians, who are enjoined to "love (even) our enemies," often find ourselves "double-binded" in this respect by some folk who are capable of putting us in "no-win" situations inter-personally, sometimes in even most charming of ways. This is not unlike what a woman I used to work with called "gettin' into a pissin' contest with a skunk." If I accommodate this person in whatever way, he is merely exploiting me, which is

15. Rom 5:3, 2 Cor 11–12.
16. Gen 4:9.
17. Luke 10:25–37, Matt 5:43–48.

not necessarily the healthiest way of loving anyone, to enable whomever to operate in such ways. I hardly have a simple answer to this dilemma, except the reminder of what I have just suggested: regardless of the decision we make, whether or not to extend ourselves to such persons, how we are defined is what is most important. In other words, in some interpersonal relationships, the best we can hope for involves merely trying to cut our losses, in terms of our own self-respect, or even an effort on our part to be respectful of certain others. Sometimes our choices in life, including dealing with certain people, get reduced to trying to decide in which direction we are going to lose. In fact, one paradox of Christian ethics, at least, as painful as it may be, is that in some situations the most respectfully loving we can be to some people is to have nothing to do with them.[18]

Such no-win circumstances may, at times, seem even more benign than malicious. Some people are, for instance, inordinately needy. No matter how much we do for them, or how much attention they get, it's never enough. A variation on this theme might even be the advice one of my veteran clergy-colleagues has been known to offer other ministers: "When you accept a call to a new place of service, watch out for the sycophants, those who seem to think you're the greatest. They're the ones most likely, later, to try to do you in." An important mentor of mine, the late Lee Swope, another distinguished Baptist minister, once said to me: "I don't trust people. I trust God. I accept people." At the time, I didn't know what he meant by that statement, but over forty years later, I think I've learned. Jesus taught us, as Christians, to be as "wise as serpents and [as] innocent as doves."[19] Finding that balance is surely one of life's most formidable tasks. Sometimes we get it right, while at other times we don't. Healthy Christian people don't keep score, even when we get the short end of the stick. It's not our successes or achievements, nor our failures or our disappointments, that are meant, finally, to define us.

If Jesus claims that in giving ourselves away we actually save ourselves, the assumption is that we have a "self" to give and to save. For a Christian, a healthy sense of self is rooted always and deeply in the grace of God. It is quite unconditional. As they say in Alcoholics Anonymous: "Whether you're from Yale or from jail, from Park Avenue or the park bench." God never loves any of us because of who we are; rather, we are

---

18. Titus 3:10–11.

19. Matt 10:16.

loved by God because that is who God is. For a Christian, it is God's love for each of us, and for all of us, that defines our lives, that tells us, ultimately, who we are. God's love doesn't seek value; instead, it is God's love that creates value. Indeed, God loves us all as though there were only one of us to love, and each of us as much as all of us. For people of Christian faith, such status, such worth, such value: it is a gift—not achieved, but received—and gratefully so. For a Christian, to be thankful is to be gracefull. In Christian terms, this is our definition of "self."

In the New Testament, the same Greek word, *charis,* serves as the root for what I believe to be the three most important words in the Bible: grace, gratitude, and gift. Each has everything to do with the other. From a Christian point of view, we can only give as we have received. For a Christian, generosity always springs from gratitude. In fact, if we are better givers than receivers, if someone has told us this is the way to be: in terms of Christian learning and living, we have been deceived. There is something wrong with this, and we may not be quite as generous as we think.

Co-dependency is, of course, a word coined in our time. It refers to anyone who isn't well defined as a person, who doesn't have adequate ego boundaries, whose sense of "self" is connected too much to that of others or another, to whatever the degree. Co-dependency is a relative concept. The caricature of a co-dependent person is one who chronically devalues himself and is often enmeshed with, perhaps even enslaved to, the needs of others. Co-dependent people "try" to take care of others, while generally not doing a very good job taking care of themselves. By definition, co-dependency implies a lack of self-worth, what some call self-esteem, perhaps even self-respect. Co-dependent people try to get their needs met by doing for others; this often takes the form of placating.

Because co-dependent people tend to be lacking in strength of "self," they may be enabling of the weaknesses, even the hurtfulness in others. In fact, one wouldn't have to be too intuitive nor extrapolate too far to see how someone with this problem could find plenty of proof-texts in the Bible to support such a pathologic way of living: as in turn the other cheek, walk the second mile, forgive seventy times seven. It is not all that hard to see how anyone with such a problem might become quite defensive, perhaps even to the point of denouncing someone like myself for writing a paragraph such as this. I frequently run across some theologian who is taking shots at such "psychologizing." And I have known any number of clergy along the way whose defensiveness, whose rather glib denouncing of "a kind of Christianity that has sold its soul to psychology" merely betrays the fact that they are such poor limit-setters, so interpersonally ill-defined. Such folk are, I'm afraid, some of the worst do-gooders, any more of which this world, not to mention God, hardly needs.

This reminds me of a family I once saw in my counseling practice. The father was triangulated between his wife and their youngest child, a teenaged son. The father was coming down hard on the kid while yet trying to placate his wife. The mother was the enabler of her drug-addicted, highly manipulative, and fundamentally dishonest "baby boy." He had her working overtime enabling him. Or was his purpose merely to create a job for his mom, to meet her needs as an enabler? She was the prettiest and sweetest, the nicest and most pious little Christian woman you could ever meet. However, she got her buttons pushed and became awfully angry at me when I dared to point out what was going on in her family. As such, co-dependency is a Christian heresy.

It is noteworthy, I think, how Jesus speaks to this matter: that we can't "love our neighbor" at least in a reasonably heathly way, apart from a "love," if you will, of oneself. For a Christian, this love comes always from loving God, even as we are loved quite unconditionally and just as un-deservedly by God. When our lives are rooted in this profound sense of grace, our way of loving and giving of ourselves to others will be quite different from when we so need to do for others as a way of trying to meet our own needs, to try to feel better about ourselves. For one thing, our way of self-giving won't be something we need or try to trade on, nor will we be forever complaining about our particular lot in life. Have you ever noticed how often it works this way? Chronically complaining about how much we do for others is usually a dead giveaway that our motives are rather tragically misplaced. Jesus claims that what's important to God, as he declares in the Sermon on the Mount, has to do with what "your Father . . . sees in secret . . . ."[20] For a Christian, at least, God measures our motives. In the divine economy, this is what finally counts.

20. Matt 6.

THE INDIVIDUAL AND THE GROUP

The distinctive quality of evangelical[21] Christianity is its emphasis upon one's personal relationship with God, through a trusting faith in Jesus, as the Christ, the commitment of one's life to his lordship. This emphasis upon the individual, upon one's "personal" relationship with God is also the most glaring weakness in contemporary evangelical Christianity, because it tends to play right into the narcissism of our age. This is likely the foremost of modern/post-modern sins: that any of us would think we are all that important, that our needs, that our particular self-interests come first. However, this seems to be the predominant heresy among many Christian folk in our time: me-ism. If it is true that God has no grandchildren, that each of us must finally decide for ourselves whether or not we are going to follow Jesus, that the choice is ours alone, and no one else can make it for us, it is also true that to be a Christian is to be a part of God's people in this world, a larger community of faith that extends quite beyond the needs or the importance of any individual or family. The "worship of family" being not uncommon among many Christians, despite such little evidence in the scriptures for even such a good priority.

For example, I grew up in the kind of Christian family where we actually competed with others to see who could be the "best" Christian. This was defined by the piety of the day in our particular religious subculture. "Good" Christians didn't do a lot of the things that other "worldly" people, or even less pious Christians did. The agenda was largely negative, and the ethic focused primarily on matters of personal piety. "Good" Christians didn't drink, dance, smoke, fornicate or masturbate, curse, swear, gamble, go to the pool hall, play baseball, or go to the movies on Sunday. I'm trying to remember if there was anything else. As I recall, those were about the only things I ever heard any preacher ever preach against in the church of my childhood, except perhaps dressing modestly enough. However, that

21. The term "evangelical" has, unfortunately, become a misunderstood and misused word these days. In popular usage, the assumption is that if one calls himself an "evangelical," that also means she is a fundamentalist, in the manner of Pat Robertson, James Dobson, and the late Jerry Falwell, as well as a dispensationalist, after John Hagee, the Scofied Reference Bible, and the popular *Left Behind* novels. Indeed, many even think that being an "evangelical" Christian, here in America, is equivalent to supporting a particular political party, social agenda, and foreign policy. When, in fact, our English word, "evangelical," comes from the Greek word, *euangelion*, which means, literally, "gospel" (Mark 1:1). In other words, anyone who believes the gospel is an "evangelical" Christian, many of whom—including myself—are hardly fundamentalists or dispensationalists.

just applied to women! In those days, few, if any, in my world had any concept of sexism as a moral issue. And the anti-sexual messages were even more implicit than explicit, which enhanced their gravity.

When I was a youngster, one minister I knew loved to watch the prize fights on Wednesday nights after Prayer Meeting. The fights featured such great boxers as Kid Gavilan and Sugar Ray Robinson and were sponsored by Pabst Blue Ribbon beer. I was at his house one Wednesday night, when the fights were on, and he made it a point to tell me why he always got up between rounds and turned off the television, so he wouldn't have to watch those Satanic beer commercials. The remote control hadn't yet come of age. It was interesting, if not ironic, that the pietistic ethic that would denounce beer would embrace the violence, much less the corruption, of boxing.

I don't want to caricature this particular minister unfairly, in reference, for instance, to college students these days, where the function of a fraternity party often has to do with who can claim bragging rights for drinking the most beer and getting the drunkest. There was surely some motive in the man's madness, strange as it may have seemed. Anyone who has experienced the destruction of alcoholism in individuals and families and other segments of society might not be all that put-off by such a caricature of this kind of Christian piety. In fact, these days there seems to be some genuine social concern over how alcohol and sex are promoted in such exploitative ways, certainly in the media, a concern that likely stems from whatever the source, other than necessarily anyone's personal piety, Christian or otherwise.

On the positive side, being a "good" Christian was still interpreted largely in terms of personal piety, not the least of which was faithfulness in church attendance, supporting the "church program," as it was called, and certainly by tithing. I don't remember anything any minister in my childhood ever said being more important than that tithing was surely the litmus test of what it means to be a Christian. In fact, if you were a "really good" Christian, you tithed on your gross, not your net worth or earnings. Believe me, I've heard any number of sermons on that subject. Also, "good" Christians had a disciplined devotional life. You read the Bible and prayed every day. I can remember reading my "daily Bible readings" in bed at night, as a youngster, trying to stay awake amidst all those vital statistics and names and ceremonial details in Leviticus and Numbers.

It's interesting that the importance of such classic spiritual disciplines aren't looked upon as being quite as quaint these days, among a good many Christians, as they may have once seemed, to me at least, in the world of my childhood and adolescence. In fact, I have come to see faithful Christian living as involving five essential Christian disciplines, not unlike those that characterize twelve-step programs. The five disciplines are prayer, worship, Bible study, tithing, and service. Not that any of these disciplines can't, of course, be misappropriated, becoming merely shallow legalisms. Each contains its own ambiguity. For example, is there a difference between praying and merely telling God what we believe God needs to know? Or how about the difference between worship and entertainment. With respect to this particular Christian discipline, there seems to be at least some confusion, these days, in the marketing of popular religion. Similarly, Bible study is likely anything but faithful when it gets reduced to the mere subjectivity of group grope. "Here's what I think it means, what do you think?"

The idea that our family would have actually been competitive with regard to our personal piety, that we may have even thought ourselves somehow better than some of our neighbors because of such dogged devotion: this was largely left unspoken. Consequently, the message was loud and clear. We were hardly underprivileged people, but if it seemed that we may have had less or gotten to do less than others around us, our consolation was in knowing that we were "better" Christians than some other folk. If it sounds like there is something wrong with this way of living, chalk it up to a legalistic, pietistic, and individualistic kind of religion, even one that calls itself Christian.

In terms of Christian ethics, the downside of so-called "evangelical Christianity" is its emphasis on personal, as against corporate morality. As in the theme of Reinhold Neibuhr's classic, *Moral Man and Immoral Society*. For example, my beloved theology professor, the late Dale Moody, told me once of forgetting his briefcase, leaving it on a platform at a train station in the Weimer County of Germany. At the time, he was studying in Europe. When he returned several hours later, the briefcase was still there. No one had taken it. Dr. Moody observed the irony: the very people who wouldn't think of taking something that didn't belong to them were the same people who embraced Adolph Hitler.

A part of the story of John Newton, for instance, is well known. Newton, who wrote the beloved hymn "Amazing Grace," was considered an evangelical Christian in the Church of England of his day. Newton was a slave trader before becoming a Christian. But what is not generally known is that Newton nonetheless continued for years to reap economic gain from his ongoing role as a prominent investor in the slave trade. At the same time, it can also be argued that evangelical Christians have contributed significantly to important social change across the past 300 years, including the abolition of slavery, the creation of child labor laws, women's suffrage, and the temperance movement. If the Baptist Walter Rauschenbusch was the father of the "Social Gospel Movement," here in America, a century ago, and another Baptist preacher, Martin Luther King, Jr., led the Civil Rights Movement in the mid-twentieth-century, their counterparts today are represented. for example, in the likes of Jim Wallis, editor of the penetrating *Sojourners* magazine, and a host of other lesser-known faithful evangelicals.

The relationship between the individual and the group creates some particular difficulties if and when Christians ever try to understand Jews. Rooted deeply in Israel's ethos is the priority of the group. One is born a Jew, whether he practices his religion or not. In Hebrew, Israel means, literally, "people of God." There seems to have been in ancient Hebrew psychology, if you can call it that, something of an inherent reciprocity between the individual and the group. The emphasis in Judaism is always upon the family, the tribe, the body, the whole, the larger community.

In terms of Christian history, when one studies the Reformation, this same issue emerges. If Calvin seemed to go further than Luther in distinguishing Protestantism from Roman Catholicism, the Anabaptists went even further still, particularly in rejecting any notion of a state or ethnic, a cultural or territorial church. For those of us who are heirs to more of an Anabaptist influence, with its emphasis on individualism: in terms of our understanding of Christian faith, this can be easily overemphasized. If one is a Jew by birth, and there are even those who would claim to be Christian by virtue of their citizenship, by the fact that they were born into a particular family or culture or nation or church, a more rigorous evangelical Christianity would surely insist that one is a Christian, not by birth, but by a "new birth."[22]

However, it is this sort of individualistic emphasis, with respect to what it means to be a Christian, that is often lacking in balance. In par-

22. John 3.

ticular, St. Paul addresses the problem in the church in Corinth, where people seem to have been competing, as it were, over things like who had been baptized by whom, who was more or less affluent, who had higher social standing, or who may have had this or that particular pedigree, in terms of ethnicity. Not to mention whose spiritual gifts were of greater value. It is true even today. Where I live it often has to do with one's family history in our particularly historic American city, extending back as it does to the days of the colonies. Even in the congregation I pastor, which is 200 years younger than some other more prestigious churches in town, the "my family has been here longer than yours" card is still sometimes played.

An individualistic emphasis in matters of Christian faith and practice often leads to a kind of competitiveness that is divisive and hurtful and sinful in the "body of Christ," as Paul says it.[23] It hinders authentic Christian witness. In our culture, Christian individualism often tends to collude with our narcissism, our me-ism. Ours is an uprooted and fragmented culture, and we are competitive to a fault, often even in terms of our religion. We hardly need any more of this. If each of us must finally "walk that lonesome valley," if "nobody else can walk it for you," as Christian people we are, finally, called and blessed to be but a small part of a larger community of faith, joined together with a whole host, "a great cloud of witnesses," as it were. This extends beyond the self-importance, the particular needs or self-interests, much less the particular "achievements" of any of us, be they moral, spiritual, or otherwise.

BEING AND DOING

Central to the Protestant work ethic, on which Protestants hardly have a corner, is the notion that "God helps those who help themselves." Dutiful Christians love to quote the Letter of James: "Faith without works is dead."[24] Consequently, the fact that the gospel speaks of God's doing for us what we could never do for ourselves, both in terms of our creation and our redemption: this creates something of a bind for most of us. It's true, I'm afraid. Most evangelical Christians can quote, or at least paraphrase any number of verses from the New Testament that insist that we can't save ourselves, try as we may; that any such attempt at self-justification is our very undoing, the kind of works-righteousness that betrays our deep-

23. 1 Cor 12.
24. Jas 2:26.

est sin. Nevertheless, since most of us tend to be pretty concrete in the ways we approach our living, we are usually looking for some quantifiers when it comes to matters of faith. Some might call these legalisms. A less pejorative term would be the "fruits" by which people of Christian faith are to be known.[25] Most of us prefer to be able to see, to weigh, to measure our faithfulness to God. Which reminds me of a line I heard years ago, I know not where, from the late Samuel Miller, a Baptist preacher who was, I believe, once the dean of Harvard Divinity School. As close as I can recall, he said: "It is not our faith in God, which may be fickle or faint, that saves, but God's faith in us."

If Christian faith is more gift than accomplishment indeed, the status that God confers upon us, in and through Christ, is quite beyond anything we could ever achieve and hardly deserve. At the same time, if Christian faith is a way of being, it is also, in a very real sense, a matter of doing. It's just that when the latter prevails, when the proverbial cart gets before the horse or the tail wags the dog, the integrity of the gospel is compromised and our lives and witness become shallow and hollow at best. Put bluntly, none of us has the power to follow Christ faithfully. We can't do it, try as we may. We will fail every time. Rather, the integrity of a Christian witness in this world comes always and only when we willfully open our lives and submit ourselves in ways that the Spirit, the Presence of Christ, might live in, through, and for us. For many of us, that may seem awfully mystical or abstract.

I remember trying to talk about this one time with my dad, years ago. It made no sense to him. He couldn't understand what I was talking about, or at least claimed not to. In fact, he became pretty defensive, and he was a much a less concrete thinker than my mother. That experience was humbling, at least for me, since I believe my dad's kind of Christianity, as well as my mother's, certainly had some integrity to it. They weren't nearly as legalistic and works-righteous as they might have been other-wise, given the culture of their religion, short of some grace at the heart of their living.

How I believe on this matter has, I'm sure, to do with some sense of the ambiguity of our lives, at least mine. Some folk seem to have quite a clear vision of right and wrong, of good and bad, of what is more or less pleasing to God. However, I have discovered that often what I think is

---

25. Gal 5:22–23.

right turns out to be so wrong, that doing good isn't always perceived, much less received as such, particularly when this would seem to be a matter of knowing and doing the will of God. My motives are seldom pure. Are yours? Who would claim such omniscience? Some folk seem to, who are always doing things for God rather dutifully. This is not to say that much of such doing isn't worthy and helpful and likely even providential, in the sense that God might likely will it and even choose to bless it. To be sure, much of God's work in this world has been given to us to do. As Christian people, we are God's partners in the work of creating, generating, and redeeming. We are called to be "salt" and "light," a source of healing and vision. It's just that over the years I've grown less self-assured that my doing is certainly, much less always, as near to what God would will and bless as I might think or wish. As a result, Christian living, at least for me, has become more of a mystery. I am called, if not to see as clearly as I might have once thought, and even today would wish, to trust: to trust my life and work to God; to believe, as a way of knowing, that God's will and purpose, in and through me and quite apart from me, that this will be revealed and accomplished in God's own way and time. Is that an oxymoron? God's own "time?" It looks like that's how it is, at least for the finite creatures we are. Surely God needs and wants the best I have to give, even as whatever that may be is after all a gift from God. Likely as not, God's will is known and done despite, rather than necessarily because of, anything I do or don't.

Is this a life of Christian faith? I think so. It is both being in the way and getting out of the way. Is it giving up? I don't think so. However, it does involve some letting go. What I am speaking to here involves a transformed understanding of power, indeed a radical Christian view of power, as a paradox: that the more power you want or need, the less you have, and likely ever will have. Even as such power is, after all, pretty pseudo and quite temporary at best. Being in control is an illusion, perhaps even a delusion. When it comes to God, letting go is really a way of holding on, or rather, of being held. For people of Christian faith, God's power has been revealed most fully in God's own vulnerability, God's own divestiture, God's own self-emptying.[26] Again, as St. Paul would say, in the cross of Christ: "lest the cross be emptied of its power."[27] How's that

26. Phil 2.
27. 1 Cor 1:17.

for irony? As Christian people, we are called to a vocation of creating, generating, and redeeming, even as God has created and is redeeming all of life, indeed, our lives. Our doing always springs from our being. God has so willed it, in and through Christ, our Lord.

THE SACRED AND THE SECULAR

For Jews and Christians, all of life is sacred. For Christians, at least, it is our very humanity that God was not ashamed to wear, to embrace fully. So then, from a Christian point of view, life cannot be so neatly separated between what we might call the secular and the sacred. Here I speak of secular as a way of living quite exclusive of God, and sacred as the deepest of convictions, to quote Elizabeth Barrett Browning, that "earth's crammed with heaven, and every common bush aglow." And not that the two aren't often confused in the minds of most modern and/or postmodern folk. After all, there are plenty of well-meaning Christian people who think little of God, who live on fairly secular terms, often even at church, at least if you've attended many church board meetings. Unless they find themselves acting particularly religious. Typically, this is at church, on a Sunday, especially at Christmas and Easter. More often, however, I suspect, even some who would claim to be Christian know it's time to catch a serious case of religion when there is a crisis or a problem in their lives. Some would call it prayer, of the kind that usually begin: "Please, God . . . ."

As for so-called secular people, there are surely some who never give in, even when they don't know or can't understand, whatever the circumstances, as casual or as painful as they may be. For such folk, their worldview is limited to natural or material explanations or interpretations. Notwithstanding, of course, the source of such a way of reasoning, which a theistic person, certainly a Christian, would call God. A thoroughgoing secularist would insist, however, that the methodologies are different. Science is science, reason is reason, and faith is faith. People of theistic faith, certainly Jews and Christians, would, however, claim that you can't so neatly separate the two. This is surely a fundamental tenet of Christian conviction, that the material and the spiritual are interwoven, and that God is the source of all that is. Not that this can be proven in any way comparable to the methods of science. As I often put it, the second-hardest thing in the world to do is to believe in God. There is only one thing harder, and that is not believing, because then you have to be God, and that's a big job! God is the source of all being, of all that is, including the ways we think and reason and try to understand or know, as well as how we feel and even what and how we believe. That is, at least, a biblical view of God, by way of Paul Tillich.

I once saw a woman in my counseling practice for at least a couple of years. When she first came to see me, she was so depressed and withdrawn, she was almost catatonic. Given her age and symptoms, particularly her confusion, I thought she might be experiencing the onset of Alzheimer's, but it was not confirmed. A few years later, however, she was diagnosed with cancer and subsequently died. In the time I saw her, I grew to know and to love her dearly, to admire her gifts, her strength, and her courage. She was quite guarded, but gradually she became more revealing of her life to me. She was a strong and proud woman, "plain and tall," a country girl who liked to hunt and fish, ride her motorcycle, drive her pickup truck, and work in her garden. She loved the NASCAR races and knew all the drivers, some of whom she liked; others, she hated. Actually, she wouldn't watch the races on television. She preferred to listen to them on the radio. Now that's hard-core! In case you didn't know, here in the South stock car racing is like football. It's a religion. She was also a smart person, and a talented seamstress and musician. However, she hadn't done much of any of that for a long time. Hers was a sad story. She had gone through a painful divorce. Emotionally, she was wounded. She carried some deep scars. She grew up in the church and was once quite active. She told me one of her ministers in the past had "come on" to her. She hadn't been to church in years.

I asked her once if she prayed. She said, "No." That is what she said and how she said it. She was not a person of many words. I asked her if she minded if I prayed for her. She said she would appreciate that. I always considered that to have been a gift from her: that she wanted me to pray for her. She wasn't one to let anyone get very close, much less do anything for her. She was way too guarded for that. She had been hurt too deeply. I prayed for her, silently, whenever I would think of her. Over the months and years, I prayed for healing in her life and thanked God for her, for her integrity and the positive things in her life, especially for her children, both of whom were responsible adults, for the health and strength in her relationship with them, until the day I gave the eulogy at her funeral. Before she died, she asked me if I would do that for her, if I would speak to her memory at her funeral. One thing I said that day was that most women I know would trade anything in their lives—their marriage, their career, their health, anything—to have their kids grow up and stand on their own two feet, to be functional and human in how they lived. It was almost as if that were literally true for this woman. Given all her losses in life, that is surely one gift she had given to her children, the gift of good mothering, even as they had blessed her with the quality of their living, as good a gift as any child could ever give a parent.

For people of Christian faith, the sacred and the secular are not nice, neat categories into which life can be so easily separated. God meets us and touches our lives where we may or may least expect it, even in some strange ways and places. Sometimes God's presence is comforting. Sometimes it is disturbing. Sometimes it's at church, or when we are being particularly religious. More often, perhaps, it is not. In the Bible, Jacob is nothing short of a scoundrel, yet God is present to him even in his scoundrel-i-ness. God is present to Moses when it would seem as though his prospects are dim, his career down the tubes. King David is as broken a man as he is successful, yet God is as present to him in the depth of his moral failure and subsequent family crises as in his notable achievements. To despairing old women like Sarah and Hannah, or to a callow young girl like Mary, God is miraculously present in the birth of their sons. God is present to Jesus' first disciples, motley crew that they are, in the toil and routine of their workaday world, where God touches their lives through the profound ministry of a Nazarene carpenter. To the Pharisee, Saul of Tarsus, it is in his zealous self-righteousness that God's presence, in Jesus as the Christ, is so transforming. To live faithfully as Christian people, we must be open to God's presence in God's world, anywhere and everywhere, lest our expectations be so limited they become idolatrous.

Occasionally a member of the congregation I serve comes to me, discouraged about our church, because it isn't living up to his expectations. I always try to encourage such folk with this advice. Don't let our church drive you away from the life to which God has called you. Churches can do that. Certainly, when your expectations are high, that the church, of all places, ought surely to reflect the joy and integrity of Christian witness and community at its best. As churches go, ours is likely above the norm. Yet we often get sidetracked on too much that is petty and little, or even hurtful, and surely embarrassing to God. There's some more anthropomorphism for you. Many would point to the church as perhaps the best argument for God. That indeed, the church must be at least some expression of the divine, otherwise how could it survive itself; that with friends like too many of us Christians, God hardly needs any enemies. All institutions in this world, however, are fallen, the church included. If we think otherwise, we are mistaken and are only worshipping false gods, of which, in this world, there are many. When we let go of our notions about the sacred and the secular, of just where it is that God may or may not be found, we are surely more open to what is truly sacred in life, to where and how God is willing and able to find us. Because, for people of Christian faith, "God so loved the world . . . ."[28]

SIN AND SINS

In the Bible, Sin is a condition. Capital S. It is separation from God, as well as from ourselves and others. To use Tillich's language, it is alienation and estrangement from the Ground of Being. In this sense, then, there is only one Sin, and that is the worship of anything or anyone other than God. All our other sins are a consequence of Sin as a condition.

I know this may sound rather theoretical, but it has its practical consequences. Here are some examples. Most of the time when we lie, steal, or cheat, we think of it quite instrumentally. That is, we don't think of lying, stealing, or cheating as somehow connected to the larger picture of our spiritual condition, our relationship with God. When we do such things, or even later, when we get caught and are confronted in some way or other over what we have done, we tend to see such sins only in their more immediate context. Most of us think of such sinning as merely expedient, something we did in the moment. Even if the action was premeditated, it was still, in a sense, expedient. In the case of stealing, for instance, we wanted something we didn't have, or perhaps just more of what we may have had too much of already. So much for stealing.[29] In the case of lying or cheating, we were just trying to defend, protect, or promote ourselves

28. John 3:16.

29. cf. *The Confessions of St. Augustine,* Trans. Rex Warner (New York: Mentor-Omega Books, 1963) 49. It is noteworthy how the mature Augustine reflects upon the habitual stealing of his youth in a manner so similar to how I, here, interpret it. This is likely why I would tend to do so some seventeen centuries later, under the influence of such a rich and deep Hebrew-Christian moral and spiritual tradition. Augustine writes, for example: "What then was it that I loved in that theft of mine . . . did I find it pleasant to break your law and prefer to break it by stealth, since I could not break it by any real power . . . a prisoner, making a show of a kind of truncated liberty, doing unpunished what I was not allowed to do and so producing a darkened image of omnipotence?"

in some way or other, if we even thought of it that deeply. Most of us tend to lie or cheat more instrumentally, in the form of expedience.

One reason I don't lie much anymore is because I have discovered that I'm not very good at it. I have a fairly high guilt quotient, which tends to betray me. Lying is, after all, a lot like Lay's Potato Chips: you can't tell just one! You have to keep coming up with more lies to cover other ones. And that gets hard after awhile. However, some people seem to be pretty good at it. I, on the other hand, tend to cave in too easily to be very good at lying, much less at stealing or cheating. As a result, I've learned to tell the truth. Not that my motive for doing so is always all that principled. It just keeps me out of even more trouble further down the road.

To be in right relationship with God is to be defined adequately: to accept God's love for oneself as something quite unconditional. This means that we don't have to try to defend ourselves, nor attack or besmirch others. Isn't that what gossip is? Isn't that what being hurtful to another is usually about, the source of most of our interpersonal power plays? Isn't that what thinking we are better than others is? Isn't this the source of negative stereotyping and prejudice? Is this not the basis for exploiting or of being exploited, when we aren't adequately defined? Something or someone gets to us, and we become threatened in some way or other, even though we may be quite unaware that this is what is going on. What happens when we agree or go along with someone against our wishes or better judgment? Is this not generally fear-based, the fear that if we don't agree or go along, this person or these people won't like us, we won't fit in, we might not be included? When we think of sinning in this way, there is an important connection between our sins and the condition of Sin in any of our lives. When we are not adequately defined, our sense of self, worth, adequacy, and value is not connected to the right source. This is the relationship between Sin and sins.

Another reason I speak of Sin and sins as I do is because of the irony that any experienced counselor has likely observed. It occurs almost exclusively in neurotic people, when whomever is obsessing about having done something wrong. Ironically, it is often their worrying and self-recrimination that is usually worse than whatever it is they may have done, whatever it is about which they are so obsessed. I once heard a priest describe the confessions of some folk as if he were being "stoned with popcorn." Such a view of sin tends to be ironic, and tragically so, in that its emphasis is misplaced. Since such obsessions typically attach too much importance to a legalistic or perfectionist image of ourselves before God. In believing that we are somehow atoning for our sins by obsessing so, we are in fact sinning even worse, in the sense of not accepting a forgiveness God can and does give only to those humble enough to receive it, a humility that hasn't become so distorted that it is, in Wes Eades' term, a "heresy." Though viewed as being humble, too much so-called "humility" is, I'm afraid, about as arrogant a posture as anyone could ever assume. As if any of our sins, yours or mine or anyone else's, are unforgivable, at least to God. For some people, however, this appears to be what they believe.

You noticed, perhaps, how I said it was neurotic people who tend to obsess about so much of what may be wrong with themselves, about even the least of their mistakes or failures. This is not the case, however, for people who have some form of character disorder. People with a character disorder tend to externalize almost everything. They are masters at shifting outward and off to others, especially the worst in themselves. It's always someone else's fault. But not for most of us neurotics. To the contrary, we often even go looking for something wrong somewhere else, in order to make it our own, as if we don't have enough troubles to tend to in the first place. For neurotic people, if there is a problem anywhere in our world—whatever it might be, or to whomever it might belong—it surely must have something to do with us, or at least we ought to be able to do something about it.

When it comes to the traditional Christian doctrine concerning hell, it is easy to see what this might be for someone who is neurotic. Hell is an awful sense of separation from God, a deeply internalized and quite as painful awareness, perhaps a sense of guilt or shame. For people with a character disorder, however, it would seem as though they remain somehow oblivious to any estrangement or alienation from anyone, even God. Maybe that *is* their hell: to be quite unconnected to anyone, including God, and just as unaware of it. Speaking to the relative nature of evil, in relation to good as an absolute, C. S. Lewis once remarked: "If an ungodly man were to go to heaven, he'd think he was in hell!" Maybe that's how it works. For neurotic folk, hell is distance. It is separation, or at least the fear of it, the tyranny of being alone, of being quite unconnected to anyone else, even their problems. For socio-paths, however, hell is likely the fear of closeness, of being near anyone, much less God. Be that as it may, you may have heard the joke about the Baptist who died and went to hell. He immediately began to protest: "This isn't right. Something's wrong. I *know*

I was saved." His friend, a Methodist, had the same experience. He died and went to hell. But his protest wasn't quite as strong: "Well now," he said, "I *thought* I was saved." But when their socio-pathic neighbor died and went to hell, all he had to say was: "It's not hot, and I'm not here!"

Meanwhile, back to us neurotics. What's that great line? "Just because you made a mistake, does that mean you are one?" Some people I encounter sometimes find this helpful, when I explain the matter this way. In the New Testament, the Greek word most commonly translated as "perfect:" it doesn't mean what we normally think perfection to be, as in never making a mistake. The word is *telos*. In fact, when Jesus says, in the Sermon on the Mount, "Be perfect, even as you Father in Heaven is perfect," that is the same Greek word he uses when he says from the cross, "It is finished." The latter translation is closer to the meaning of *telos*: complete, fulfilled, finished. You might recognize this idea from our English word telescope, where that which is far away is brought near. Therefore, if there is any such thing as being "perfect," for a Christian, it has to do with a kind of growth or maturity, a fulfilling or completing. This suggests something quite different from any sort of legalistic, never-make-a-mistake kind of perfectionism. Indeed, folk who may have been tyrannized by the "curse of perfectionism" sometimes tell me they find it comforting to realize: "God isn't finished with me yet!"

In a remarkable novel by Peter DeVries, *The Blood of the Lamb*, Don Wanderhope's wife, Greta, is such a tragically mistaken and troubled soul.[30] Before she finally commits suicide, she has an adulterous affair, which would seem not quite as pathologic, nor perhaps even as sinful as the kind of religious quackery she latches onto in her desperate search for some definition of her "self." Her minister, who is every bit the exploiter—in the name of the Lord, of course!—he calls on her and her husband and asks to pray for Mr. Wanderhope. It is because he is willing—and that is not a typographical error. Wanderhope is *willing* to forgive his wife. Yet both the minister and Greta denounce him for such a "sinful" gesture. Not that he is being glib about such forgiveness, not at all. And neither is God. In the words of the Letter of 1 John: "If we confess our sins, God is faithful and just to forgive us . . . ."[31] When it comes to sinning, even God can't forgive the arrogance, an unwillingness on the part of any of us to accept God's

---

30. Peter DeVries, *The Blood of the Lamb* (Boston: Little Brown, 1961).
31. 1 John 1:9.

forgiveness, much less that of another. When we don't understand the relationship between Sin and sins, our religion will tend to be as sick and
sinful as that of Greta Wanderhope and her fraudulent minister, because
we will always be trying to solve the wrong problem.

Our sins are forever the result of Sin as a condition of separation
from God. Nonetheless, it is God, in Christ, who has reached down and
out to repair the breach, to touch and heal such brokenness, our condition of alienation and estrangement, certainly from God, as well as from
ourselves and others. Becoming a Christian hardly makes anyone mistake-free. It does call us, however, to accept God's acceptance of us. And
whenever we are willing to do this, we will, perhaps, at least be humble
enough to know for sure that we're not God. For God would never treat
any of us the way some of us often treat ourselves, if not others. Indeed,
when it comes to being "perfected," in the biblical sense, this seems to be
closer to what it means.

In terms of the relationship of Sin to sins, I have surely been far too
distracted, self-conscious, and self-seeking throughout my life. Not that
this is some rare moral or spiritual disease. I expect there are others who
might say the same. The clue to this for me, however, has come with my
awareness of just how defensive I can become when someone criticizes
me, the power I often give to others to define my life, to confirm my
worth, much less to devalue me; the approval of another I may so desperately seek, the rejection or lack of acceptance I too often fear. Whenever I
find myself living with such anxiety or resentment, I know my priorities
in life are misplaced. To put it more bluntly, this kind of sinning is but a
symptom of my Sin, my condition of estrangement, of alienation from
God, from myself, and from others. In this case, I am being an idolator.
I am worshipping some false god, when I give such power to anyone or
anything, the power to define my life, to confer or deny status, to tell me
who I am. Eventhough most of us would not tend to think this way, at
least in the moment.

We are usually too caught up in our own drama of defensiveness, in
our anxiety, our obsessing, even our paranoia. If we want to be glib about
it and rationalize the situation, when this happens, what we are doing
and how we are doing it may merely come off looking like just more bad
form on our part. We just lost our poise or perspective for the moment.
We lost our "cool," or perhaps our bearing. Even those words, however,
can be helpful in understanding what is really going on with most of us at

such times, certainly when we lose perspective or lose our bearing. These seem to be rather apt images of what it means for our lives to be rooted deeply in the defining presence of God: to have perspective and a sense of bearing in our lives, to be focused in the right direction, to know what is most important. If this means resting our lives in grace alone—the grace of God—then this is surely the antidote to much needless fear and worry, to the sort of distractions, self-consciousness, self-seeking, and defensiveness that can be such a tyrannous way of living for any of us.

6

Developmental Stages, Values, and Theological Reflections

"More people will attend your funeral if it's a pretty day."

—Coach John McKissick

IN THIS CHAPTER, I AM DISCUSSING VARIOUS DEVELOPMENTAL MOD-
ELS and certain values implicit in a kind of psychotherapy I would
encourage. Finally, I am offering some theological reflections on the
counseling process.

DEVELOPMENTAL MODELS

One of the most important books I have ever read is Erik Erikson's
Childhood and Society, first published in 1950.[1] In chapter 7 of his book,
entitled "Eight Ages of Man," Erikson interprets the process of human development from infancy into old age. His language, to me, is nothing less
than inspired. It is elegant. There are, of course, specialists in developmental psychology, of which I am hardly one. I have, however, read, studied,
and worked with various interpreters of Erikson and other developmental
theorists. My colleague of many years, Dr. Fances Welch, is a gifted child
psychologist from whom I have learned much. She has often been my
teacher concerning matters of child development. I am also indebted to
Professor Donald Capps at Princeton Theological Seminary. He has been,
for me and others, an important interpreter of Erikson.[2] For many years

1. Erik Erikson, *Childhood and Society* (New York: W. W. Norton and Co., Inc. (2nd
edition), 1963).

2. Donald Capps, *Life Cycle Theory and Pastoral Care* (Philadelphia: Fortress Press,
1983).

now, I have been paying particular attention to where people seem to be developmentally. I have found this especially important in my work as a therapist. I here offer my observations on Erikson's various developmental stages, some of which I have had occasion to observe, clinically, to a greater extent than others.

"Basic Trust vs. Mistrust." How safe is the world? If mother leaves the room, will she return? Can I trust these people I live with to take care of me? Such is the view of an infant in the first eighteen months of life, although obviously such a sense is pre-cognitive for a child of this age. My wife became a mother as a teenager. From what I can tell, she rose to the occasion and did an exceptional job. She tells me that at least one thing she remembers thinking when her first child, a daughter, was born was: "Wow! I must take really good care of her." She obviously did.

That is not, however, the case with many parents and their children. There are lots of kids born into this world to parents who hardly have a clue about how to take care of themselves, much less a child, and certainly an infant who is totally reliant upon a parent in order to survive. What is remarkable is how many people seem to do so, in spite of such poor parenting. Similarly, there are many people deeply scarred, emotionally and otherwise, for the lack of adequate parenting at the most vulnerable and fragile of times in their lives. The Erikson view of human development suggests that these various stages are like a series of building blocks. Succeeding stages build upon the adequate completion of the previous developmental tasks. When such tasks are not completed, a person is often "stuck," as we say, in a particular developmental stage. In Erikson's scheme, this first stage is the foundation of what I consider reasonably sane living. Indeed, when life is fearful or hurtful, so tentative and uncertain to an infant in this stage, as it surely is to many unfortunate children, the consequences in later life are usually quite serious. Psychotherapy that addresses such developmental problems is unusually demanding and difficult. Exceptional gifts and skills on the part of a therapist are required when a person's fundamental view of the world is distrustful in proportion to the harshness of whatever circumstances he may have survived.

I speak to the next two developmental stages together because of a particular interest that has emerged for me over the years. Erikson call the next eighteen months of life "Autonomy vs. Shame and Doubt." This corresponds to a child developing language and getting toilet training, since by now a child whose physical development is normal has learned to walk. Autonomy suggests a struggle of the will between parent and child around any number of issues, not the least of which is learning to use the toilet. The less anxious the parent, the less stressful this developmental stage tends to be for both parent and child. For the more psychoanalytically oriented counselor, the power struggle between parent and child in this stage is of highly symbolic value.

The succeeding developmental stage, which Erikson calls "Initiative vs. Guilt," continues up through approximately age five. The focus of this stage involves infantile sexuality, where it is normal for children to be intrigued that males and females have different genitalia.

In my experience, shame seems to have a more primitive quality to it; guilt may appear a bit more sophisticated. Shame seems more concrete in people's experience; guilt appears to be more abstract. John Bradshaw, a recovering alcoholic who has written several popular books, speaks of "shame-based families."[3] Most experienced therapists have observed how "shaming" is often a prominent parenting style for many people. The implication seems to be that we parent in ways similar to how we were parented, which may or may not be something good. One might think it reasonable for someone to correct the mistakes of her parenting when she becomes a parent herself. However, such logic does not appear to be the norm across generations in many families. Instead, the more common pattern appears to be a tendency toward replicating the parenting styles of previous generations, often quite unconsciously. Most research seems to indicate this pattern in particular as it concerns notable forms of family dysfunction, including patterns of violence, addiction, and abuse. Shaming, as a predominant parenting style, would seem apparent often enough for Bradshaw to speak of a culture of "shame-based families." This caricature is certainly common in my clinical experience.

What has struck my interest in particular, over the years, is how few people ever say to me, "I'm ashamed" of whatever. In contrast, hardly a day passes that someone doesn't tell me how "guilty" he or she feels about this or that. Is this a factor of acculturation? As they say, "guilt is the gift that keeps on giving!" Is this, as I've suggested, because shame is a more primitive experience, while guilt is in some way more sophisticated? If so, does guilt serve as something of a hedge, does it somehow protect us

---

3. John Bradshaw, *Healing the Shame that Binds You* (Deerfield Beach: Health Communications, 1988).

from a deeper sense of shame and so serve as one of our more common emotional defenses?

I was talking about this one time with my colleague of several years, Mark Deaton, who is a Presbyterian minister and a talented therapist. I was sharing the observations I have made here: how hardly anyone ever says to me, "I'm ashamed," while most folk seem to talk quite readily about how "guilty" they feel.

Mark said: "Shame is about what someone does to you; guilt is about what you do to someone else." That sounds right to me. Certainly, shame might be better understood as a verb (shaming) than as a noun. If verbs tend to be more concrete, more visceral than nouns, which are more abstract, then my idea that guilt, as a noun, which functions in some emotionally protective ways, versus shame: this would seem to make sense. It is interesting that in his discussion of shame, Erikson speaks of this experience in terms of being exposed, as in being "caught with your pants down." He continues to describe the sense of being shamed: " . . . this, I think, is essentially rage turned against the self. He who is ashamed would like to force the world not to look at him, not to notice his exposure."[4] My clinical experience suggests that shaming is not uncommon in families and that many people are indeed the most emotionally vulnerable at this point, in terms of how they may have been shamed. It strikes me as no accident that this stage and its functional tasks are rather primitive in the process of human development, such that it is here many people may be quite as emotionally fragile as they are vulnerable.

"Industry vs. Inferiority." There is nothing more beautiful than a third-grader who is on task. Conversely, there is nothing more painful than to observe a child of similar age who appears to be falling off the power curve. I say it this way because this developmental stage, which encompasses roughly the elementary school years, is where children develop such basic competencies as the academic and social skills learned in school. These include being able to read and write, follow instructions, complete tasks, and get along with others. If home schooling can promote most of these skills, it is the last one that such a setting would likely minimize. Erikson's language here could not be more apt. On-task kids in this age group are industrious. Work at this age is play. It's an adventure. There is an innocence about it all, not unlike that story in Genesis of

---

4. Erikson, *Childhood and Society,* 252.

those mythical children who are tasked with gardening. Work has yet to become toil, for it is good work, purposeful work, celebrative work. On-task elementary school children are energetic, enthusiastic, and inquiring. Teaching and supervising children at this age requires an abundance of energy and patience. At my age, when I am involved with children of this age, I am reminded of why I had children when I was considerably younger. I'm more patient these days, but hardly as energetic.

Likewise, children who are not successful at these developmental tasks may develop a sense of inferiority. So much of life has to do with such fundamental and necessary academic and social skills that become a basic building block for developing later job skills and social functioning, both of which are a necessity for most people. I say it that way because I have known at least one person who, despite not completing this developmental stage adequately, inherited a home and a trust fund, and so was able to survive in rather minimal ways, even as an adult, without living parents to care for him. In fact, some of his friends seemed to provide a certain network of support for him, even as some weren't above exploiting him.

Take, for example, reading. If a child can read, she can proceed to many other tasks in life and likely develop other competencies. Conversely, when someone can't read, or even read very well, he has to compensate in ways that are often debilitating. In my lifetime, much attention has been paid to children's learning disabilities, and much has been accomplished in diagnosing and treating such problems on the part of both educators and the medical community. Many people have benefited from this effort, and the work continues. When one does not complete this important developmental stage, the alternative to industry is as painful as it sounds. Feelings of inferiority are awful to live with. They don't contribute to health and growth and a sense of well-being. I have worked with many parents facing such problems with their children. Unfortunately, I have also seen many children who it would appear were born into the wrong family, when it came to the positive qualities of patience, kindness, and gentleness, the encouragement and persistence needed for parenting children with difficulties in this developmental stage.

"Ego Identity vs. Role Confusion." I often say that teenagers live in a house of mirrors. They are constantly checking themselves out in terms of how they look in relation to their peers. Conformity, acceptance, and belonging are essential characteristics of this developmental stage. Indeed, the adolescent discovers who he is by comparison. That's why having the right kind of Nike sneakers or Polo shirt, or perhaps even having your body pierced, is so important to people in this age group. Those who market all the stuff out there to buy certainly know the value of such appeal. My children grew up in a highly stratified community, with respect to the many teenagers who lived in our town. The social stratification was referred to as "the jocks, the preps, and the heads." Being in the band or on the football team was a big deal. If you couldn't compete on those terms, then you might dye your hair purple, get a ring in your nose, and hang out with "*your* crowd," smoking on the parking lot at school. If you're a teenager, then or now, whenever or wherever, you are going to belong somewhere, whether it's on a team, in a band, in a club, in a church youth group, or in a gang.

I'm remembering a family I once saw in my counseling practice. The older daughter and her friends seemed to style themselves as political activists. She was probably sixteen. And she was really miffed at her younger sister, who was around fourteen, because the younger girl appeared to be horning in on the older sister's current political cause.

"Who does she think she is?" the older girl exclaimed to me. "She can't support Greenpeace! She doesn't even know what it is. She's always trying to steal my ideas." When I questioned the older girl further, however, she wasn't clear either as to who or what Greenpeace was all about. If belonging is important to teenagers, belonging in a somewhat exclusive way may be even more important. It is likely one of the reasons why kids in this age group can be so cruel to one another around issues of exclusivity, whenever the fairly fragile and rather tentative image of oneself would seem to be threatened so easily.

Of all the many reasons we implore teenagers not to get married and not to have babies, surely none is more important than the fact that you can't relate to anyone else in a very mature or responsible way when you don't yet know who you are. Unfortunately, too many teenagers in our society have babies as a way of trying to confirm some sense of worth or importance in themselves and/or to try to get away from a dysfunctional, even abusive family. This is hardly the best of reasons for having babies. No child should ever be expected to do so much for a parent, since making anyone else, especially a parent, feel OK about himself is quite an impossible task. In this respect, nature tends to play a trick on many people of this age, since most teenagers are usually more mature biologically, or even socially, than they are emotionally. As a parent, it is much easier if your child is thirteen going on thirteen (or even eleven), than if she is thirteen going on eighteen.

As a teenager, I was physically and socially mature quite beyond my emotional maturation. Not that I realized it at the time. That understanding would, unfortunately, be many years later in coming. By some positive stroke of fate, however, both of my children, a son and a daughter, were relatively "late bloomers," as we say. Both their physical and their social maturation process seemed to be somewhat slower, certainly slower than that of their father or of many other children I have known. This is a gift to most parents, and it is usually better for children as well. It takes some pressure off both the child and the parent. It allows a child's growth process to be more measured and likely creates better balance in his life.

The primary developmental task of adolescence involves the search for one's "self." This seems to be expressed largely in terms of interpersonal relationships. A major factor in this stage has to do with one's sexuality, one's sexual identity, one's essential maleness or femaleness, and all that this entails.

Clinically speaking, given the importance of peer relationships, of belonging, and since adolescents tend to be largely a mass of exploding hormones, teenagers often function primarily in terms of emotions. They can be easily exploited by peers, and certainly by adults. Teachers, coaches, and youth workers of various kinds are morally obligated to understand how true this is and not exploit the youth they work with. The advertising and entertainment industries do quite a good (or is it bad?) enough job at this already! It is tragic whenever purveyors of religion fall into the same trap.

As a minister and a counselor, I commonly talk with people regarding their religious development, or lack thereof. By that, I mean people are often revealing of such matters to me, wittingly or otherwise. I have been listening rather carefully now over many years. It is noteworthy to me how many adults appear to be stuck somewhere back in their adolescence in terms of their religious or moral-spiritual development. This may, unfortunately, merely correspond to where they are, developmentally, in terms of their emotional life.

People often describe to me some "peak" experience when they were at church camp or in a youth group as a teenager, as if this has become normative for them. It often seems as if they are in fact trying to live, chronologically, as an adult with just such an adolescent religious framework, one that is primarily emotional. Such folk are often highly exploit-able as adults—"in the name of the Lord" no less!—because their religious development is anachronistic. As cozy and nostalgic as it may seem, it doesn't fit with where they are chronologically. As a result, such normative religion will not tend to serve such people well. It will often be the source of dis-ease and dysfunction in their lives.

Erikson speaks of the young adult years in terms of "Intimacy vs. Isolation." Some might consider this developmental stage as including the years between roughly eighteen and thirty. I would suggest that in more advanced, industrialized, and technological societies such as our own, this stage might be extended significantly for many people. For example, if one compares contemporary life with certain other cultures and earlier historical epochs, there have been previous times and places where it was likely that most people would have been married by the time they were fifteen and dead by the time they were thirty. That is hardly the case in our culture. These days, people obviously live longer. Growing up, as it were, the process of maturing seems to be far more complicated. For example, both of my children have married in recent years, in their thirties. When I was ten years younger than they, I was both married and a parent. That was only thirty-some years ago, and it's not that I was any more mature in my twenties than they were at the same age.

There are at least three primary developmental tasks in this stage. These tasks include leaving one's family of origin, choosing or creating a life's work, and establishing, with another person, a new family. These are rather monumental tasks. It seems important to me that people in this stage of life be given ample support for what they are facing. This includes a fairly high level of tolerance for errors in judgment, for the stop-and-start character of this developmental stage. In fact, our society seems to be more supportive than ever around matters of career choice and development. Seminaries and medical schools, for example, are full of second-career people. I taught an ethics seminar at the local medical school several years ago, and the average age in the seminar was roughly thirty. Only two of the students had recently graduated from college. The others were nurses, dentists, engineers, PhD's in chemistry, and the like.

From the perspective of most family counselors, there is an impor-tant connection between adequately differentiating, in relation to one's family of origin, and marrying responsibly. The two somehow go to-gether. When people who get married are poorly differentiated, a higher level of dysfunction in their marriage is likely. Differentiation here suggests a significant level of maturity, becoming more of one's own person, in the sense of not being so connected emotionally to others, including one's parents or other family members. Some families, across generations, seem to promote differentiation to a greater degree than others, where people often remain fairly "stuck" to or with one another in a pattern of emotional dependency, and often, as well, with subsequent resentment. It strikes me that, for increasing numbers of people in our society, the process of differentiation may only begin in their thirties. Often this has to do with economics. I've noticed, for example, how many young adults seem to still want continued parental financial support, but without any strings attached: "Shut up, dad, and just write the check!" It doesn't, however, usually work that way. People who become more adequately differentiated often start by untying some of the financial strings. Indeed, many highly trained professional people are still in school into their thirties. Having been one of these myself, I can testify to how such circumstances tend to retard the important process of maturing, emotionally or otherwise.

Generally speaking, women in this developmental stage tend to be ahead of men in terms of emotional maturity. Some would claim that many of the traditional sex-role stereotypes in our culture tend to perpetuate this. The caricature here is that of the "woman behind the man," where the wife is long-suffering, where she "covers" for him, where her job in life is to make her husband look good, often at her own expense. In this caricature, the wife "winks" at her husband's "indiscretions." She looks the other way, and in operating in rather executive fashion behind his back and often taking care of the important functions required of more mature people, she tends to promote his somehow managing to stay a little boy. This is a common caricature of sex-role stereotyping where I have lived and worked throughout my career as a counselor. As one woman I know declares, "My husband is a high maintenance man!" Some men would claim that the reverse is also true, and I have certainly seen it to be so. In addition, such patterns in families often tend to be perpetuated across generations.

Over the years, I think some of my best work as a therapist has been with men, often in this developmental stage. Such therapy is hardly sophisticated. To the contrary, it is actually pretty crude. I sometimes call it a "come to Jesus" meeting, where I talk to guys like a proverbial Dutch Uncle. In essence, I say, "Listen here, bubba. If you don't grow up, one of these days your wife is going to stop putting up with your crap!" I've noticed a pattern.

Often, a bride of twenty-one is so tolerant of her husband's immaturity, until she gets to be about thirty. Then it is no longer quite as cute.

I have always tried to make my own appointments in order to survey who calls for counseling. Almost always, it is the woman. After all, isn't that her job? Unless the horse is out of the barn. That's when she tells him she's in love with the preacher or the mailman or her therapist. That is when he goes ballistic. The male ego seems rather incapable of tolerating much of anything that doesn't fit within his typically rather narrow purview, and hardly another man! When it comes to this, have you ever noticed how many men seem to have quite a double standard? All of a sudden, he is on the phone, the most compliant client any counselor has ever heard from, quite willing to "do anything" to make his marriage work. How different from the more common caricature of males in therapy, at least where I have lived and worked: "I agreed to come for her. It's OK, if this is what she wants. She probably needs it. But I can't see where talking to someone else about your problems does any good." Here in the South, we affectionately call these guys "good ol' boys." Down here we clone 'em!

Erikson calls the primary developmental task of adult midlife, "Generativity." Its alternative is "Stagnation." In the chapter on "Balanced Religion" I spoke of how Christians are called to participate with God in creating, generating, and redeeming or reclaiming. The second of these qualities comes from Erikson's concept of generativity, which is the passing on of values and skills to succeeding generations. This occurs both in families and in the larger culture, through various forms of parenting, teaching, coaching, and mentoring. In its most practical terms, generativity is when parents stop competing with their kids. It is when you, as a mother, don't need to try to go to the prom through your daughter because you got to go when you were a teenager, because you have completed such a developmental task and aren't still stuck back there somewhere in your adolescence. Another common caricature in our culture involves little league sports. Much of the coaching is done by the kind of fathers I sometimes refer to as "has-beens" or "never was-es." These are dads who are way too caught up in the drama of their child's life around sports because, from the experience of their youth, they remain still quite unfulfilled. To live generatively in one's more mature adult years is to have moved past the normal developmental tasks of childhood, adolescence, and younger adulthood in ways that allow a person to share his or her wisdom and experience with succeeding generations in genuinely constructive, even nurturing ways, rather than in projecting onto or in competing with our youngsters.

It doesn't take such profound insight to realize that ours is a culture in crisis around issues of generativity. Unlike some cultures where growing older is respected, even revered, ours tends to be a culture of planned obsolescence, a throw-away culture, not just with things, but also with people. The optimal American lifestyle is to be young and energetic and "with it," on the go and able to keep up with the Joneses. When people are no longer able to compete on these terms, we have all sorts of schemes to warehouse them, most commonly in nursing homes. When people get older, they slow down and become a bother. They encumber our more normative pace, our consumptive and competitive ways of living. In our culture, we so glamorize youth and vitality, a certain image of so-called "freedom," which undermines both the normal tasks of adolescent development and the significance of the aging process. Consequently, in America today we have a culture of sixteen-year-olds (if not thirteen-year-olds) trying to be thirty and just as many forty-year-olds trying to be sixteen!

There are few things in life more painful to watch than a chronologically mature adult still casting about in search of his or her "self," trying so desperately to be someone other than who he or she is. It is as pathetic as a middle-aged person who seems "stuck" back in high school or college, as if that was surely the high point of her life, that nothing much of importance has happened since.

Having been watching and listening rather carefully, over a number of years, it strikes me that each of us faces something of a crisis somewhere along the way. Most of us don't get all of everything we need to develop most fully from our family of origin. As a result, for most people, some borrowing and acquiring and adapting occurs, likely from the time we first move out of our home environment to go to school. In today's culture, where both parents normally work out of the home and children spend most of their preschool days in child development centers, this process may begin even before the traditional kindergarten or first grade.

Then, sometime later we face what I consider to be something of a watershed in our lives. For some, it may be in the teen years. For others, it may be in young adulthood. My sense is that for most of us it is around or in our thirties. For some people, it may come even later. It is here that we often realize more clearly than ever before that we both need to make some changes in ourselves and that we can, that we have both the freedom and the responsibility to take more of ourselves into our own hands, to become more of our own person, less dependent upon and/or resentful of anyone else.

This may involve changing or modifying our values or our attitude; it may be even more internalized than external. It may involve major decisions concerning marriage or career or childrearing, of how and where we are going to live. Indeed, it may be quite externalized. Whatever or however it may be, it would seem that there is, during this period of our lives, whatever the chronology, a "window of opportunity," and that most people make major changes in their lives here, if they ever make any at all. If they don't, it is as if that opportunity passes, and they tend to live out the rest of their lives in pretty much whatever direction they have set upon. Often this may be a way of life that has become pretty negative or unfulfilling. It strikes me that this is the developmental crisis of midlife. Am I going to continue on in the direction and the manner in which my life seems to be headed, or am I going to make some changes? Whether I do or don't, am I going to accept and be at some peace with who I am and who I'm not, with myself and my life as it is? Am I going to live out my days in bitterness or resentment, in envy or regret?

Erikson speaks of the senior stage of human development as "Ego Integrity vs. Despair." Traditionally seen as beyond age fifty-five, this stage, at least the chronology of it, seems to have become more ambiguous in recent times. On the one hand, most people live longer, and many work productively into their seventies or beyond. Indeed, the senior United States senator from South Carolina, Strom Thurmond, continued to represent our state into his nineties! At the same time, many people are able to "retire" from necessary, life-sustaining work at a fairly young age, and it is interesting to note how some folk seem to adapt to this era of their living far better than others.

Some men, especially, seem primarily defined by their work and often lose some sense of themselves when such a role is laid aside or taken from them. Women generally seem to have a more balanced self-concept, between their personal and professional lives, between their role in their family and any other apart from it. When I interview women in the workplace, outside of the home, they almost universally claim a deeper loyalty to and a greater sense of purpose and fulfillment from their personal and family roles, as opposed to their work outside the home, however much pride they make take in it.

I once had a conversation with Will Campbell in which he challenged the traditional Calvinist value of meaningful work. He claimed that this was an anachronism in a highly industrialized society, and that people today should try to find a job or career that provides maximum material benefit for the minimum contribution of oneself to the job. He argued that meaning in life is to be found avocationally, apart from the workplace. I doubt that my father approached his life and work from such a conscious philosophical or theological premise. In actuality, as I reflect upon his life, however, this seems to have been how he lived. He always told me that his mother wanted him to be a teacher and a coach. But he could make more money in fewer hours working at a coalmine, so that is what he did. As loyal a worker as he surely was and as positive an attitude as he always seemed to have—he wasn't a chronic griper and complainer, even about his job—it was still patently obvious that the greater joy and meaning of his life came, not from his job, but from his role in his family, working around the house and playing with his children, from being a deacon and the Sunday School superintendent at church, from coaching little league baseball, from serving on the school board and supporting the local athletic teams. In this sense, then, he seemed rather actualized avocationally, ironically, in the very ways his mother had wished for him.

I had a good buddy named Cape Harney, who was a mentor to me. He died a few years ago, in his eighties. During his career, he was a top-level manager in industry, both in the United States and in Europe. We used to have lunch together regularly, so I could pick his brain. In his retirement years, his life was so full, with his photography hobby, his tutoring in a literacy program, and his church work. He was like a lot of retired people I've known, who wonder: "How did I ever hold a job and still take care of all this other stuff?" Cape was so talented, vital, and capable, and his knowledge and wisdom invaluable.

I asked him once why he wasn't still working. He replied, "I can't justify it morally. I would be taking a younger person's job, and I have a good retirement income. Someone else needs my job."

That is when I asked him which was harder: his life in retirement or in his midlife, when he seemingly had more responsibility, when more people were counting on him, when if he got half the items on his "to do" list crossed off he had had a good day or week. Without hesitation, he replied, "Oh, today is much harder! That's why I make things count, my hobbies and my volunteer work, whatever. I tell myself they do make a difference. How I choose to spend my days is at least keeping me alive." My friend used to fix breakfast for his wife each morning. "I serve it to her in bed," he explained. "I sit at the other end of the bed, and we talk. It's our time together each day, because she's as busy as I am." Then he added, "It's only fair. She fixed my breakfast every morning for many years. Now it's my turn to do that for her."

Before I accepted a call in my midlife to pastor a church, I noticed in my counseling practice that I was spending more time with families caring for aging parents, grandparents, and other family members. Part of my sense of call to my current ministry had to do with this interest, since this is an important part of my life and work these days, looking after older members of our congregation. I visit folk in their homes, in the hospital, and in nursing homes and assisted living facilities. It may be the best part of my job. I think of it as preparation for my own obsolescence. If I live long enough, I will someday be dependent upon others to care for me, and not necessarily a loved one or a member of my family. If I live long enough, will anyone want to spend time with me, will anyone choose to pay me any attention? It's true for all of us, if we live long enough. Slowing ourselves down at least long enough to spend time with older people is good for most of us; it helps us put our lives in better perspective. When I walk through a nursing home, and I visit in several regularly, I silently pray for the staff and speak encouraging words to them, thanking them for the important work they do.

Think about this caricature. Here's an old man or woman who is paying, or their family is paying, a good sum of money for someone to provide care for them in a nursing home. That someone, who is making minimum wage and entrusted with their care, sees to it that they are clean and fed, changes their bed, dresses them, and is hopefully nice to them. I think of this often these days when I walk through the corridors of a nursing home, offering pastoral care to all who are involved. I pray for the best in these situations: for the children and other relatives of such aging persons; for those entrusted with the caregiving, that they will rise to the occasion, that they will be considerate and kind, that they won't be abusive or neglectful. I pray for those who are growing older, who are often quite infirmed, and who have become so fragile and vulnerable. That is not now how it is for some of us. However, if we live long enough, it likely will be. This caricature is only one variation on the theme of aging, because many older people I know and serve live in even more distressing circumstances. Sensitivity to and consideration for the elderly is one way we can prepare, emotionally, morally and spiritually, for our own terminal aging.

The congregation I serve is blessed to be balanced age-wise. We have our share of little kids, plenty of old folks, and the rest of the human family in between. So many of our senior adults remain quite vital. We have eighty-year-olds who still function as if they were fifty! I can't expect this to always be so. If I live long enough, I will conduct even more funerals.

Most old people I talk with aren't afraid of death. In fact, many who are suffering so either tell me they want to die, that they are praying to die, or they ask me if it's OK to want this, to think this, or to pray this way. I bless their will and their need to die. Because our culture in America is so youth-oriented, most of us want to look the other way when it comes to aging, to subsequent fatal illness and death. We tend to treat such matters, particularly dying, so euphemistically. A far healthier attitude is to bless the process of aging and illness and death as an important part of the human journey. The great fear for most older people is not dying, it is outliving their money. Most older people dread the thought of having to go to a nursing home or having to live with one of their children. For many such folk, this is a fate worse than death, not being able to live in their own home and not being able to take care of themselves.

Facing the end of one's life with more gratitude than regret is the developmental task of old age. That is why, as I have suggested, I am quite certain that some preparation for this stage in life is important. Some anticipation of one's own obsolescence seems necessary. It is important to acknowledge, somewhere along the way, that anyone's ultimate worth is more than merely performance-based. Over the years, this pattern has presented as likely the most painful, among clients and families I have seen in counseling, or in my more general pastoral ministry: when someone is facing a crisis in his or her life, and it is apparent that he or she isn't the least bit prepared for it, as though it never entered the person's mind that such a crisis might ever occur. One has to be discounting at a fairly significant level, you have to be in some pretty major denial to never look around at what is so common among others in this world and never suspect that you, as well, might someday have to face some of the same things in your life.

I was present for both of my parents in their aging, in their fatal illness, and in their dying. I was able to bless them in that stage of their living. I sometimes wonder whether they could receive such a blessing, since both were better givers than receivers. The process of getting old and sick and dying, for both of my parents, was particularly stressful because neither would ever want to be a bother to anyone, certainly to their children. I'm sure that both of my parents saw themselves as being in this world, not to be taken care of, but to care for others, and certainly to take care of themselves. For Erikson, the final stage of human development is essentially moral and spiritual, as well as emotional, and I doubt I will ever read more inspired words than these: "Webster's Dictionary is kind enough to help us complete this outline in a circular fashion. Trust (the first of our ego values) is here defined as 'the assured reliance on another's integrity,' the last of our values. I suspect that Webster had business in mind rather than babies, credit rather than faith. But the formulation stands. And it seems possible to further paraphrase the relation of adult integrity and infantile trust by saying that healthy children will not fear life if their elders have integrity enough not to fear death."[5]

As important as Erikson's model of human development is, it is strengthened even further by its cyclical nature, as compared to the hierarchical pattern in other developmental models I have studied. For example, James Fowler's stages of faith development, which are patterned largely on Lawrence Kohlberg's study of moral development, tend to be hierarchical.[6] They proceed, essentially, from more concrete to more abstract ways of thinking. The same is true for a similar developmental model, that of the late Scott Peck. I heard Dr. Peck present this material first in a lecture some years ago at a local university, which was later published in his book, *A Different Drum*.[7]

I point to these examples because such developmental models as those of Peck, Fowler, and Kohlberg, from the critique of Christian orthodoxy, all tend to be fairly Gnostic. Implied is some notion of ascending upward to increasingly higher levels of spirituality or morality, a pattern that reflects, as I've mentioned, some movement from more concrete to more abstract thinking or conceptualizing. An example is the difference between a morality of reciprocity and a more principled moral framework. The former is logical: if I treat you the way I want to be treated, there's a good chance you will reciprocate. However, in principled moral-

5. Ibid., 269.

6. James Fowler, *Stages of Faith* (San Francisco: Harper and Row, 1981).

7. Scott Peck, *A Different Drum* (New York: Simon and Schuster, 1987).

ity, making a decision in one direction is apt to be just as costly in or from another. It's called "the horns of a dilemma."

As significant as hierarchical developmental models may be, they remain questionable in terms of Christian faith. In orthodox Christian thought, one does not proceed upward toward God, toward a higher spirituality, even morality. Rather, God is revealed in a downward pattern, if you will, in God's own divestiture, God's own self-emptying.[8] Contrary to the dominant ethos of our culture, even at church, the gospel is about downward mobility! This critique of Christian orthodoxy seems important given the current cultural climate, which would appear to be incipiently, if not notably Gnostic. After all, whether in the first century or in our own, it is a Gnostic view that tends to promote a kind of spiritual or moral elitism. It is as if some people are somehow so accomplished or work hard enough so as to ascend to higher levels of spirituality and morality than their less accomplished or devoted peers.

This may or may not be so. It is, however, alien to the more radical nature of Christian faith. As Jesus would say, "Suffer the *little children* to come unto me, for such is the Kingdom of Heaven" (meaning, or course, not "child-*ish*-ness," but "child-*like*-ness").[9] In Hebrew-Christian thought, moral and spiritual development are meant always to go together. In a biblical way of believing moral and spiritual development function ironically, as essentially a paradox. The more you need to try to climb such a ladder, the less likely you will succeed, since the gospel frames the process of moral and spiritual development on quite different terms. To paraphrase Garth Brooks, some of God's best friends are in "low places." Even as there are certainly some feminists who would also have plenty to say about the symbolic nature of such hierarchical developmental models. For example, I was attending a conference some years ago, and at one point the group was singing spirituals and camp songs, as though we were back at church camp. Instead of singing, "We Are Climbing Jacob's Ladder," we sang, "We Are Dancing Sarah's Circle." From a Christian way of seeing things, there's something to that.

It is also worth keeping this in mind when considering various models of human development, and certainly when considering moral and

8. Phil 2.
9. Matt 19; Mark 10; Luke 18.

spiritual development.[10] They are, I believe, better understood descriptively, rather than prescriptively. Otherwise, you tend to get what I have, in chapter 1, referring to various counseling theories, called the "Procrustean Bed" syndrome, where people are often fitted to this or that developmental model, as against the other way around. In the words of Jesus, "The sabbath was made for man, not man for the sabbath."[11] This is another way of saying that people should always come first. Developmental models can be helpful when they suggest and anticipate general patterns. In this respect, they are held to with a relatively light touch; they are taken seriously, but not too seriously. This is different from some sort of iron-clad adherence to any developmental model, a kind of caricature which would insist that this is precisely where someone should be developmentally, according to some prescribed chronology, or some other definitive pattern. In my judgment, this is simply too rigid a view.

VALUES

In the counseling process, certain values are implicit. Not that therapists, be they theorists or practitioners, are necessarily conscious of what value implications are inherent in the work they do. Nor should values be reified. Values aren't vegetables, for example. If "they" exist, they "exist" as abstractions, not in necessarily any concrete way, and are thus better understood implicitly, rather than as some explicit "thing." Given this caveat, I would suggest that implicit in a kind of counseling I endorse is the following value orientation: an emphasis on awareness, autonomy, spontaneity, and intimacy.

A premise of more psychodynamically oriented counseling is the idea of bringing the unconscious into one's consciousness. Even therapists whose theoretical orientation may be quite different would likely claim that increased awareness on the part of the client is an important function, even a goal of counseling. When people describe positive change in their lives, their report often begins with, "I wasn't aware that's what I was doing," or perhaps "I didn't realize I was giving so much power in my life" to so and so, or that "I had any choice in the matter."

---

10. cf. Daniel J. Levinson, et. al. *The Seasons of a Man's Life* (New York: Ballantine Books, 1978).

11. Mark 2:27.

An example of the kind of heightened awareness that may come through therapy, an intervention commonly used by family counselors, one that generally carries with it a fairly low threshold of threat is Bowen's genogram. Here the therapist will interview clients, asking questions about their families, across multiple generations. As they talk together, the counselor will diagram in rather graphic and symbolic fashion the information presented. Often what emerge are certain prevailing patterns in families, of which clients may not be aware. For example, there may be a pattern of hard-drinking husbands and long-suffering wives, or perhaps a pattern of strong, dominating females and weak, passive males. In response to a genogram, clients will often say something like, "Gosh, I didn't realize that I was doing pretty much what all the men (or women) in my family have done before." This is but one example of the value and function of awareness in the counseling process.

Or again, when clients may identify a problem belief or behavior in their lives, I will often ask, "I wonder where you learned that?" In the process of trying to answer such a question, clients often become aware of something quite significant in their lives, which heretofore they may have never even thought about, something they may have taken for granted or assumed was just the way things are. Often such awareness may bring relief. Conversely, it may be quite threatening. Gestalt therapists speak of the "Ah Ha" experience as a moment of revelation, of insight, of awareness. I'm remembering a client in group therapy years ago. He was talking to the introject of his mother in his own head, a common two-chair technique, when he turned to me and said, "You know something, I just realized. I really did want to go to college. But I'd be damned if I would, because that's what my mother wanted me to do. It's like I screwed myself trying to get back at her."

A common characteristic of clients who seek therapy is that they are symptomatic. In other words, they are usually hurting or failing in some way or other. That's all they know. Often they are asking why. The process of effective counseling is hardly that of giving easy answers to such questions, since this often results in clients becoming even more defensive or perhaps helpless. Effective therapists construct their work with clients in ways that help clients come to their own realizations, their own discoveries of what is likely going on in their lives. This is awareness, of which the client may have had little or none when she came to see the counselor. In this sense, then, awareness can be threatening. Some folk would prefer their symptoms, their pain, to any understanding of what it's about, especially if such awareness might suggest the person's complicity in his own problems. That awareness may also often provide options, alternatives, and choices, and it implies responsibility for what is going on and how this can be changed, how the person's life can be different. The idea here is that awareness, in the counseling process, is always connected to personal responsibility, to other possibilities, and certainly to the client's capability.

This leads to the next value implicit in the counseling process: autonomy. Autonomy is a word rich in meaning, for it implies two things at the same time: freedom and responsibility. Freedom means you have choices, that you're not locked in, despite however limited your options may be. This, of course, raises quite a philosophical question: what are the limits of human freedom? I won't try to answer that here, except it is my observation that those who think they don't have much freedom likely have more than they realize. Conversely, those who think that their freedom is somehow unlimited usually have less than they are often willing to accept. This is particularly true when it comes to freedom of choice. From the perspective of Hebrew-Christian faith, human freedom is fundamentally a paradox. Those who are always wanting or needing more generally end up with less. From a Christian way of seeing things, it is only in embracing the limits of human freedom that we end up freer than we might ever be otherwise. For people of Christian faith, this is always in relation to God. That's why, when you read the great Christian confessions, the saints are always talking about being "in bondage," or of being "a slave" to Christ or for Christ's sake, and that bondage is the source of their notably radical sense of freedom.[12]

In my experience, freedom and responsibility go together, because the freest people seem always to be those who take greater personal responsibility in and for their lives. If I had to pick one issue about which most therapists are most often concerned about with most people, it would be the matter of personal responsibility for whatever. Some people take too much responsibility for others. Most people don't take enough responsibility for themselves.

Personal responsibility works in both directions. It is not letting others shift the responsibility for their lives to us, nor taking too much

12. cf. Seward Hiltner, *Theological Dynamics* (New York: Abingdon, 1972), Ch. 1, "Freedom and Destiny."

responsibility for others. At the same time, it is not shifting outward or off to anyone else that which is our own personal responsibility, our responsibility for whatever it is we believe, think, or feel, and certainly for how we behave. Autonomy, the important inter-relationship of personal freedom and responsibility, is a significant value implicit in a constructive counseling process.

Spontaneity suggests flexibility, as against being too rigid, or merely reactive. It is not necessarily being inconsistent, since consistency may be a virtue, in the sense of being reliable. Often, however, people are too predictable. We're not talking here about those who aren't consistent enough. That's a different problem. A lack of spontaneity can create problems for any of us when we are locked in to only one way of seeing or doing almost anything. As I have suggested earlier, this can be but another example of "crazy": doing the same thing habitually, while expecting different results. When people are more spontaneous, they tend to evaluate a situation on its own terms, rather than merely dealing with it stereotypically. Was it Emerson who said, "A foolish consistency is the hobgoblin of little minds?" If, for example, I chronically nag my spouse about his drinking, I may discover that I don't "have" to do that. Whether it makes any difference or not in his drinking, I have at least chosen to stop being a nag. I am not merely reacting so predictably to something/someone over which I have such little control. Again, if my predictable response to my sister-in-law's patronizing of me is to be so cordially adapted, I may choose to distance myself some from her. Even when I'm around her, I may discover that I don't have to be nearly as open and vulnerable to her as I may have been, that I can change my "normal" response, that I have some capacity to not let her "get to me" as she might have otherwise been able to do. Some would call this "boundary-setting."

Anyone who has modified her code of ethics in the context of an overriding situation or circumstance; anyone who has changed a prejudicial or stereotypical response; any parent who has backed down and agreed to pay for his daughter's college tuition, even "if she does get married"; anyone who has stood by a pregnant teenager, not to mention loving and accepting and caring for a child who wasn't planned or expected, or perhaps even "wanted"; any "straight" person who has embraced, affirmed, and supported a gay or lesbian child, relative, friend, colleague, or employee, upon realizing that one does not choose one's sexual orientation, and that this is hardly the defining criterion of anyone's morality or worth as a person: this is, in the fuller impact of what it means, an expression of spontaneity, particularly when it involves accepting or doing something we may have said we never would.

The last of the values implicit in effective counseling concerns intimacy. Intimacy is an increased capacity to be close with another or others. Contrary to the popular notion in our culture, intimacy may or may not be sexual. In fact, much sexual activity, even between spouses, is often anything but intimate. It may, unfortunately, tend to be even more exploitative. Intimacy involves a high level of trust between those who share it. It is feeling secure enough in oneself and with another to be more honest, open, and revealing. In an intimate relationship, there is a deeper level of both disclosure and acceptance. When we share an intimate relationship with another, we mutually "say" things to one another we would not likely say to someone else, even of a negative sort, just as we are more open to one another to "hear" what the other may have to say to us, what we may not choose to hear from someone else. As a client once said to me, there is "a silver lining of care" in such engagement. That is how he described the giving and receiving of criticism in a more intimate relationship, within a context of mutual respect, trust, and acceptance.

Less intimate relationships are characterized by a greater degree of guardedness, even attempts at manipulation. When we share an intimate relationship with another, we are respectful of each other's person. We don't invade or violate the personal space of another, be it physical or emotional. There is a certain delicacy to more intimate relationships, a special-ness that is mutually respected and preserved. In this sense, then, intimacy is a paradox, one of life's most significant both/ands. Intimacy is both comforting and sustaining, as well as challenging. In an intimate relationship, we are both confirmed, and we are also called upon to respond and to grow.

Years ago I read Thomas Oden's *Game Free*, in which he described psychotherapy as "surrogate intimacy."[13] I agreed with Oden then, and I agree with him now. This is surely one valid and important way to understand a constructive counseling relationship: between therapist and client(s), there develops a relationship characterized by the level of intimacy I have just described, one of honesty, openness, trust, respect, affirmation, confrontation, confirmation, change, and growth. It is surrogate in the sense

13. Thomas C. Oden, *Game Free: A Guide to the Meaning of Intimacy* (New York: Harper and Row, 1971).

that such a relationship is not spontaneous or informal. If a client chooses a counselor and a therapist agrees to work with a client, that mutuality is defined, contracted, and circumscribed. For one thing, there is a financial arrangement concerning what the client agrees to pay for the counselor's time and professional services. The relationship is limited to agreed-upon counseling sessions, including necessary phone conversations. In this sense, then, such an intimate relationship is highly circumscribed. It is formalized. When it is not formalized, if the relationship between therapist and client becomes too casual, or is compromised by what is considered a "dual relationship," involvement with one another apart from the counselor-client context, then the relationship ceases to be the appropriate surrogate level of intimacy it is designed to be. If or when this happens, the counselor is responsible, since it is her clinical, ethical, and legal responsibility to define the limits of the counseling relationship.

As an implicit value in and of counseling, intimacy is promoted as something good. All research, not to mention common sense, would suggest that appropriate intimacy is good for one's physical, emotional, moral, spiritual, and social health. At the same time, developing and sustaining appropriate intimacy in one's life is often the most difficult of tasks. This highlights the value of a kind of psychotherapy designed, through this surrogate process, to promote and develop a client's increased capacity for and capability of developing such intimacy apart from his therapist. In this respect, much of what the therapist is doing may rightly be considered "modeling." Even though I once heard the late Ed Friedman claim that modeling is of little value, research on the effectiveness of counseling suggests that modeling on the part of the therapist is an important ingredient. In this respect, when a counselor is both appropriately affirming and confronting with a client, when she is appropriately revealing, and at the same time sets clear boundaries and models how one takes good care of himself with another, she is modeling the dynamics of how reasonably healthy people develop and sustain a fairly significant level of intimacy.

THEOLOGICAL REFLECTIONS

I think of the person and work of a counselor and the therapeutic process primarily in theological terms, especially, Hebrew-Christian theology. Perhaps this is because I am a Christian minister. Then again, if I were not a minister, I still might do so. Conversely, I know any number of ministers who seem never to think of much of anything theologically, in terms of counseling or otherwise. The point is moot: I am a pastoral counselor. I was seminary-trained. I understand and interpret the person and work of a therapist and the counseling process from a particular theological perspective. I am organizing these reflections in three parts: around a distinctive Hebrew-Christian worldview; the worth, value, and significance of persons in such a faith and values tradition; and a uniquely relational dimension to Hebrew-Christian theology.

I have previously mentioned various distinctive characteristics of a Hebrew-Christian worldview, all of which have important implications for the practice and value of psychotherapy. From such a perspective, this world is real, not illusory. Nature and history have meaning and purpose. This world had a beginning, and it will have an end. We are not on a treadmill, going nowhere. In such a worldview, the physical creation is seen, not as a mistake, but as something good. Likewise, the spiritual and the material dimensions of life are somehow bound together in a unique and special way. Jews and Christians do not see the world as dualistic, where spirit is good and flesh is bad, where the goal of life is to somehow transcend one's created-ness. To the contrary, from a Hebrew-Christian perspective, the ultimate purpose of our living is to embrace fully the gift of our human-ness. For Jews and Christians, our sin is never in being human, but in being in some way less or other than human. The irony of this, tragic as it is, is that when we think we are or try to be somehow more, that is when we usually end up being somewhat less.

If, at least for people of Christian faith, this world is created good, it is also fallen. In a Christian view, we have all sinned, which is to say that we human folk have willfully rebelled against God, and in our own way, we have sought to be God. Thus, we are estranged from the Ground of our Being, and as a result, from ourselves and from each other as well. However, the Christian view is that in our fallen-ness, in our bent or brokenness, in our estrangement, we have been reconciled to God in the historical person of Jesus, as the Christ. For people of Christian faith, all of creation has and is being redeemed in him, in Christ. So then, we live as it were "in the meantime," between the fallen nature of ourselves and this world and the completion of our redemption, including all of creation, which is yet to be fully realized in this life. Indeed, it is a redemption that will be completed beyond this life. This is the perspective of Christian faith.[14]

Because of the incompleteness of this created world and its ultimate redemption, and because of the interrelationship of the material and the spiritual dimensions of life, there is suffering in this world. From a Christian perspective, such suffering is not to be denied anymore than it is to be sought after. It is, rather, the human situation. As such, it is to be embraced, in faith, as ultimately a part of our redemption. For Christians, this is what it means to "share in the sufferings of Christ."[15] To live with integrity, at least for a Christian, is not to rise above this world, unencumbered by its burdens and cares. It is, rather, to embrace this world in its, as well as our own, fallen-ness, as a means of sharing in God's redemptive purpose for all of creation. In the Gospels, Jesus faces his own death on terms quite different from those of Socrates. When his friend Lazarus dies, our Lord does not preach a neat and tidy sermon about the advantage of anyone escaping his physical embodiment. Rather, he weeps.[16]

A uniquely Christian worldview, then, is fundamentally paradoxical. This world is created good. It is also fallen, yet being redeemed in Christ. Christians live in and embrace both a material and a spiritual world at the same time. Suffering is ultimately redeemed as it is embraced, not denied. For a Christian, life is characterized by choice, not fate. Christians share with Jews and Muslims a revealed religion of ethical monotheism. In this view, the oneness and the character of God is revealed in terms of wholeness and integrity, as against a projection of fragmentation and mere capriciousness.

My Jewish cardiologist tells me that he is privileged to practice medicine, and he considers the work he does a sacred trust and calling. That is also my understanding, as a Christian, of my work as a therapist. From such a perspective, people are held in high regard. They are special and important; they have inherent worth and value because they are the fullest expression of God's creativity, not to mention, for a Christian at least, God's redemptive purpose in Christ. From a Christian point of view, this is the highest status God could ever confer upon anyone. In the incarnation of Jesus as the Christ, God was not ashamed or afraid to embrace the

14. Rom 8:18.
15. 2 Cor 1:5.
16. John 11:35.

fullness of our humanity, even to the point of sharing redemptively in our own and very human way of not only suffering, but also dying.

It is also noteworthy that, from a Hebrew-Christian way of seeing things, we humankind are not merely the victims of blind fate; that in the sovereignty and providence and grace of God, we are afforded a remarkable sense of freedom and all the responsibility that goes with it. This is so, even if, for most of us, it would seem that such freedom and responsibility can be awfully intimidating, the kind of gift many of us are tempted to return, something we may experience as more of a burden than a blessing.[17] Yet, this is, after all, inherent in the status God accords us, at least from a Christian point of view. This includes being created in God's own image; being granted such freedom and responsibility; and sharing with God in the good work of creation, redemption, and generativity, the incomparable truth of Christian faith, the incarnation, the fact of God's own humanity, with us and for us in Christ, our Lord.

I don't know when it began to dawn on me, maybe when I was in seminary, or perhaps in my training and work as a counselor, but somewhere along the way I began to notice the remarkably relational nature of Christian faith. Throughout the scriptures, this seems to be a basic paradigm. In what we Christians call the Old Testament, God's covenant with Israel—as a people, the people of God—is relational.[18] Indeed, even in a patriarchal culture, this relationship is interpreted with all the tenderness and sensitivity of the relationship of a mother and an infant child.[19] In the Christian witness of the New Testament, it seems no accident that Jesus, in the Gospels, consistently speaks to the relationship of humankind with God in terms of interpersonal and family metaphors and related images. Jesus uses the most intimate of Aramaic words in reference to God as Loving Father, "*Abba/* daddy." He likens the God-people of God relationship to that of a mother hen and her chicks, and in surely the best known and likely the most beloved of Jesus' parables: in one he portrays the relationship of a father and his two sons to interpret how it is between God and such similar children, be they rebellious or compliant in over-

---

17. cf. Reinhold Neibuhr, *The Nature and Destiny of Man* I (New York: Charles Scribner's Sons, 1941) 251.

18. Exod 6:7.

19. Isa 66:7–14.

adapted ways; while in the other, the "outsider" is the model of friendship, the good neighbor.[20]

Somewhere in the course of my training and work as a counselor, it became clear to me that the interpersonal process of psychotherapy is both a vivid and important paradigm, as well as a practical means of "doing" theology. I use a verb here in quite the same way that faith, in the Hebrew-Christian tradition, is more of a verb than a noun. In the Bible, faith is existential; it is not an abstraction. Faith is believing, or even more concretely, trusting—trusting ever in God's faithfulness toward us human folk and to all of creation. In the same way, I think of the counseling process as "doing" theology in its most practical terms. The great Baptist preacher, Harry Emerson Fosdick, whom I referred to in the "Introduction" to this book, actually defined preaching as "mass counseling." I don't necessarily agree with him, totally, even though counseling is surely at least one important dimension of preaching.

Thus, any number of Hebrew-Christian theological images are both evoked in and out of and through the therapeutic process, as well as being evocative for an understanding of what happens in counseling from such a faith perspective. Those I speak to here include the concepts of intimacy, acceptance, empathy, and congruence.[21] I have spoken to the matter of intimacy in various ways throughout this book, the paradox of a healthy and respectful openness and closeness interpersonally. From a Christian perspective, the closest we ever experience intimacy in this life is but a paradigm of the relationship God wishes to have with each of us in Christ. Just as people of Christian faith understand human intimacy, limited as it inevitably is in a broken world: indeed, the value and nature of personal intimacy, for a Christian, is understood always in terms of one's relationship with God.

The central symbol of Christian faith is a cross, which extends both vertically and horizontally, calling the Christian to both reach up and to reach out. According to the Letter of John: "He who says he is in the light and hates his brother is in the darkness still."[22] From a Christian understanding, if any of us would claim to have an intimate relationship with God, yet seem so unable to develop and sustain much intimacy with any-

---

20. Mark 14:36; Matt 23:37; Luke 15:11 ff. and 10:29 ff.

21. cf. Thomas Oden, *Kerygma and Counseling* (Philadelphia: Westminister, 1966).

22. 1 John 1:9.

one else, we are deluded. In Christian ethics, there is always a connection between our vertical relationship with God and our horizontal relationships in this life, and vice versa. Healthy people, Christian or otherwise, are never emotionally isolated. This is an explicit Christian value. When we become cut off from others, we are borrowing as much trouble in our lives as when we are too needy and dependent upon others. Intimacy is strengthening; it helps promote balance in our lives, because intimacy is based upon emotional strength, not weakness; it reflects the balance of interdependence and reciprocity. Christians are called always to live in community, in vital and responsible relationship with others.

For many Christians, marriage is understood as a sacrament, in that it is the consequence even more of God's willing than of anyone's choosing. Even Christians, who might not understand or interpret marriage in quite the same way, would likely agree that there is hardly an experience known to humankind more revealing of God's grace, more sacramental, than the intimacy of a good marriage. It is a gift to be prized and nurtured. Many would claim much the same for the gift of deep and sustaining friendship apart from marriage.

Acceptance is a cornerstone of counseling in its most practical terms. Therapists who are helpful to their clients create an environment, context, and relationship of acceptance. There is an unconditional quality to it. Put in the simplest of terms, it goes something like this: I may not agree with you, with what you believe, think, or feel, much less with how you behave, or perhaps have behaved; I may not even like you. However, I accept you as a person of worth and value. This may be about as close as any counselor can get to an unconditional acceptance of another. Christians would claim that only God can accept any of us unconditionally, and that the rest of life is full of conditions, as blatant or subtle as they may be. A Christian critique of the counseling process is wary of any therapist who is too glib about his "acceptance" of others. From a Christian perspective, then, acceptance functions as something of a paradox as well: that the less you need to be so accepting, the more genuinely accepting of others you may likely be, within reasonable human limitation. For a Christian, accepting another has its roots in God's acceptance of any of us. However, if God's acceptance of us is quite unconditional, our acceptance of others is always approximate; it is never quite as absolute as some might so naively think. In Romans 14 and 15, in fact, Paul addresses this delicate issue among Christians who find it difficult to be very accepting of other Christians' differences.

Two of the terms for love in the Greek New Testament may be helpful at this point. One is *agape*. This is the Greek word for what we might call regard. It carries a fairly general connotation; it is not wishing ill toward another. It is interesting that the King James Bible translates this Greek word as "charity" in 1 Corinthians 13. That Elizabethan idiom seems appropriate to an understanding of acceptance in the counseling relationship. By contrast, *phileo* is more particular, in the sense of what we might call "liking" someone, or liking something about someone. This kind of love is characterized by all sorts of conditions, compared to the more unconditional nature of *agape*. When counselors talk about the importance of accepting others, the concept of *agape* comes perhaps a bit closer to what is involved. At its most practical, the best therapists seem to have a quality of accepting others more unconditionally than might generally be true for many folk. Both the research and the testimonies of those who claim to have been helped through counseling insist that this more unconditional nature of acceptance is fundamental to the process.

Some would likely make a distinction between judging and condemning. We all make choices and value judgments all the time, and we don't always agree with everyone and everything. Is this different from condemning? Is this what Jesus is suggesting in the Sermon on the Mount, when he says, "Judge not, lest you be judged?"[23] Indeed, in the setting of this same catechism in the Gospel of Luke, such a suggestion is made just that explicit.[24]

The non-judging, or at least non-condemning spirit of effective counseling, the level of positive regard, and the degree of acceptance which is so important in such a relationship: this sounds a lot like what Christians call grace. In a Christian way of understanding, grace is God's unconditional acceptance of us all, in Christ. As a Christian, I seek to grace the lives of others, even as I have been graced, just as such relationships suggest something of what our relationship with God is like. I think I would stand among many who would claim that their lives have been graced relationally, that it is here, in the acceptance of another, and in being accepted, even more for being than for doing or not doing whatever,

23. Matt 7:1–5.
24. Luke 6:37.

that we likely get our best glimpse, or perhaps our fullest understanding of grace, at least in this life.

Not everyone would likely see it as so. I'm remembering talking with a client one time. She was describing her relationship with her father, who had recently died, about her sense of his love for her being quite unconditional. To which I replied, "It sounds like your dad was grace-full."

She responded, "Oh yes, he was a wonderful dancer." Now, of course, this woman was a pretty concrete thinker; she tended to see things in fairly literal terms. However, it also struck me that, even though she was a regular churchgoer, she seemed to have little understanding of how I had just interpreted grace: as an acceptance at the heart of life, the richest of God's gifts to any of us, a level of regard that we actually can and do give to and receive from one another in this life as God's children, to whatever degree. Such an interpersonal relationship, as a paradigm of grace: from a Christian way of thinking, this seems to point to what Paul Tillich speaks of in some famous lines about "accepting our acceptance." [25] In the case of the woman I just mentioned, she had experienced such acceptance, indeed the blessing of such grace, quite concretely in her relationship with her father, surely the best gift any parent could ever give a child.

Empathy and congruence need to go together. Empathy means to "walk a mile in my shoes." Empathy involves some capacity to share the experience of another, literally or in some way similar. When we empathize, we draw and are drawn close to another, even as we allow others to draw close to us when we are willing to accept their capacity to empathize. Those who report being helped in and through counseling consistently describe this as an important quality of the therapist. Counselors often comment on how some people discount at such a level as to essentially reject whatever genuine empathy may be extended to them.

Whenever people experience emotional healing in their lives, however, they open themselves up to accept the gift of empathy, that someone else really does understand and care about what they may have faced or are going through; that others have experienced similar problems or crises in their lives as well. To reject empathy is a form of grandiosity that cuts us off from others, as though no one else has ever experienced anything quite like this before, that our problems are either not nearly as bad or far worse than those of anyone else. I call this playing either "one-up" or

25. Paul Tillich, *The Shaking of the Foundations* (New York: Charles Scribner's Sons, 1948) 162.

"one-down." Whenever any of us do this, we discount and devalue the significance of empathy for emotional healing in our lives. The Christian belief in the incarnation, the humanity of God, is analogous to empathy in human relations, in the sense that God, in the person of Jesus, as the Christ, has fully embraced our human experience, that God has indeed "walked a mile in our shoes."

As I've explained earlier in this book, in chapter 4, congruence means something "fits." For example, when someone is telling me about something painful in his life and he is smiling, perhaps giggling or even laughing, this is incongruent. The emotion being expressed contradicts the content of what the person is describing, narrating, or interpreting. I know this sounds like a caricature, yet it is perhaps the most common incongruity any of us ever encounter, since humor is likely the most socially sanctioned way of trying to deny or defend ourselves against emotional pain. Any experienced counselor has surely observed how smiles and tears can be so close to each other in one's emotional spectrum. Most good therapists are apt to confront such an incongruity, usually in a gentle manner, yet firmly. However confronted, the message is still, "That's not funny," or "What are you smiling about?"

There are other common incongruities, such as fear expressed as anger, or perhaps anger expressed as sadness, even as niceness. My mother used to say, "Kill 'em with kindness." Now there's an oxymoron for you! It's incongruent. What is apparent, or should be, is the connection between congruence and empathy if the empathy is, in fact, somewhere close to accurate. Otherwise, it isn't helpful. Just as sometimes sympathy tends to be more patronizing than genuine or empathic. Sympathy is feeling sorry for someone, which may, in fact, be helpful. Often, however, feeling sorry for whomever is the last thing the person needs. Reasonably emotionally healthy people are capable of empathizing with others without losing their own sense of "self," of who is ultimately responsible for whom. As I explained in a portion of chapter 5, such folk tend to be rather well defined. They don't take on too much of what belongs to another, even another's pain. This is at least an important characteristic of an ethical and capable counselor.

What may look caring can be patronizing; it may merely be putting someone down, and often is. Instead of lifting them up, by leading to their strength, it may be reinforcing their weakness, and likely their dependency. It can also be disrespectful, in the sense of trying to take from another something that is uniquely his, even his emotional pain and what he may choose to do with it. Short of protecting anyone from hurting or killing herself or another, this is an important consideration for responsible therapists, both clinically and ethically. It is a matter of considered judgment. Too often, when any of us are too willing, or perhaps even eager to take on another's emotional suffering, it has less to do with trying to provide comfort for the other person than with trying to accommodate our own sense of discomfort in the presence of another's pain.

The synoptic Gospels of the New Testament, in particular, bear a consistent witness to the integrity and authenticity of Jesus as the Christ. When they say of our Lord, "He speaks, not as the scribes and Pharisees, but as one having authority," this is the believing community's way of saying, in essence, that this guy is the real deal, that he isn't a phony.[26] In the language of a counselor, the emphasis here would seem to be on the importance of congruence. This, then, is the standard by which we Christians measure our motives.

In T. S. Eliot's *Murder in the Cathedral*, the Archbishop, Thomas Beckett, who is about to die for his faith, speaks these disturbing words: "The last temptation is the greatest treason, to do the right deed for the wrong reason."[27] Christians certainly acknowledge the possibility of mixed motives, on the part of any of us, as fallen people in a fallen world. For a Christian, however, the motive counts more than the outcome, particularly with respect to acts of charity and caring. In reaching out to others, or even in holding back, we simply trust our efforts to God, regardless of how we may be perceived or received. Consequently, there is a humbling dimension to such care giving. It is not calculated. It is not a means to an end; it is, rather, an end in itself.

For a Christian, empathizing is sacramental, a vehicle of grace. A sacrament is not only where we meet God, but also where God meets us most deeply. This, then, is motive enough. "When, Lord, did we see thee hungry and feed thee, or thirsty and give thee drink? And when did we see thee a stranger and welcome thee, or naked and clothe thee? In as much as you have done it unto one of the least of these," says Jesus, "you have done it unto me."[28] Beyond their literalness, these are powerful

---

26. Mark 1:22; Matt 7:29; Luke 4:36.

27. T.S. Eliot, *Murder in the Cathedral* (San Diego: Harcourt, 1963).

28. Matt 25.

images of empathy, of extending oneself to touch the needs and hurts of others, or of merely drawing near and standing by, alongside, in a spirit of genuine caring. For a Christian, the motive is always its own end: as unto him, Jesus, our Savior, our Lord.

Someone has said that God offers support, not protection. Even among the most well-intentioned Christians, such an assertion might evoke some disagreement, but not likely among the more effective of caregivers. If there is a sense—and a real one at that—in which our lives, in all their joy and sorrow, are finally gathered up into the very heart of that love who is God, there is also a sense in which God is like a good parent who, in relation to her children, is forever working herself out of a job. In providing support, good parents know that sometimes this means standing aside, as hard as it may be, even (if not especially) when their child may be floundering. It is a balanced expression of a mature way of loving. Effective caregivers, at least from a Christian way of seeing things, embrace this analogy in the work they do. It informs their understanding of what helping may or may not be. They are careful not to presume on others, even to the point of trying to take away another's pain, much less doing for someone what she can and might well need to learn to do for herself.

This raises a question for anyone who seeks to help others from a Christian faith perspective. It is as important as it can be troubling. Put bluntly, what makes counseling Christian? Is it more explicit than implicit? Those who promote the former might insist that Christian counseling is when the therapist, for example, prays with clients, or cites biblical references to support her interventions. Not that there is anything wrong with this. Except it can be contrived. For that matter, what kind of praying counts? I say this because I recently had a conversation with an Episcopal priest who claimed, "I don't want anyone praying one of those spontaneous Baptist prayers over me. If it's not out of the Book of Common Prayer, it won't do any good." Indeed, for many, such symbols or rituals carry a great deal of credibility, just as there are those for whom even the best-written prayers may seem lacking in authenticity.

I'm remembering a rather accomplished and affluent woman I once saw in my counseling practice. She was deeply troubled about her marriage. I gathered that her husband was rejecting her, and she presented as quite emotionally fragile and vulnerable. In fact, she seemed rather desperate. In our conversation together, she remarked, "If you want to pray for me, that's OK."

I suspected this meant, "Please do so." To which I replied, "What do you think I've been doing?" It was, of course, precisely what I was doing as we talked together. I was consciously invoking God's healing presence in the life of this woman, her husband, and her family. And even if I weren't quite as consciously aware of interceding on her behalf, would my sincere engagement of her constitute, in its own way, a prayer? Some would say, "Yes," while others would say, "No." For many, I suspect, if one isn't praying overtly, one isn't praying. Not that I necessarily agree. In fact, much of the praying I observe—the kind where someone is telling God all sorts of things God apparently doesn't know—strikes me as something other than prayer.

It's not that I don't understand and interpret the counseling process from an explicit and rather radical Christian point of view. It's just that the ministry of Jesus, when one reads the Gospels, suggests that our Lord seems to have valued the implicit above the explicit as reflecting an important Christian distinctive, a certain integrity, perhaps even a necessary congruence. If one takes the scriptures seriously, and certainly the prominence of Jesus as their interpreter, one wouldn't have to go beyond the Sermon on the Mount to see what I'm claiming. "Beware of practicing your piety before men," says Jesus. He continues, ". . . when you pray, go into your room and shut the door and pray to your Father who is in secret . . . ." [29] Throughout the Gospels, Jesus consistently challenges the outward expression of even the deepest of spiritual yearnings, in particular among the more explicitly religious.[30]

For some years, I have had a plaque hanging in my office. It is said that Carl Jung had this same inscription carved above the front door of his house in Zurich, Switzerland. It reads: *VOCATUS-atque-non-VOCATUS-Deus-aderit.* Translated: "Bidden, or not bidden, God is present."

Reasonably well-integrated caregivers, however explicitly Christian or otherwise, seem to have a feel and an appreciation for the irony that the deeper and more genuine one's faith, the less one will necessarily need to trade on it quite as overtly. Even St. Paul confesses, " . . . for we do not know how to pray as we ought, but the Spirit . . . intercedes for us in sighs too deep for words."[31] I would submit that this is the rationale for valu-

29. Matt 6.
30. Matt 23.
31. Rom 8.

ing what is even more implicit than explicit in a ministry of authentic Christian care giving. In this context, I'm remembering a quaint legend of the Quakers, members of the Friends Service Committee, helping to repair a bombed-out Berlin following World War II. A facetious German was heard to say, "The problem with you Quakers is that you don't preach what you practice!" My hope and prayer is that my preference for a faith so deeply integrated into the counseling process and the person of the therapist reflects, not a lack of Christian commitment, but rather a genuine faithfulness to the witness and presence of Jesus as the Christ, the human face of God.[32]

32. John A. T. Robinson, *The Human Face of God* (Philadelphia: Westminster Press, 1973).